CREATE A CELEBRATION

CREATE A CELEBRATION

Ideas and resources for theme parties, holidays, and special occasions

ACTIVITIES FOR ALL AGES

Ellen M. Pals

Illustrated by Karen Novess

fulcrum resources

FULCRUM PUBLISHING

GOLDEN, COLORADO

Library of Congress Cataloging-in-Publication Data

Pals, Ellen M.
    Create a celebration : ideas and resources for theme parties, holidays, and special occasions : activities for all ages / by Ellen M. Pals ; illustrated by Karen Novess.
       p.   cm.
    Originally published: Littleton, CO : Aladdin, © 1990.
    Includes index.
    ISBN 1-55591-949-9 (pbk.)
    1. Entertaining. 2. Games. I. Title.
 [GV1471.P17   1996]   96-12612
 793.2—dc20   CIP

                    Printed in the United States of America

                    0 9 8 7 6 5 4 3 2 1

                         Fulcrum Publishing
                    350 Indiana Street, Suite 350
                    Golden, Colorado 80401-5093
                    (800) 992-2908 • (303) 277-1623

LEGEND OF THE COVER ART

The jester that appears on the cover of this book symbolizes the fun and laughter that are a vital part of our lives. Clowning has always been intrinsic to human nature as a way of expressing the foolishness and good humor that bubble up from our inner selves and sparkle on the surface of our beings. Unfortunately, we sometimes forget the importance of simply having fun. In today's world, an element of competition seems built into almost every aspect of our lives. Not only must we "get ahead" in the workplace, but we emphasize elements of "win and lose" or "goal achievement" even in our recreation and leisure time. Volumes have been written about the negative effects this kind of stress has on our physical and mental health. In a pragmatic, scientific society we look for complex remedies to stress-related ailments when what we really need to understand is the value of laughter and good times. Clowning allows us to release our frustrations and take a good-natured look at ourselves in a way that helps us heal whatever troubles mind or body. It's the most basic "therapy" of all and is available to everyone!

Remember to keep fun and laughter, joy and high spirits the best part of all life's celebrations!

ACKNOWLEDGMENTS

My thanks for the assistance I needed to complete this book go to the following people:

To Amanda and Albert Beermann, my parents, who created celebrations in our home as we were growing up and who always found a place at the table for someone who might otherwise be alone.

To Linda Beermann who edited and proofread the text and offered design suggestions.

To Karen Novess who so beautifully created the visual images for the text.

To my family, Jim, Justin, and Tara, who helped plan, execute, and enjoy countless parties and celebrations and gave counsel when needed.

Special thanks to many friends and relatives who have patiently and generously shared ideas, advice, encouragement, and enthusiasm.

CONTENTS

PREFACE

Games! Dances! Music! Drama! They've all held a special place in my heart since childhood. Integrating these interests into "celebration" just seemed to come naturally as I was growing up. Over the years, creating special events for loved ones, organizations, schools, and businesses has resulted in countless fun times for my family, friends, and me. Now I'd like to share some of these ideas that have been so enjoyable for us. The result is *Create a Celebration*.

Holidays and other celebrations are times when people connect and traditions are born. These bring precious memories, but they're important to our lives in other ways as well. According to child psychologist Dr. Lawrence Hartman of Harvard Medical School, "Healthy families have a respect for tradition. Tradition helps order the universe and ensures that things are safe, that children and adults can count on certain events happening." These traditions are also vital to society as a whole. Noted literary scholar Joseph Campbell says that certain rites of passage are significant to our society, and kids growing up today (especially in cities) do not have these rituals and myths. Many experts agree that young people who do not experience rites of passage and rituals in their own families or from other traditional sources will instinctively create initiations and ethical systems of their own. The result is seen in troubled youth struggling in a society whose values they never learned and do not share. For the individual, the family, and all of society, the importance of tradition cannot be overemphasized.

Another important part of celebration is its teaching aspect. Many of our celebrations are re-enactments or re-creations of important events. Religious rituals are obvious examples—for instance, the songs and games of Hanukkah celebrate the Jewish victory over persecution centuries ago and the miracle of the oil lamp; Christmas gifts represent those given to the infant Jesus. All-American holidays like Thanksgiving or the Fourth of July re-enact important moments in our nation's history. "Acting out" can give us real insight into life in other times and other cultures. We better understand frontier living through Tom Sawyer escapades or singing songs of the cowboy. We also learn the ways of the Eskimo, the African, or the Pacific Islander by playing their games and celebrating their cultures. This insight and understanding is invaluable to us as citizens of an increasingly global society.

Fortunately, creating a special event—and thus helping build a tradition or learning about other cultures—can be a rewarding activity for you and your family or group. *Create a Celebration* emphasizes the philosophy that planning and executing a party can and should be an intergenerational experience shared and enjoyed by young and old together. This is a "how to" book for involving all party guests and taking into consideration a variety of ages, interests, and personality types. When everyone celebrates together, groups are bonded and a sense of community develops among friends, in neighborhoods, and within organizations.

The 26 thematic parties, holidays, and special occasions contained in this book include a quick, easy, and complete reference guide for busy party lovers. An outline format is timesaving, but there are also detailed preparation plans. Even the procrastinator or the never-a-spare-minute person can put together a great event in limited time! Hosts have at their fingertips everything they need for that special party or celebration. But remember, there's no reason to limit your creativity. Use this book as a starting point, then …

CREATE A CELEBRATION!

Introduction:

General Party Procedures

CELEBRATION! The word has a joyful, almost magical sound. For some, it may conjure visions of New Year's Eve revelers. Others may think fondly of family and friends gathered around a Thanksgiving table or of children's birthday merriment. Whatever the reason for celebration, fellowship, food, and fun are sure to be part of it! Celebration means good times, not just for guests, but for hosts as well. There's excitement, anticipation, and the pleasure of staging a special happening. The atmosphere of celebration is electric. Theme parties are especially fun and easy to plan and develop. Once a theme is chosen, imagination has free rein. Ideas are everywhere! Of course, pre-planning for any party is imperative. A carefully prepared and well-executed event means less stress for hosts and insures an enjoyable experience for all participants. A theme, a plan, preparation … and the party! For adults as well as children, these are the ingredients for celebration!

Planning the Party

Share the party with your children—involve them in as many ways as possible

- Anticipation is as exciting as the celebration itself.
- Consult family members on all decisions.
- Consider opinions and feelings.
- Allow children to help create invitations, decorations, etc. and allow for imperfections.
- Planning is a valuable learning experience.

Plan ahead

- Choose the party theme.
- Decide on the date, time, and location. Determine the beginning and ending time. Be sensitive to nap times and children's schedules.
- Surprise parties are of little value to children.
- Be sensitive to the availability of guests.
- Develop a guest list. How many? For young children a good rule of thumb is to invite the same number of children as the age of the child—four years = four guests. The host and hostess must feel comfortable with the number of guests attending the party. Consider space and the kind of party. Consider party theme and environment.
- For a more intimate gathering, it is important that the space is not too large.
- Advantages of your home: Secure and convenient. Gives confidence to the host and hostess. Supervision of children is easier.
- Advantages of the out-of-doors: More freedom. Less mess. Affords a setting for livelier kinds of games or activities.

Create the Invitation

- Write the invitation as opposed to phoning
  Send them 7 to 14 days in advance
  R.S.V.P. by a specific date
  It is best to deliver invitations by hand or by mail. Do not deliver at school or group activities! Those not receiving one feel left out.
- Be imaginative
  Hand-created invitations
  Purchased invitations
- Include these things in your invitation:
  Time and day
  Location (may include directions)
  Beginning and ending time. (Preschool-age children's party should not exceed 1 ½ hours. Elementary-age children's party should last about 2 ½ hours if a meal is included.)

Budget

- Food is most expensive, especially when purchased already prepared
- Entertaining at home cuts many costs
- Planning ahead also cuts many costs
- Improvise

Developing a Checklist and Time Line

- Date, time, theme, and location
- Activities
- Invitations and guest list
- Supplies
- Menus/recipes/ice
- Partyware

- Shopping list
- Deadlines
- Decorations
- Cleanup
- Available help

Thinking of Your Guests

- Plan your party around the guest(s) of honor. Talk with them to learn about their hobbies, interests, etc.
- Prepare food that guests will like.
- Have all details of the party finished well ahead of the party time. A relaxed host will enjoy the party.
- Make a party schedule, but let it be flexible.
- If you feel you need extra help at the party, ask a competent teenager.
- Be sensitive to age, sex, and personality of guests.
- Use discretion—think through all activities well.
- If guests include children and adults, provide activities for both and ask an older child to assist you by helping entertain the younger children present. Favorite baby-sitters may assist.
- If extra parking is needed, arrange with neighbors to use some of their space. When necessary, use parking signs with arrows.
- For large parties, identify the party home with a sign, banner, balloons, or flags.
- Have sufficient quantity and variety of beverages.

- Be sensitive to people with allergies. Board out your dog or cat.
- Pick up and put away unusual items (tripping hazards, extension cords over the floor, antiques, and "breakables") the day before guests arrive.
- For a large reception or open house, stagger arrival times on the invitations.
- Adapt to children's schedule and age. Activities must be appropriate.
- It is always special to have a party take-home favor for the departing guests. This eases the party letdown for children. Use bags to carry home favors.
- Have a trash bag or box ready for disposable items.
- Portable plastic files are great to keep ideas and resources at your fingertips.
- Keep guest lists.
- Complete important things first. If time runs out before all details are finished, forget one or two less important details.
- Remember: plan ahead—a relaxed host will be more at ease with guests.

ORGANIZING GAMES AND ACTIVITIES FOR YOUNG CHILDREN

- Organization of preschoolers should be kept at a low level. They are not capable of elaborate teamwork. Preschoolers are not interested in competition. They are not able to wait in line. Game formations must be simple: circles and free formations (no set patterns). Keep rules to a minimum and directions simple as well. Games/activities should appeal to individual achievement rather than group or team achievement.
- Guidelines, rules, and restrictions are very important for guests to know. Children need structure for cooperative behavior and a successful party.
- Reach children at their own level verbally and physically.

ORGANIZING GAMES AND ACTIVITIES FOR ALL AGES

- Arrival should be a time to familiarize and explore. Activity should be unstructured and relaxed.
- Any treasure hunt needs to have the boundaries well defined, especially if the hunt takes place indoors.
- Use a treasure hunt to hide articles needed for another activity. For example, a bubble gum cigar is needed for a bubble-blowing contest.
- Keep everyone busy, entertained, and having fun.
- Have extra activities in mind as a back-up when needed, especially if you must move indoors because of inclement weather.
- Keep the length of games short, but long enough to be interesting. End when everyone is still having a good time.
- Keep relay lines short—four or five guests in one line.
- Avoid germ-spreading games. For example, use blindfolds with discretion.
- Avoid making one person a spectacle. Be thoughtful!
- Allow guests to choose not to participate.
- Activities that involve everyone simultaneously are best.
- Teens and adults especially like the freedom to move in and out of activities spontaneously.
- Avoid elimination games unless the elimination time is short and participants rotate back into the game quickly.

- Avoid having only one winner! Give everyone a certificate, ribbon, etc.
- Sometimes an activity may not be going well. Go on to another activity.
- Post schedules of activities for larger groups.

RENTING RESOURCES

Almost anything you might need for a successful party/celebration can be rented. Check the index in the back of your Yellow Pages! Here are a few samples of things that can be rented or hired: hot tubs, silver serving pieces, tables and chairs, clowns, musicians, magicians, karate demonstrations, balloons, ethnic music groups, drama groups, straw bales, animals, plants, etc.

Yellow Pages Index

- Animals
    - Circus
    - Feed stores
    - County extension services
    - Entertainment
    - Ranches
- Balloons/banners
- Bartending
- Butlers/maids
- Calligraphers
- Caricature art (see entertainment)
- Caterers/food
- Clowns
- Comedians (see entertainment)
- Carnival equipment/concessionaires
- Costumes
- Dance floors
- Decorations
- Entertainers
- Entertainment consultants (see entertainment)
- Ethnic dance, music, and song (see entertainment)
- Flags
- Florists
- Graphic designers (for invitations and signs)
- Jugglers/unicyclers (see entertainment)

- Magicians
- Mexican goods/piñatas
- Mimes
- Music (see entertainment)
- Musicians
- Orchestras/bands
- Party planners/supplies
- Party equipment rental
- Photographers/video
- Portable toilets (see toilets)
- Puppets and marionettes
- Reunion planning services
- Schools and universities
    - Art and Drama Dept.
    - Foreign Language Dept.
    - Music Dept.
    - Physical Education Dept.
    - English Dept.
- Sound systems and equipment
- Tents
- Theater

Note: Check references and preview entertainment. Make sure entertainers have the space needed to perform. Help arrange the audience for the show. Entertainers appreciate being paid in cash.

DECORATING WITH A FLAIR

Decorations set the stage for the drama which will unfold. Adornments are the elements of surprise. Personalize; simple touches can be very effective in creating moods. Colors and textures are also important to successful decorating. Costumes create moods especially when a lot of decorating is not possible. Below are some general formats that may be helpful to you as you decorate.

Backgrounds and Ceilings

Using wire and streamers, fabricate tents, canopies, and a multitude of designs, structures, or backgrounds. Colored butcher paper is excellent for giant backdrops. It can be purchased at a teacher's supply store. Foam core insulation (4 x 8-foot sheets) is another good medium that can be used as a backdrop for waves or for balloon dart throws. Create a giant animal or heart with balloons.

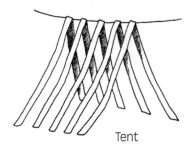

Tent

Teepee

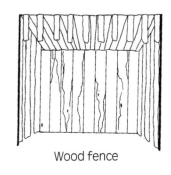

Wood fence

Umbrella—use a pole,
wire, and Hula Hoop

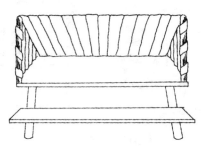

Canopy—build over a picnic table

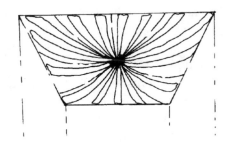

Ceiling—keep working streamers
to the center

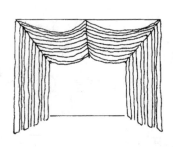

Room canopies

Ribbons

Ribbons are a beautiful decoration medium for parties and celebrations. Decoratively wrap poles, railing, posts, banisters, and mailboxes. Dangle ribbon pieces from trees, doorways, wires, arbors, etc. Hang long pieces (4 feet) or short pieces (8 inches). Dangle them high or dangle them low. Serpentine ribbon can hang from a patio umbrella or a chandelier; it can lie casually around the table centerpiece along with metallic confetti. Let ribbons give your next special occasion a bit of drama.

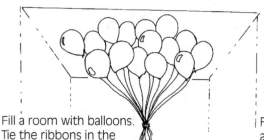

Suspend from a wire

Wrap poles

Flags

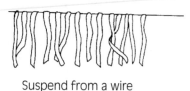

Flags are great fun for celebrations. There are hundreds of thematic and national cocktail flags available. Choose an appropriate cocktail flag and place it in each dessert. If you are having international guests for dinner, they will be delighted to see their national flag flying alongside your flag. Also available are whimsical theme flags just for fun.

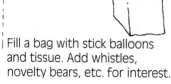

Balloons

Balloons have been around forever, almost! In Pieter Brueghel's painting of *Children's Games* in 1560, we see children playing with a balloon—of course it wasn't colorful and made of latex. Balloons are very festive and give the feeling of excitement and surprise.

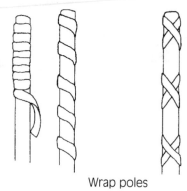

Fill a room with balloons. Tie the ribbons in the middle.

Fill a bag with stick balloons and tissue. Add whistles, novelty bears, etc. for interest.

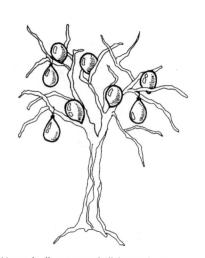

Hang balloons and ribbons in trees.

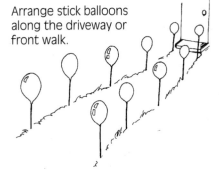

Attach lots of helium-filled balloons to the mailbox (8 to 10)!

Float large helium-filled animals, space ships, vehicles, etc. around the party room.

Arrange stick balloons along the driveway or front walk.

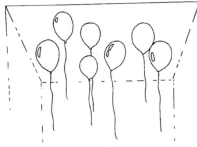

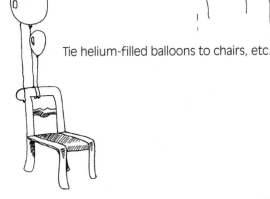

Place a dollar bill or a winning number inside helium balloons. Tie colorful ribbon on each balloon, long enough so they can be reached by the guests. Let them drift to the ceiling. Each guest may pick a balloon and receive a surprise.

Tie helium-filled balloons to chairs, etc.

Candles/Lamps/Torches

Use candle chimneys or hurricane shades in air conditioning or breezy settings. Lighting kerosene lamps, torches, and votive candles creates a dramatic setting for any party.

BUILDING A GROUP

Whenever we are in groups—whether immediate family, friends, or unfamiliar faces—individual personality types become integral to the group's interaction. Knowing "who people are" is an important social dynamic for both the partygiver and the guests. For example, some individuals are most comfortable in a one-on-one situation while others are energized by large groups of people. Meeting people is effortless for some but watching/observing comes more easily for others. The amount of time an individual needs to become involved in an activity is another variable. Remember, people (including children) react differently in group settings depending on their comfort levels. It is important to acknowledge and be sensitive to personality types. Support each individual's style.

USING THIS BOOK

- Tailor all resources and ideas to your party
- Theme terminology is given so you can easily create invitations, signs, banners, etc.
- Select only the games/activities that are appropriate for your party

Remember your video recorders, cameras, flash, and extra film!

Section One

PARTIES BY THEME

1: Backyard Sports Fest

Games are as old as humankind, evolving to give pleasure and to train the young. Young pages in Medieval times played games that imitated the skills of knights. Young Native Americans played games that prepared them for adulthood. Fascinating stories can be told about these remarkable pastimes. It is also interesting to note that many games throughout the world are similar in nature even though the cultures never interacted. Spear or stick throwing, dominoes, and marbles are a few examples of these similarities.

Games generally evolved from play. A young child may have tossed a pebble at a tree. A friend would come by and soon the play became a contest. They made up rules and a winner and a loser resulted. There are also games with no winners or losers. Playing by rules, however, is the important ingredient in all games. For most people the fascination of games is the joy of playing. It is this pleasure that distinguishes a true game from sport. In a sport, winning rather than playing is important. The evolution of lawn tennis is a good example. Early in the 1900s, women donned little straw hats and played tennis in skirts. It was a social event and lots of fun. Today, tennis is played by trained athletes and involves stiff competition. This is far from the leisurely game it once was. Put some fun back into games and create a lighthearted sports event.

INVITATION

CONTESTANT: _____
You are invited to a
SPORTS FESTIVAL
Stadium: 5582 West Golden
Saturday, June 12, 1997
Opening Ceremony: 1 P.M.
Closing Ceremony: 4 P.M.
Torchbearer: Guest of Honor

DECORATIONS

- Hang **flags** and **athletic posters** around the "stadium."
- **Athletic equipment** is great for table centerpieces.
- Use **flags** from many countries on the table or hanging.
- Create a **reviewing stand** on your front porch or stoop with colorful streamers or red, white, and blue bunting.
- Display **posters** of famous athletes on fences, etc.
- Officials may wear **black-and-white striped shirts** with a **whistle**. Less serious referees may wear something clownlike.
- **Balloons** create a festive atmosphere.
- Create a centerpiece of **balloons, flags,** and **whistles** attached to balloon sticks and stuck into a flower oasis.
- Tack up old **pennants** and **flags**.
- Place cards may resemble **balls**—soccer, baseball, football, etc.

SPORTING TERMS

Athletics	Defense	Olympic
Running	Offense	Official
Balancing	Catching	Sportsmanship
Flaming torch	Torchbearer	Goal
Jumping	Dash	Umpire
Throwing	Photo-finish	Referee
Player	Stadium	Coach
Spectators	Go get 'em	Rhythmic
Score	Gold medal	Hurrah
Climbing	Medalist	Nice play

REFRESHMENTS

- Trail Mix
- Oranges
- Hot dogs
- Gatorade
- Popcorn
- Peanuts

FAVORS

- Gold medals made with gold chocolate coins and blue ribbon
- Plastic sports equipment
- Sports paraphernalia—whistles, lanyards, etc.
- Baseball cards may also be used as a place card
- Softballs on which guests may exchange signatures

ACTIVITIES/GAMES
Opening Ceremony

Ages: 6–teen
Time: 15 minutes
Materials Needed: "Bugler's Dream" or "Chariots of Fire" (sheet music or tape), tape player, torch to carry and a torch to light, burlap, string, wax, dowel, coffee can for melted wax, flagbearer, torchbearer, narrator, and a script for the ceremony.
Advance Preparation: Organize the music for the opening ceremony. With adult supervision make torches for the opening ceremony:

1. Wrap burlap around a dowel or stick five times.
2. Tie the burlap in place with string.
3. Dip in hot wax (be very careful).
4. Repeat this process several times.
5. Make two torches—one to carry and the official torch to be lighted. The official torch may be larger for a

longer-lasting flame. A short stick for handling is all that is needed for the main torch.

Activity: The narrator welcomes everyone to the Summer Sports Fest, and introduces the athletes as they parade into the stadium and sit down on either side of the main torch (for safety reasons keep a safe distance from the torch). As athletes march in, a recording of the "Bugler's Dream" is playing. After all athletes are seated, the flagbearer is introduced and enters the stadium. The torchbearer is introduced, runs in, and lights the main torch from his burning torch. Music contin-

ues until the torch is lighted. The narrator makes closing remarks and then gives participants instructions about the games. It is important to have the narration and procedures written.

Variation: Use a flashlight with orange or yellow tissue paper to create torches. Create a flame with dry ice and water using a birdbath as the brazier.

Miniature Golf

Ages: 7–teen
Time: 20–30 minutes
Materials Needed: Tunnels, flags on dowel sticks, sand, cardboard boxes (assorted sizes), large baking pans, shoeboxes, tuna cans, carpet pieces, lawn edging, bricks, putters, and golf or rubber balls.
Advance Preparation: Build a miniature golf course. Let your imagination run wild!
Activity: Play miniature golf.
Variation: In a large field or park, set up a large golf course. Use flags to mark each "green." Give

each athlete a Frisbee. Score by the number of throws it takes to touch a flag. Score as in golf. Lowest score wins or make up your own rules!

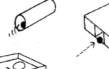

Obstacle Course

Ages: 7–teen
Time: 20–30 minutes
Materials Needed: Bicycle tires, boxes (assorted sizes), marking cones, tumbling or exercise mats, Hula Hoops, stools, barrel, large log, broomstick, an 8-foot 2 x 4 board, soccer ball, stopwatch, wooden ladder, sawhorses, rope, and bean bags or balls.

Advance Preparation: Gather all the materials needed for the obstacle course. Set up an obstacle course.
Activity: Athletes run through the obstacle course competing for the best time. A timer stands at the finish line and gives guests their time through the obstacle course.

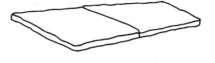

Do two forward rolls across tumbling mats.

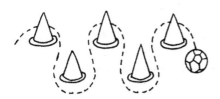

Jump from one bicycle tire to another.

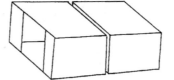

Crawl through a tunnel of boxes.

Dribble a soccer ball through several marking cones.

Jump into a Hula Hoop from a stool.

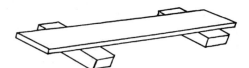

Hop on one foot across a 2 x 4 board.
Heighten with two bricks.

Jump over a broomstick
resting on two stools.

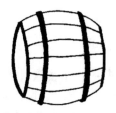

Crawl through a barrel.

Walk a log.

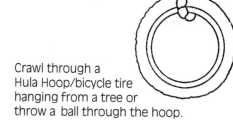

Crawl through a
Hula Hoop/bicycle tire
hanging from a tree or
throw a ball through the hoop.

Walk the rungs of a wooden ladder.

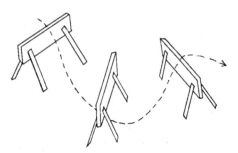

Climb over and under sawhorses.

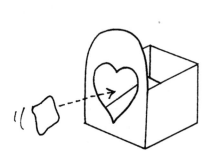

Tie a rope to a tree limb.
Climb up and swing.

Toss a bean bag/ball through a large hole in a box.

FINISH LINE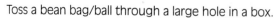

Athletic Events (Crazy Olympics)

Ages: 7–teen
Time: 30–40 minutes
Materials Needed: Tumbling or exercise mats, football, Hula Hoops, soccer ball, Frisbee, orange cone markers, wooden planks, tape measure, inflatable boats and paddles, jump ropes, trumpet, stilts, music for gymnastics, plastic water gun, and stakes.
Advance Preparation: Gather equipment and set up athletic events.

Activities:

1. **Stilt Race**
   Athletes race 60 feet (walk quickly). The first one to cross the finish line—heavy cord—wins. Use stilts or modified stilts made from cord and cans—coffee cans.
   Note: See Event XII in "May Day."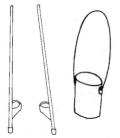

2. **Floor Exercise**
   Athletes create a dance or gymnastics routine on the mats or on the lawn. Accompany routines with music played on a tape recorder.

3. **Football Throw**
   Athletes throw for distance or accuracy through a hoop. Each contestant has three throws.

4. **Discus Throw**
   Athletes throw a Frisbee/paper plate for distance.

5. **Soccer Goal**
   Athletes kick a soccer ball through two markers or cones to score a goal. Adjust distance for age of contestant.

6. **Javelin Throw**
   Athletes throw a dowel or yardstick for distance.
   Variation: Throw a soda straw for distance.

7. **Standing Broad Jump**
   Athletes stand behind a toe line and jump for distance. Measure the distance jumped or have predetermined distances marked with a little marker at the side.
   Variation: Divide into teams and line up. The first member of each team makes a standing broad jump. The next team member jumps from where the first person landed and so on. Measure the collective jumps to determine the winning team.

8. **Rope Skipping**
   a. Athletes may create a routine (most unique, most creative, etc.).
   b. Athletes jump a set number of jumps in one minute.
   c. Athletes jump as long as possible without missing.
   d. Race to a finish line while jumping.

9. **Hot Air**
   Athletes play a trumpet or bugle. The player who holds a note for the longest time wins.

10. **Fitness Test**
    a. Athletes do sit-ups for one minute.
    b. Athletes do push-ups for 30 seconds.
    c. Athletes do toe-touches for one minute. Winners are the contestants with the best record in the time allowed.

11. **Marathon**
    Athletes run around a block or park. When finished with the run, contestants lie down in a prone position and shoot a water gun/Ping Pong gun at a target. Guest with best score in both events wins.

12. **Regatta**
    Athletes race inflated paddle boats in a pool or lake.

13. **Shot Put Throw**
    Athletes throw water balloons. Farthest throw wins. This works well on a street or hard surface.

14. **Backward Bound**
    Run backward to a finish line.

15. **Hot Shot**
    Basketball throw from designated spots. Best score wins.

16. **Twenty-Five Foot Dash**
    Divide contestants into several teams. Team members measure their feet and all the foot measurements are added together. The longest team measurement of feet wins.

17. **Kick Up Your Heels**
    Contestants line up on a straight line and unfasten their right shoes. On "Go," contestants kick their shoes for distance.

18. **Best Time!**
    Players line up at a starting line. On the signal "Go," walkers begin the race toward the goal line which is about 100 feet from the starting line. The object of the race is to cross the finish line in exactly one minute. The person finishing closest to the one-minute time is the winner. All players must keep moving and may not check their watches.

19. **Log Roll**

Participants lie on the grass in a long row with their bodies parallel to a finish line 24 feet away. On "Go," they begin rolling toward the finish line. First person to reach the finish line is the winner. **Note:** Keep space between participants to avoid their running into one another.

20. **Peanut/Candy Scramble**

Place treats along the finish line. Guests line up on the starting line and on "Go" run to the goal line to snatch as many treats as possible.

21. **Pillow Joust**

Two contestants joust with pillows or soccer boppers while balancing on a log. The one remaining on the log is the winner.

Grand Finale

Ages: 6–adult

Time: 20 minutes

Materials Needed: Several pairs of wood stilts or stilts made from cans; soft pretzels or marshmallows.

Advance Preparation: Hang sweet morsels from cords dangling from a rope strung across a room or from trees in the yard.

Activity: Participants must balance on their stilts while attempting to bite off a tempting morsel—without using their hands.

Note: Vary the height of the cords appropriate to the height of the participants and stilts.

Awards

Character sketch badges

Handle awards with much care and thought. Everyone wants to be a winner and, in a child's world, all should be winners in some way. Awards should reinforce a positive image. Here are some ideas for award winners (in addition to ribbons for athletic prowess): Sportsmanship, Wettest, Funniest, Best Form, Worked the Hardest, Most Considerate, Kindest, etc. Also see gold medals under "Favors" in this chapter.

PLAY BALL!

2: Bear Affair

Bears have always held a special place in fairy tale, folklore, and myths depicting divine and natural strengths. In Europe, ancient legends reveal the fear people had of bears. North American Indians hunted bears but also worshipped them as gods. Mishka, a favorite bear in Russian folklore and legends, served as the mascot for the 1980 Olympic Games in Moscow. The familiar "Teddy Bear" is another powerful symbol—one of comfort and solace especially for the young but also for the lonely or elderly. "Teddy" was born in 1902 when a Russian immigrant, Morris Michtom, saw a newspaper cartoon of a bear cub kind-hearted Theodore Roosevelt could not bring himself to shoot. Michtom fashioned a Teddy Bear depicting this cute little cub. Shortly after that, the Teddy Bear craze began. Today, the cuddly bear continues to be the world's most popular soft toy.

INVITATION

Attach an invitation with ribbon to a small stuffed bear or cut a bear from construction paper.

BEARER Of A Special Invitation
Date:_____
Time:_____
Place:_____
R.S.V.P._____

DECORATIONS

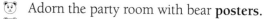

- Greet guests in a **bear costume** or **bear mask**.
- Have **bears, bears, bears** sitting all about the party room.
- Seat **bears** at a child's table with a **miniature balloon** centerpiece on the table.
- Hang **balloons/streamers/serpentine**.
- Snuggle **bears** in **baskets**.
- Place a **bear** on a **unicycle** or a **child's tricycle**.
- If the party is outside, put **bears** up in the **trees**.
- Make **bear paw tracks** coming up the walkway to the front door.

- Adorn the party room with bear **posters**.
- Wrap a gallon jug with rope to look like a **beehive**.
- Stick **bees** on the **hive**.
- Display **mini bear flags** created with stickers and hors d'oeuvre picks.

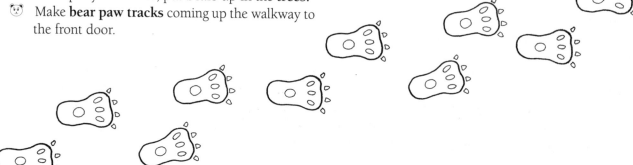

TERMS

Cuddle
Sweetest
Hunt
Bear up
Soft
Grin and Bear It
Bear facts
Teddy power
Snuggle
Fuzzy-Wuzzy
Bearer of
Smokey

Berry/Beary nice
Cub-ble up
Unbearable
Friendly
Grizzly tales
Hug a bear
Hibernate
Teddy Bear
Honey
Bear's den
Bearaphernalia
Bear hugs

Shakesbearian
Ambling
Bear tracks
Bear paws
Rambling
Lovable
Limbering
Wooly
Bitzy Bear
Frolicsome
Bearish adventure

KINDS OF BEARS

Black bear
Grizzly bear
Koala bear

Brown bear
Polar bear

Panda bear
Kodiak bear

FAMOUS BEARS

Rupert (British)
Smokey (American)
Albert (British)
Corduroy (American)
Paddington (British)
Barney Bear (American)

Sooty (British)
Teddy Bear (American)
Winnie the Pooh (British)
Yogi (American)
Boo-Boo (American)
Bre'r Bear (American)

Billy Bluegum (Australian)
Mr. Bear (Japanese)
Bussi Bar (German)
Mishka (Russian)
Bimbo (Spanish)
Nounours (French)

REFRESHMENTS

- ☺ Bear cake or encircle a round cake with Teddy Grahams
- ☺ Bit-O-Honey candy
- ☺ Have a Teddy Bear Picnic (put refreshments in a large basket lined with a red-and-white checked cloth)
- ☺ Berry juice
- ☺ Serve honey in bear shaped dispensers
- ☺ Gummi Bears

FAVORS

- ☺ Small antique bears
- ☺ Bear paraphernalia
- ☺ Storybooks about bears
- ☺ Bear stickers or pencils
- ☺ A book about Teddy Roosevelt
- ☺ "Gummi Bears"

ACTIVITIES/GAMES
Musical Bears

Ages: 2–5 years
Time: 20 minutes
Materials Needed: Disc/tape player and the recording, *My Teddy Bear and Me*. Resource: *My Teddy Bear and Me*, KIM 7039, and *The Teddy Bears' Picnic*, VHS RS88605V Kimbo Educational, 800-631-2187.
Advance Preparation: Purchase the disc/tape.
Activity: Guests enjoy favorite bear melodies and do simple actions. Assume a bear walk position by placing the hands on the floor with arms and knees straight. Guests sway rhythmically from side to side like lumbering bears.

Bear Hunt

Ages: 4–12 years
Time: 15 minutes
Materials Needed: Small bears (antique bears or erasers).
Advance Preparation: Hide bears throughout the party room or among trees and bushes.

Activity: Guests go on a bear hunt. When they find a bear, they may keep it as a favor. If you hide more than one bear, tell guests in advance how many bears they will hunt.
Variation: Guests search for hidden bears, but they must count rather than collect the bears.

Let's Go on a Bear Hunt

Ages: 3–12 years
Time: 20 minutes
Materials Needed: The old "Bear Hunt" story.
Advance Preparation: The leader should practice this story until he/she can tell it easily. Have your children practice it with you.
Activity: Take the guests on a Bear Hunt! Guests sit on the floor in a semicircle with the leader facing the guests. This is a storytelling activity which involves action and participation. The guests repeat words and actions of the bear hunt leader.

Leader: Have you ever been on a bear hunt?
Guests: No.
Leader: This is how it goes. Say and do everything that I do. Is everyone ready? (Place your hands on your knees— make sure all guests have hands on their knees.)
Leader: Let's go on a bear hunt.
Guests: Let's go on a bear hunt.
Leader: (Pats one knee and then the other several times, to imitate slow walking.)
Guests: (Guests imitate the leader in unison.)

Leader: Oh, look! (shades eyes with hand and peers into the distance).
Guests: Repeat and imitate action.
Leader: I see a wide river.
Guests: Repeat.
Leader: Can't go around it.
Guests: Repeat.
Leader: Can't go under it.
Guests: Repeat.
Leader: Let's swim across (makes crawl stroke motions).
Guests: Repeat (after seven or eight strokes, leader resumes knee-patting).

Leader: Oh look! (hands over eyes and peering again).
Guests: Repeat.

This is the beginning of the bear hunt story. Continue with the story using many obstacles and motions—fence, wheat, cotton or cornfield, cave, mountain, forest, etc. Helpful words for your story may be: *explore, dark, damp, rugged, bright, warm, soft, furry,* and *over.* Finish by telling the story backward! End with "Whew!"

Parade of the Teddy Bears

Ages: 3–4 years
Time: 15 minutes
Materials Needed: Guests should bring their favorite teddy bear (indicate this on the invitation). A tape with marching music and a tape player.

Advance Preparation: Listen to the music and have your child practice with the tape for appropriateness.
Activity: Guests parade their bears to music.

Favorite Bear Stories

Ages: 3–6 years and teen girls
Time: 15–20 minutes
Materials Needed: Polaroid camera and favorite bears brought to the party by the guests.
Advance Preparation: Indicate on the invitation that

guests should bring their favorite bears. Purchase film and flash for the camera.
Activity: Guests share a short story or remark about their favorite bear. After the stories, all gather for a group picture of guests and bears.

Teddy Bear Style Show

Ages: 4–12 years
Time: 15–20 minutes
Materials Needed: Guests should bring their bear in a favorite costume (indicate this on the invitation). Background music for the style show, someone to narrate the style show, and a tape player. The record *Teddy Bears' Picnic* is a cute song.

Advance Preparation: Find music for the style show. Select the style show narrator and have tape player in place for the style show.
Activity: Guests parade bears in a style show. You may give certificates for the most handsome, smallest, most winsome, largest, fuzziest, sweetest, prettiest color, cutest, most Victorian, funniest nose, etc.

Honey for the "Bears"

Ages: 4–12 years
Time: 15 minutes
Materials Needed: Small bags made of tissue paper and netting, Bit-O-Honey pieces, and ribbon.
Advance Preparation: Create tissue bags to resemble honeycombs or decorate a bag to resemble a jar of honey.

Fill with Bit-O-Honey pieces and hang on tree branches that can be easily reached by the "bears." The tree should be easy to climb. Smaller children will need to be helped by an adult.
Activity: Bears climb the tree for a "bit of honey"!

Puppet Show

Ages: 3–8 years
Time: 20 minutes
Materials Needed: Characters from the story of "Goldilocks" or another favorite bear story. A puppet stage made from a large box and tapes for background music. Remember the tape player.

Advance Preparation: Ask older children or teens to develop the puppet show for the guests.
Activity: The guests view a favorite bear puppet show.
Variation: Guests work the puppets to a previously taped puppet story narration. This can be very effective. Keep the story simple using some repetition.

Where Are Those Bears Hibernating?

Ages: 5–12 years
Time: 15–20 minutes
Materials Needed: Bears, bears, and more bears hidden about the party room. Some can be disguised in pictures and posters, partially hidden behind a pillow, sitting on a picture, etc. Use cookie cutters, stickers, pencil erasers, or whatever comes shaped as a bear.

Advance Preparation: Hide bear paraphernalia and collect all materials needed.
Activity: Each guest is given a paper and pencil. Guests search the room for 10 minutes trying to find all the bears. They need only to write down the number. The winner must show the guests where all the bears are hibernating.

"Shakesbearian Production"

Ages: All ages
Time: 20 minutes
Materials Needed: Character bears for the production and children's storybooks or plays based on Shakespeare's works. *Favorite Tales from Shakespeare* or *Shakespeare* by Charles and Mary Lamb are two excellent resources.
Advance Preparation: Stage a short play using bears as actors.

Activity: With bears, dramatize excerpts from Shakespeare's plays. Shakespeare often used jesters or fools in his plays—stage some of their antics. Since music was very important during the time of Shakespeare, many of his plays have music in them—use background music.
Note: In England, on the afternoon of the performance, one of the actors would stand at the entrance to the innyard/courtyard (forerunner of the playhouse) to collect an admission fee. A child in a bear costume might collect the "fee" at the party.

Teddy Bear Tea

See "Tea Party" in the Doll Party chapter.

Scavenger Bear Hunt

Ages: 12–teen girls
Time: 30–45 minutes
Materials Needed: $5.00–$10.00 for each group of guests.
Advance Preparation: Develop guidelines for the scavenger hunt. Include some shopping safety hints for young girls.

Activity: Take the girls to a shopping center and give each group of two or three the same amount of money. They must purchase bear paraphernalia—as many as possible but none can be alike (one sticker, one eraser, etc.). Guests are given a time limit and must meet at a designated spot at the end of the time limit.

Teddy Bear Picnic

Ages: 3–12 years

Time: 45–55 minutes

Materials Needed: Picnic packed for all the guests. Remember Bit-O-Honey pieces, red-checked paper goods, and plaid blankets on which to sit.

Advance Preparation: Prepare the food and purchase paper ware for the picnic. Determine the location and consider walking to a park nearby.

Activity: Guests have a picnic with their favorite bears.

HAVE A "BEARY" GOOD TIME!

3: Clown/Jester/Carnival

The art of clowning goes back thousands of years. It's a part of human nature. More often than not, when a group of people gather, there is someone to make them laugh. The kinds of jestering have varied through the ages as has the costuming. Tumbling, juggling, mimicry, witticisms, pranks, poking gentle fun, dancing, music making, mock-preaching, mime, and making mischief were among the talents and antics used to amuse and charm people. Funny makeup and elaborate costumes were also very important to the acts. Many royal courts and noble houses employed jesters and similar entertainers. They thrived in circuses at medieval celebrations, and also performed literature and drama. Today's art of buffooning owes much to the jesters and merrymakers of the past.

INVITATION

Draw and cut clown faces from brightly colored paper. On the clown's collar, write out the party details and use clown stickers to seal the invitation envelope. Create an invitation with balloons. Write the message on the balloon or on a piece of paper that can be put inside the balloon.

It's a Party!
June 15, 3:00 p.m.
Christy's House
12 South Union Street

DECORATIONS

🤹 Purchase or make **large clown posters.** There are many clown resource books in your library. Also check "Posters" in the Yellow Pages.

🤹 Hang **large bells** throughout the party area.

🤹 Purchase or make **large banners or flags.**

🤹 Purchase **confetti** and sprinkle it on the serving table.

🤹 Place a **safety mirror** in the center of a **large clown face poster** with the caption "Who's this clown?"

🤹 Fill a basket with **juggling items** for the centerpiece.

🤹 Purchase **clown/jester music** at a record shop.

🤹 Cascade **balloons** or attach **balloons** to sticks and insert them into the ground.

🤹 Cut **pleated clowns** and use as table decoration.

Mirror

🤹 Hang **plastic flags** around the party area.

🤹 Highlight your house or yard with dangling **ribbons.** String wire and cascade **streamers**, creating a tent look.

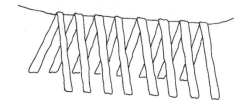

TERMS

Bamboozle
Comics
Hoodwink
Baffle
Clever
Jesting/joking
Fool
Mimic
Jeering
Thrilling
Dazzle
Hocus-pocus

Charming
Witty
Amuse
Cut-up
Entrancing
Funny
Entertainment
Pantomime
Antics
Greedy
Mischievous
Jokes

Wit
Charm
Carnival
Goofy
Silly
Crazy
Calliope
Playbills
Marquees
Trickery
Zany
Waggish

CHARACTER ROLES

Villain
Medicine man
Enchanter
Jester/court fool
Comedian/actor
Harlequin mime

Juggler
Minstrels
Magician/conjurer
Clown
Buffoon
Sorcerer/wizard

Ventriloquist
Tumblers
Dwarf fool
Mischief maker
Comic
Joker

FAMOUS CLOWNS

Bozo
Grimaldi
Coco
Pulcinella (Punch)
Buster Keaton
Pierrot (Pedrolino)
Charlie Chaplin
Popov

W. C. Fields
Sancho Panza
Three Stooges
Don Quixote
Marx Brothers
Howdy Doody
Leporello
Abbott and Costello

Jean-Baptiste
Laurel and Hardy
Marcel Marceau
Tom Sawyer and Huck Finn
Tweedledum and Tweedledee
Sexton and Patch
Emmett Kelly
Lou Jacobs

REFRESHMENTS

- Candy circus peanuts (use as candleholders)
- Clown ice-cream sundaes
- Popcorn
- Peanuts
- Punch

FAVORS

- Trick items (disappearing ink, etc.)
- Puzzles
- Juggling bags/ bean bags
- Tennis balls (decorate and use for juggling)
- Clown makeup (Caran D'ache)
- Books on clowns

ACTIVITIES/GAMES
Clowns, Magicians, Jugglers

Ages: 3–adult
Time: 15–40 minutes
Materials Needed: Professional clown, magician, or juggler. Scarves for beginning jugglers.

Advance Preparation: Arrange to hire a professional or a talented teenager. Create a stage area for these people.
Activity: Watch a clown, magician, or juggler. Guests attempt simple juggling tricks using scarves.

Pick-a-Pocket

Ages: 4–adult
Time: Spontaneous throughout the party
Materials Needed: A clown outfit with many pockets sewn on the suit. Coupons, prizes, and a redemption center.

Advance Preparation: Sew pockets on a clown suit and fill pockets with coupons.
Activity: Guests pick-a-pocket for a coupon and redeem the coupon for a prize at the redemption center.

Clown Band

Ages: 3–adult
Time: Spontaneous
Materials Needed: Rhythm band instruments for small children, disc/tape of clown music, or an adult clown band. Resource: Preschool Playtime Band, KIM 9099C Kimbo Educational, 800-631-2187.
Advance Preparation: Gather equipment if you are cre-

ating a child's clown band. If using an adult clown band, create the band using friends who play instruments or hire a clown band.
Activity: The clown band plays spontaneously throughout the party. Young children parade up and down the sidewalk or around the backyard with their rhythm instruments.

Juggling

Ages: 4–adult
Time: 15–30 minutes
Materials Needed: Juggling balls. If possible, hire a teenager who will do a routine and also help teach a beginning juggling technique. Scarves work well for beginners and young guests.
Advance Preparation: A few weeks before the party, find a juggler who will perform and teach juggling. Gather juggling equipment for the party guests.

Activity: The juggler gives a performance with a simple "how-to" after the routine. All guests participate in learning an easy juggling technique.
Variation: Clowns/guests gather in a circle with three small Nerf balls. Pass the balls in and across the circle while calling the names of the recipients. Keep adding balls until it become crazy!

Balloon Sculpture

Ages: 9–adult
Time: 20–30 minutes
Materials Needed: Sculpture balloons, directions for making them, and a clown who can make and teach balloon sculpture. Check "Magicians" in your Yellow Pages.

Advance Preparation: Purchase balloons and/or arrange for a professional clown who does this as part of his act.
Activity: Create balloon animals for all the young children. Older children and adults may learn how to make them.

Magic Show

Ages: 4–adult
Time: 15–40 minutes
Materials Needed: Provide a small stage or stage area. Each guest can perform a magic act or two. Tricks can be purchased or use magic books from your library. A master of ceremonies will make this activity seem more professional.
Advance Preparation: Have all guests prepare one or two magic tricks. Indicate this on the invitation. Have a few additional tricks ready in case a guest did not prepare a magic trick.

Activity: Guests present a magic show on stage. A few tricks can be done spontaneously during the party. Some samples of tricks: Flash paper (paper that burns instantly), squirt flower, rubber cigars, rubber pencils, squirt cameras, pipe cleaner sponge ring (tie a small wet sponge on the underside of a pipe cleaner ring and shake hands), etc.

Face Painting

Ages: 4–adult
Time: 20–40 minutes
Materials Needed: Mirrors, paper towels, sponges, water, terry cloth towels, table and chairs, and Caran D'ache Paints (water-base makeup).
Advance Preparation: Check your library for clown books and display sample clown faces. Have all materials gathered and ready for face painting.

Activity: Create all types of clown faces. For older children and adults, this can be done as a contest. Award prizes for the funniest, most creative, most intricate, cleverest, etc. Award funny giant certificates.

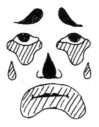  

Puppet Sideshow

Ages: 6–12 years
Time: 10–15 minutes
Materials Needed: Clown puppets, puppet stage (card table turned on its side or a sheet placed at half height across a doorway), and a short script.
Advance Preparation: Write or use a storybook to produce a short puppet show. Practice the show. If this is a large group, use a speaker system to amplify the voices. Add sound effects for an even more professional sideshow.

Activity: Present an extraordinary puppet show for all the guests.

Parade of Character Balloons

Ages: 6–12 years
Time: 20–25 minutes
Materials Needed: Scissors, large balloons, felt-tip markers, curl ribbon, tissue paper, colored tag board, clown/marching music, and tape player.
Advance Preparation: Gather all materials and make a sample balloon character.

Activity: Guests blow up a large balloon and decorate it as a favorite character. Cut out shoes from tag board and slip shoes onto the end of the balloon. When all the guests have finished their balloon characters, parade the balloons to circus or marching music.

Cut here
↓ and insert balloon.

Clown Basketball

Ages: 6–teen
Time: 10–15 minutes
Materials Needed: Tennis balls, a round wastebasket, and masking tape.

Advance Preparation: Set up a basketball-throwing contest. Use tape to designate the throwing line.
Activity: Each player has five throws. Guests bounce a tennis ball into a wastebasket from about 10 feet away. Adjust distance for smaller guests.

Hoop de Loop

Ages: 6–teen
Time: 10–15 minutes
Materials Needed: Card table, 4 throwing rings (10 to 12 inches in diameter) made with heavy cardboard, and masking tape.
Advance Preparation: Turn a card table upside down. Place a strip of masking tape on the ground about 10

steps away from the target (card table legs).
Activity: Players take turns pitching the rings onto the table legs. The closer legs are worth 5 points and the farther legs are 10 points. Prizes are based on the number of points earned. Younger children do this as an activity and do not keep score.

Pick-Up

Ages: 6–adult
Time: 10–15 minutes
Materials Needed: Several tall cola bottles, large piece of cardboard, flat plastic ring, bamboo fishing pole, and string.
Advance Preparation: Set up the activity on a large

piece of cardboard. Make a fishing pole with string attached to the flat ring. Lay the bottles on their sides.
Activity: The object of this activity is to loop the ring around the bottle neck and set the bottles upright. Points can be given for the number of bottles picked up.

Ball/Bean Bag Throw

Ages: 4–adult
Time: 15–20 minutes
Materials Needed: Bean bags or tennis balls, bucket or box, and markers.
Advance Preparation: Make bean bags and decorate a

box with a big clown face. Tennis balls can be decorated with permanent magic markers.
Activity: Throw bean bags or balls through the holes in a box or into a bucket. When younger children are playing this activity, do not keep score.

Tattoo the Circus Lady

Ages: 6–teen
Time: 15–30 minutes
Materials Needed: Two pieces of tag board taped together, fine-tip felt pens, markers, and masking tape.
Advance Preparation: Gather materials and draw a circus lady on the tag board (trace around a child lying

on the large piece of tag board). Give the lady some hair, an attractive face, and a cute bikini. The circus lady poster is now ready for hanging and special tattoos.
Activity: Guests draw tattoos on the circus lady.

Cloudburst

Ages: 6–adult
Time: 15 minutes
Materials Needed: Two or three large boxes filled with balloons; two or three tubs filled with water balloons.
Advance Preparation: Blow up balloons and fill the boxes with them. Each box should contain the same number of balloons.
Activity: Divide guests into two or three groups. Groups gather around their box and, at a starting point, begin to break balloons by sitting on them. The first group to break all the balloons plucked from their box wins.
Variation: Guests form two or three relay teams. Each team member passes 20 water balloons backward over his head to the next team member. The last member of each team places the water balloons in an empty tub. The team with the most unbroken water balloons in their tub wins.

"Goin' Fishin"

Ages: 3–9 years
Time: 10 minutes
Materials Needed: Washtub, bamboo poles, string, magnets, tag board, contact paper, large paper clips, scissors, permanent marker, and prizes.
Advance Preparation: Cut fish, old cans, and boots from heavy paper. Decorate and put a paper clip on each. Make several fishing poles with bamboo sticks, string, and magnets. Write a prize number on each fish, can, and boot and place them in a large tub.
Activity: Each guest goes fishing and receives a prize for each catch.
Variation: Cover both sides of the fish, etc. with clear contact paper to make them waterproof and place them in a tub of water. Remember to write the prize numbers with permanent marker.

Target Clowns

Ages: 4–12 years
Time: 15 minutes
Materials Needed: Paper plates, Ping Pong balls, markers, yarn, construction paper, basket, and string.
Advance Preparation: Have children draw six comic faces on paper plates. Decorate the faces with construction paper, curl ribbon, etc. Hang the characters at different levels from a door frame or a tree limb. Fill a basket with Ping Pong balls.
Activity: Guests throw Ping Pong balls at the clown faces. Three hits win a prize. Modify for younger children.

Dance Like a Clown

Ages: 3–8 years
Time: 15 minutes
Materials Needed: Recordings for clown/circus songs and rhythms for children and a tape/disc player. Resource: Kids Circus All Time Favorite Dances, KIM 7032C Kimbo Educational; Ball, Hoop, and Ribbon Activities, KIM 9126C Kimbo Educational, 800-631-2187.
Advance Preparation: Purchase recordings and preview activities.
Activity: These recordings have a variety of do-it-yourself circus activities. Choose those that are most appropriate for your party. Don't try to do too many in one setting! Dance or march to recordings you already have on hand!

Pitch a Ball

Ages: 4–teen
Time: 10 minutes
Materials Needed: Plastic swimming pool, three Styrofoam rings, 6 plastic balls in a bucket.
Advance Preparation: Fill the swimming pool and float Styrofoam rings. Collect plastic balls and keep them in a bucket.
Activity: Guests throw balls into a Styrofoam ring. The most successful pitches win. Young children play as an activity and do not keep score.

Goofy Golf

Ages: 4–teen
Time: 5 minutes
Materials Needed: Giant plastic toy golf clubs or newspapers, water balloons, and marbles.
Advance Preparation: Purchase toy golf clubs or make clubs by rolling newspapers (like a stick). Blow up balloons and place a marble in each balloon. Decorate a large box and cut a hole for the target—adjust the hole size to the size of the ball or balloon.
Activity: Guests attempt to putt the balls or balloons into the hole. Best score wins. Small children play without scoring.

Poster Review

Ages: 4–teen
Time: 5–10 minutes
Materials Needed: Posters, plastic dart guns (suction type) or bean bags, masking tape, tacks, and an old wastebasket.
Advance Preparation: Hang several posters on a fence or wall. With masking tape, mark a throwing line about 10 feet from the posters. Roll extra posters and place in a wastebasket.
Activity: Shoot dart guns or throw bean bags at the poster you want. If you hit the poster you win it. Have a supply of prize posters rolled in an old wastebasket (award a corresponding rolled poster so you do not take down the target poster).

Disappearing Quarter

Ages: 6–teen
Time: 20 minutes
Materials Needed: A bucket of water, a quarter, and 100 pennies.
Advance Preparation: Fill the bucket with about 6 inches of water and place a quarter on the bottom. Give each guest about 15 pennies.
Activity: Players each take a turn dropping a penny into the bucket of water attempting to cover the quarter with pennies. Guests win if they cover the quarter before the pennies run out. If they are unsuccessful, the bucket wins.

Mood Music

Play circus music or calliope music during the party.

CLOWN AROUND!

4: Detective/Mystery

People are fascinated by the mysterious and the unknown. They enjoy danger, especially when not putting themselves in real jeopardy. Mystery games and stories are an ideal way to satisfy this spirit of adventure and passion to discover the unexplained. Many enjoy the mental gymnastics and socializing involved in solving the puzzle elements in a mystery game. Mystery stories, on the other hand, provide the more solitary enjoyment of reading about colorful characters, exotic settings, and complicated plots. Some detectives (Sherlock Holmes is probably the most famous) are subjects of a whole series of adventures. In mystery stories, the reader has the reassuring feeling that the detective is in control and will, in the end, set things right. This assurance is something real life seldom provides. No wonder Ellery Queen called mystery stories "fairy tales for grown-ups."

INVITATION

Create a magnifying glass invitation. Cut black construction paper in the shape of a magnifying glass leaving the center open for the message. Glue clear cellophane on the back of the glass. Behind the cellophane, glue a circle of white paper a little larger than the center opening. Before gluing, write your party details on the white paper.

A PRIVATE EYE DETECTIVE
PARTY FOR SUPER SLEUTHS
Saturday, April 3
Scene of the Crime:
5500 East Yates
R.S.V.P. 555-8590

DECORATIONS

- Cut many **footprints** from black construction paper. Place them up the walkway to the front door.
- Hang **black balloons** around the party area.
- Cut **giant magnifying glasses** from large pieces of black construction paper.
- The host may dress as a **super sleuth** carrying detective bag, camera, trench coat, deerstalker hat, and large magnifying glass. Spontaneously, throughout the party, the host snaps Polaroid pictures (mug shots). A "Wanted" sign may be pinned on each guest for the mug shots.

- Display **detective paraphernalia** as a centerpiece for the party table.
- **Clue paraphernalia**—a rope, candlestick, toy revolver, and a knife are also fun for decorating.
- Place **mystery books** about the party area.
- Create **giant signs** using the **characters** in the game "Clue," super sleuths (mentioned below), and "Whodunit" signs.

SLEUTHING TERMS

Crime spotter	Messages	Suspect
Mysterious	Trickery	Alibis
Cleverness	Camouflage	Thriller
Super sleuth	Scotland Yard	Investigate
Lurking	Thief/crook	Deerstalker hat
Disguise	Clues	Cryptic
Private eyes	Witness	Keen power
Caper	Assignment	Deduction
Briar pipe	Detectives	Crime busters
Secret	Undercover	Interrogate
Loot	Scene of the crime	Observation
Fingerprinting	Whodunit	

SUPER SLEUTHS

Dick Tracy	Hardy Boys	Perry Mason
Nancy Drew	Sherlock Holmes	James Bond
Kojak	Miss Jane Marple	Ellery Queen
Batman	Columbo	Encyclopedia Brown
Poirot	Nero Wolfe	

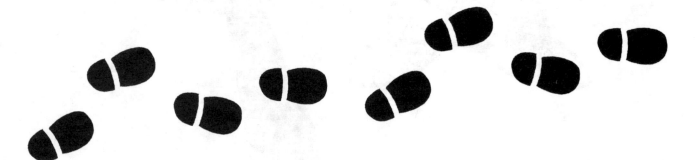

REFRESHMENTS

🔍 Mystery cakes—put a clue in the bottom of each cupcake. Use pieces of recipe cards and a ball-point pen to write out the clues. Place the writing away from the batter.

🔍 Shape a birthday cake like a magnifying glass. Use brown and white frosting.

FAVORS

🔍 Detective storybooks
🔍 Plastic water guns
🔍 Invisible ink
🔍 Badges
🔍 Bobby whistles
🔍 Washable ink pads

🔍 Detective kit:
    Notebook
    Ink pad
    Magnifying glass
    Plastic container
    Pencil
    Flashlight/penlight

ACTIVITIES/GAMES
Pickpocket

Ages: 7–adult
Time: Spontaneous
Materials Needed: Coat and deerstalker hat, fabric pieces, thread, needle, and prizes/certificates.
Advance Preparation: Sew little pockets on the coat and hat. Fill with prizes/certificates.
Activity: The guest of honor/"Super Sleuth" wears the coat and hat with added pockets. Each guest picks a pocket for a prize.

Telltale Fingerprints

Ages: 8–adult
Time: 15 minutes
Materials Needed: Washable ink pad, unruled index cards, notebooks, pencils, and a small table near the party entry.
Advance Preparation: Have all materials gathered and ready.
Activity: As guests enter, have them quickly write the word "detective" on an index card and then put their right thumbprint on the same index card. An adult or teen should then take the index card and secretly identify it with the guest's initials written in pencil on the back of the card. This will insure identities of the cards (guests are not aware of the initials). When all the guests have arrived, pass out the index cards making sure the guests do not have their own cards. Now the guests go around with their stamp pads, notebooks, and pencils gathering samples of handwritings and thumbprints. From their clues, they can identify the owner of the index card they are holding.
Note: If the party has many guests, you may use colored index cards. The men use blue and the women use yellow cards. This will shorten the activity time.

The Careless Crook

Ages: 9–adult
Time: 30 minutes
Materials Needed: Someone acting as a crook, her fingerprints, a strand of wool from the crook's sweater, a chewing gum wrapper, a strand of hair from the crook, and the crook's shoe print (use tempera paint).
Advance Preparation: Before the party select a guest or any adult attending the party to be the crook. Collect all the clues needed for this activity.
Activity: Detectives, using their detective kits, begin solving the mystery of the careless crook. When they solve it, the detectives show their proof to the party host.
Note: The crook must wear the shoes and sweater that correspond to the clues gathered earlier.

Seize the Loot

Ages: 7–14 years
Time: 15–20 minutes
Materials Needed: Bag of chocolate coins placed in a loot bag and a whistle.
Advance Preparation: Draw a starting line with a stick or cord.
Activity: Guests line up on the starting line. The object of the game is for each guest to advance toward the loot bag and seize it. But while advancing, a detective will blow a whistle every few seconds. When the guests hear the whistle blow, they must stop on a dime without moving a muscle. If they move, they must return to the starting line and begin again. The first guest to advance to the loot bag is the winner and then shares the loot with the other guests. The detective should be an older child or an adult.
Note: Introduce the game with a story about a police chase. The thieves became so excited in their escape from police that they dropped their loot bag. Now all the police/guests are hurrying to fetch the loot bag. You may also have more than one loot bag.

Mystery Objects

Ages: 7–10 years
Time: 15 minutes
Materials Needed: Five to ten objects placed in a mystery bag. One bag of objects for every five guests. Pencil and paper for each guest.
Advance Preparation: Put together the mystery bags. Make them all identical.
Activity: Guests sit in a circle and a mystery bag is given every five guests. The guests then pass the mystery bags, feel the objects in the mystery bag, and write down the items they can identify. For younger children, list many items. Let them circle the items they feel in the bag. Winners are those who have identified the most mystery objects.

Spot the Clues

Ages: 7–teen
Time: 15–20 minutes
Materials Needed: Pencil and paper for each guest, needle, thread, button, thimble, cellophane tape, movie ticket stub, note with a telephone number, rubber band, pencil, dollar bill, candy wrapper, top of a ballpoint pen, ring, stamp, matchstick, coin, hairpin, or any object that can be disguised in a background object.
Advance Preparation: Hide objects throughout the party area in a camouflaged background. Place a white thread on a wheat-colored drape, a rubber band around a doorknob, a pencil lying on a picture ledge, a dollar bill around a flower stem, etc. Make a master list of all the objects and where they are hidden. Make a list of all the objects for each of the guests.
Activity: Guests/detectives search for all the objects on their lists. When they find the object (but do not disturb it), the detectives must write down its location. After 20 minutes stop the activity and have guests count the number of clues they have successfully located.

Find the Loot

Ages: 7–10 years
Time: 10 minutes
Materials Needed: Small cloth bags filled with chocolate coins.
Advance Preparation: Hide the loot bags throughout the party area.
Activity: Little detectives search for the loot bags.

Detective Print Lifting

Ages: 7–adult
Time: 20 minutes
Materials Needed: Baby powder or pencil dust, feather or soft brush, transparent tape, and black or white paper.
Advance Preparation: Gather materials and practice the activity.
Activity: Learn to lift a fingerprint. Guests rub a finger around their nose or forehead to make it oily. Press the print finger carefully on a clean surface to make a print. Dust the print with the powder or pencil dust. Brush carefully with a feather or soft brush. Lift the print gently with transparent tape. Sticking the tape on black or white paper will reveal the print.

Secret Codes

Ages: 9–adult
Time: 15 minutes
Materials Needed: Prizes, clues written in code, copies of the secret code, and pencils.
Advance Preparation: Type or print clues in code. Type the official code below the clues. Make enough copies for each guest. A sample code could be numbers equalling letters:

1 — C
2 — F
3 — G
4 — A
5 — T
6 — R
7 — Z
8 — W
9 — S

Activity: The guests/detectives decode the clues and discover the solutions to finding the treasure.

Super Sleuths

Ages: Teen–adult

Time: 1 ½–2 hours

Materials Needed: Polaroid cameras for each group, film, and flash bulbs.

Advance Preparation: Have all equipment and supplies ready. Make a list of subjects to be photographed and list the number of points earned for photographing each. Examples of subjects:

1. A Burger King employee with french fries sticking out of his mouth. (20 pts.)
2. Someone sunbathing. (20 pts.)
3. Team member standing by a statue or monument. (20 pts.)
4. Team standing by a cemetery stone. (30 pts.)
5. Team member standing by a police officer holding up her hands. (80 pts.)
6. Someone wearing a baseball cap. (10 pts.)
7. Your team sitting on a fire truck. (20 pts.)
8. A sign with the letter "Z" in its message. (10 pts.)
9. Personalized license plate. (60 pts.)
10. Child riding an electric horse in a grocery store. (30 pts.)

Activity: Each team is given a camera and film for 10 pictures. The object of the game is to accumulate the most points. If you want to do less driving, limit subject possibilities to a designated area.

Note: Additional prizes may be awarded for the funniest picture, the most creative, etc.

"Clue"

Ages: 9–teen
Time: 30–40 minutes
Materials Needed: The game "Clue" and pencils for each guest. "Clue" can be purchased at any toy store.

Advance Preparation: Have the game ready.
Activity: Play "Clue."
Variation: Turn your house into a live gameboard and have guests come in "Clue" character's costumes.

Mysterious Weekend

Ages: 10–adult
Time: 1–2 hours up to an entire weekend
Materials Needed: A company that produces plots for private parties and fund-raisers. Check your Yellow Pages under "Theatrical Agencies" or "Entertainment."
Advance Preparation: Locate and make arrangements with such a company.

Activity: Guests spend several hours or an entire weekend sleuthing. They sort through hidden clues to solve a play-acted crime. Often guests will be asked to come in appropriate costumes.

Who's the Imposter

Ages: 12–adult

Time: First 30 minutes of the party

Materials Needed: Prizes for those who best disguise themselves.

Advance Preparation: In the invitation, explain to the guests that they should come disguised well enough so other guests will have difficulty identifying them. This should be a disguise, not a costume.

Activity: Guests disguise their identity throughout the first 30 minutes of the party. They can alter their appearance and also their voice, walk, etc. Prizes/certificates may be awarded to the best-disguised guests.

Note: Disguise can be achieved by stage makeup obtained from a theatrical supplier (see your Yellow Pages).

Mystery Games

"How to Host a Murder" (role-playing series)

"Murder Mysteries Party Games" (role-playing series)

"Just Games" (role-playing mysteries)

"Jamie Swise Games" (role-playing mysteries)

"Sherlock Holmes Consulting Detectives" (game)

"221 B. Baker Street" (game)

"Crime Busters" (game)

"Clue" (game)

WHO DUNIT!?

5: Doll Party

Dolls are ageless treasures. Since the dawn of time, they have been used in worship and ritual and cherished by children everywhere. A doll can be anything from a small stick or stone to an elaborate piece of beautiful art. Kings and queens sent fashion dolls to one another. Fashion dolls were even sent by the British to Colonial India to show women how to wear their English clothes. The Japanese celebrate a doll festival for girls when all the finest dolls are displayed in a special room for friends to admire. Some of the dolls are passed down from generation to generation and young Japanese girls consider them their greatest treasures. Of course, sometimes dolls are purely whimsical. Whatever their appearance, dolls are companions of children, adults, collectors, and historians. They are amusing and have a way of lifting the admirer out of herself and into the doll's world. Dolls are images of humankind and reflect time, places, and cultural heritage.

INVITATION

Paper doll with detachable dress or pleated paper dolls. (See directions under "Pleated Paper Dolls" in the activity section of this chapter.) Give your party a name using the doll your child enjoys.

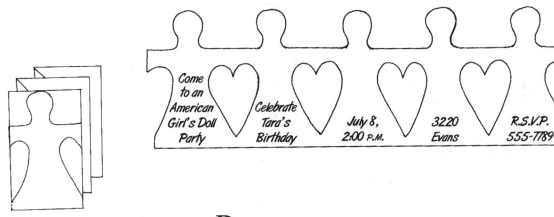

DECORATIONS

* Display a **large paper doll** on the front door and **smaller dolls** throughout the party room.
* **Pleated paper dolls** can be used as a table runner.
* Assemble all the **doll paraphernalia** your child has including stuffed animals.
* **Balloons** and **streamers** add a festive touch.
* Feature **baby pictures** of all the guests. Use a copier to enlarge.
* **Display dolls** (a Japanese custom on Doll's Day).

TERMS

Rock	Coo	Da Da
Crawl	Tea party	Basket
Play house	Stroller	Wardrobe
Buggy	Rattle	Pacifier
Nap	Bib	Ma Ma
Laugh	Cuddle	Papoose
Baby	Bye-bye	Bambino
Toddler		

KINDS OF DOLLS

Baby	Cornhusk	Sock dolls
Kachina Indian	Paper-mache	Fashion
Bisque	Costume/character	Trouble
Novelty	Rag/cloth/kid leather	Tin soldiers
China	Doll houses/dioramas	Flower fairies
Paper		

REFRESHMENTS

- Doll cut-out cookies
- Giant doll cookie (may decorate as an activity)
- Encircle the sides of the birthday cake with a row of pleated dolls (see page 32)
- Japanese candy rice cakes

FAVORS

- Paper doll books
- Doll accessories (capes, ties, ribbons, etc.)
- Bag for doll clothes
- Handkerchief dolls
- Small dolls
- Silhouettes created at the party
- Baby doll prescription (little jar of tiny candy)

ACTIVITIES/GAMES

Buggy Parade

Ages: 3–7 years
Time: 20 minutes
Materials Needed: Guests bring decorated doll buggies.
Advance Preparation: Indicate in the party invitation to bring a decorated doll buggy and a favorite doll. Make neighbors aware of the time and date of the parade—some may enjoy watching.

Activity: Children parade colorful doll buggies along the street on the sidewalk.
Variation: Provide festive music for the parade.

Dollhouse

Ages: 6–10 years
Time: 30–40 minutes
Materials Needed: Boxes (all sizes), poster board, spools, caps, foil, magazines, cloth scraps, old wallpaper, wallpaper books, old combs, clothespins, straws, paper towel rolls, buttons, yarn, glue (hot glue gun for older children), broken dowels, wooden matchsticks, bottle caps, old handkerchiefs for sheets, small plastic restaurant jelly containers, pipe cleaners, thread and needles, Scotch tape, small cans, scissors, etc.

Advance Preparation: Gather materials needed and make a few samples—dolls made out of clothespins, pictures from magazines for wall decorations, small stove, beds, sofa, table, and refrigerator.

Activity: Guests create a dollhouse. Younger children can make one room together. Older children may create three or four rooms. If you have plenty of time, create clothespin dolls, otherwise scale dollhouse rooms for small dolls you have on hand.

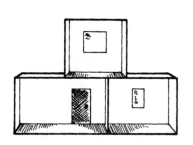    

← yarn

← pipe cleaner

← wide ribbon or cloth

Silhouette Portrait

Ages: 3–12 years
Time: Throughout the party
Materials Needed: White drawing paper, large pieces of construction paper, lamp (shade removed), pencil, masking tape, chair, scissors, and markers.
Advance Preparation: Set up portrait area. Guests should be seated so their heads are just a few inches from the wall. Place a lamp about 10

feet from the wall at the same height as the guest's head—you will want a sharp shadow around which to trace the silhouette.

Activity: An adult or teen helper traces the silhouette of each guest. Guest can then fill in her silhouette with a markers or crayons, or the silhouette can be cut out and mounted on contrasting colored paper.

Create a Baby Doll

Ages: 7–12 years
Time: 15–20 minutes
Materials Needed: Square fabric pieces or a pretty white handkerchief.

Advance Preparation: Practice making doll with your child to establish good directions for the activity.
Activity: Create baby dolls.

1. Roll sides to middle

2. Fold handkerchief in half.

3. Pull top rolls to sides, fold up. Wrap ends around and tie in a knot to create doll's head and arms.

4. Optional: Stitch simple eyes.

Another version of a handkerchief doll.

To create the doll's head, tie a small ribbon at the neck. Stitch simple eyes. Tie knots at the corners to make the arms.

Story Time

Ages: 3–6 years
Time: 10–15 minutes
Materials Needed: Doll story
Advance Preparation: It is always best to "tell" a story,

so practice doing so. If this isn't possible, read the story to the children.
Activity: Tell a story about a doll, for example: Raggedy Ann and Andy.

Pleated Paper Dolls

Ages: 5–10 years (younger guests need more assistance)
Time: 30 minutes
Materials Needed: Long strips of paper in assorted colors, glue, scissors, newspapers, yarn, buttons, old fabric pieces, crayons, markers.
Advance Preparation: Cut strips of paper 6 by 24 inches long. Pleat/fold paper and make a few samples of dolls and clothes. Have your own child make a doll to give you a better feel for giving directions to the

guests. Patterns for clothes can include crown, hair, dresses, hats, belts, boots, shoes (use slits for shoes and hats).
Activity: Make paper dolls and clothes. Fold strips in half, fourths, eighths, and sixteenths (makes 8 dolls). Draw or color the faces.
Note: Small children enjoy watching pleated dolls being made.

Doll Hide-and-Seek

Ages: 3–10 years
Time: 15 minutes
Materials Needed: Small dolls, handkerchief dolls, or paper dolls.
Advance Preparation: Hide dolls in well-defined areas or rooms.

Activity: Guests look for the dolls. If you are giving dolls as favors, have children keep the dolls they find.
Variation: Have children hide one another's dolls.

Special Names

Ages: 8–adult
Time: 5 minutes
Materials Needed: Books on name origins from your public library. Place cards, pen, ink, and stickers or drawings.

Advance Preparation: Look up derivations of all the guests' names. Type or print the derivation on the name card.
Activity: Guests must locate their place setting by finding their name derivation.

Make a Life-Sized Rag Doll

Ages: 4–12 years (younger children will need more adult help)
Time: 1 ½ hours
Materials Needed: Old sheets, stuffing (rags, foam chips, tissue paper, poly fill or newspapers), markers, straight pins, scissors, fabric glue, and sewing machines with adult or teen helpers.
Advance Preparation: Make a sample doll with your child. This will help you to anticipate what needs to be

done. Have guests bring extra clothing to outfit the new rag doll.
Activity:

a. Each guest creates a real life-sized rag doll—a twin! This activity will need adult assistance and should be done with a small group (four guests). Guests lie down on the double thickness of a sheet lightly spreading arms and legs.

b. A child then draws an outline with a marker around her friend's body, keeping a good margin for body thickness and a seam allowance (2 inches). Do not outline fingers and toes.

 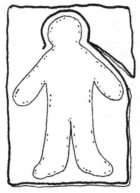

c. Pin the two sheets together inside the outline.

d. Using a sewing scissors, cut the figure a half-inch outside the outline (to allow for stitching).

e. Stitch all around the outline with the sewing machine or use fabric glue. Leave the seam open at the top (head) for stuffing the rag doll.

f. Remove the pins and turn the rag doll inside out. Stuff the feet and arms first. Shape your doll and then close the seam at the top.

g. Decorate your doll's face at the party (if there is time). You may want to design your face on paper first. Your rag doll is now ready to be named and dressed in your favorite outfit!

Yarn Doll

Ages: 6–12 years
Time: 20–30 minutes
Materials Needed: Four-ounce skeins of yarn, scissors, and a book (determine size by the height you want your doll to be). Buttons and felt pieces are optional.
Advance Preparation: Make a sample doll.
Activity: Create yarn dolls by wrapping yarn around a book lengthwise approximately 75 times. Cut a few lengths of yarn for tying-off pieces. Tie the strands together at the top of the body to hold them and then cut the loop at the other end. Remove the "body" from the book. Now create the doll's head by tying the upper part of the body. To make the arms, divide the body in half, and then divide each half again. The outside bunches are the arms—tie each arm at the wrist. Trim excess yarn. The two remaining halves will form the legs (boy) or skirt (girl). For a boy doll, tie each bunch at the ankle. Tie the waist for a boy or girl. Decorate with buttons and scraps of felt if time permits.
Note: When tying the doll, make sure all the knots are on the back side of the doll.

Doll Collection

Ages: 8–adult
Time: 30–40 minutes
Materials Needed: Antique or international doll collection.
Advance Preparation: Locate and make arrangements for someone to come in and tell about her doll collection.
Activity: Guests hear the stories behind a doll collection. Be sensitive to the care and handling of dolls in a collection.

Doll Fashion Show

Ages: 8–12 years
Time: 30 minutes
Materials Needed: Scraps of material, lace, needles, thread, scissors, and simple patterns for doll clothes. Tape and tape player for background music.

Advance Preparation: Make up a sample skirt, cape, or jumper.
Activity: All the guests design a garment for their dolls. They sew them and then have a fashion show. Narrate the fashion show with music playing in the background.

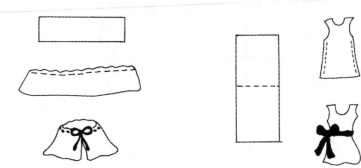

Baby Picture Puzzles

Ages: 3–adult
Time: 10 minutes
Materials Needed: Tag board, baby pictures of guests, glue, envelopes, and scissors.
Advance Preparation: Collect and copy baby pictures of guests. Glue picture copies to poster board. Draw puzzle parts on the back of the picture, cut, and place each picture puzzle in an envelope with a name on it.
Activity: Give each guest a puzzle with instructions to put it together. Guests must then try to identify the person in their puzzle picture.

Tea Party

Ages: 3–adult
Time: 20 minutes
Materials Needed: Fancy dresses, old hats, old jewelry, long skirts, small tables and chairs, toy tea services, tea party refreshments, stuffed animal companions, and dolls.
Advance Preparation: Set tables for the tea party. Decorate with miniature flower arrangements.

Activity: All guests dress up in fancy tea party clothes. They then bring their baby dolls and have a tea party. If weather permits, let the birds, butterflies, and rabbits in your backyard create a wonderful tea party ambience.
Variation: Adults, too, enjoy the nostalgia of their childhood. Celebrate with friends a "nursery tea" with old companions, antique toys, and dolls.

ENJOY THE MAGIC OF YOUR DOLLS!

6: Fiesta

Fiestas are favorite celebrations for the people of Mexico and other Latin countries. It is a time of merrymaking, eating, drinking, dancing, gambling, parades, cockfights, and amateur bullfights. Carousels and puppet and peep shows are all a part of a child's activities at a festival. The day of the fiesta is often announced with fireworks at dawn. In Spain, fiestas were held to entertain the royal court.

INVITATION

Place a serape invitation in a bright red envelope. Possible party captions might include "Fajita Fiesta" or "South of the Border!"

OLÉ! COME TO A MAGNIFICO FIESTA
TIME:
DATE:
PLACE:
R.S.V.P.:
Fiesta Dress—Poblanas, Charro Suits,
Serapes, Lace Mantillas, and Huaraches.

DECORATIONS

- Fly colorful **fiesta flags.**
- Remember **confetti.**
- Hang festive **Mexican hats.**
- Drape **serapes** around the party area.
- Decorate with lots of **fresh** or **silk flowers.**
- **Balloons** are great for the fiesta celebration.
- **Piñatas** are decorative as well as fun for the party.
- The **eye-of-god** is a very old art piece. They range in size from very small to large elaborate masterpieces.
- String **red, green,** and **white streamers, garlands,** and **fiesta pennants.**
- **Ivory-colored fans** add a nice touch to the fiesta theme.
- Display **bullfight posters** (your travel agent may have some).

- Burn new or old **candles** placed in **Tequila bottles.**
- Use **baskets** whenever possible.
- Hang **pepper strings (*ristras*)** and **pepper Christmas lights.**
- Adorn the serving tables with **red tablecloths, castanets, small guitars, maracas,** and **bongo drums.**
- Hang a few **hammocks** and borrow a few **palm trees.**
- Children will love **iguanas** or **lizards** (plastic or live).
- Arrange giant, colorful **tissue flowers** (*see instructions on following page*).

Creating a Tissue Flower:

1. Stack four pieces of tissue paper 20 inches by 20 inches.

2. Accordion pleat (³/₄ inch) the pieces like a fan.

3. Find the middle by folding in half and tie a string at the middle.

4. Round the corners of the fan.

   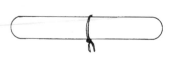

5. Spread open like a fan and pull up each layer of tissue paper gently to the center string.

 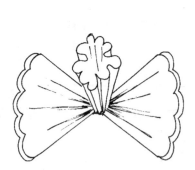 

Note: The size of tissue may vary but pieces must remain square. Mix and match tissue colors. Tie smaller tissue flowers inside large flowers.

SPANISH WORDS

Adobe—house of sun-dried brick

Amigo—friend

Arcades—series of arches

Bebé—child or baby

Bronco—rough, wild, and spirited horse

Bolero—loose, waist-length jacket

Bravo—well done or excellent

Buenas noches—good night

Buenas tardes—good afternoon

Cascarones—confetti fun maker

Chili con carne—chilis stewed with chopped meat

Gracias—thanks

Fiesta—feast day

Desperado—bandit or bold, desperate criminal

Hacienda—large estate

Lariat—rope with a noose used to lasso

Magnifico—magnificent

Mantilla—shawl

Matador—bullfighter who has the principal role

Mucho—much

Por favor—please

Rodeo—cowboy's circus

Señora—married woman

Señorita—unmarried woman

Tornado—thunderstorm

Foods

Avocados	Corn	Rice
Beans	Jicamá (hee-ca-ma)	Salsa
Chili tomatillos	Limes	Tapas
Coconut	Papaya	Tea/hot chocolate
Coffee	Peppers	Tortillas

Favors

Mexican jumping beans (nutlet containing a live larva)

Fans and mariachi shakers

Miniature serapes used as bookmarks

Balloon sculptures

Cascarones (bonkers)

To make cascarones, you will need hollow eggshells, confetti, brightly colored tissue paper, glue, and newspapers. Blow out the eggs early, using the contents for cooking.

- Dye eggs and fill with confetti.
- Cover hole with masking tape.
- Cut newspapers into rectangular pieces 10 inches by 12 inches.
- Surround eggs in a cone of newspaper.
- Festoon the cone with colorful tissue paper … cascarones are now ready to bonk a friend on the head.

Activities/Games
Jarabe Tapatio (Mexican Hat Dance)

Ages: 8–adult
Time: 30–40 minutes
Materials Needed: Sombreros, "Jarabe Tapatio" recording and a disc/tape player. Resource: *All-Time Favorite Dances*, KIM 9126, Kimbo Educational 800-631-2187.
Advance Preparation: Purchase sombreros, maracas, and the hat dance recording.

Activity: Guest participate in the Mexican hat dance and keep the beat with maracas. This dance has become very popular in Mexico. Most people are familiar with this dance.

Folk Music and Dances

Ages: All ages
Time: Varies
Materials Needed: Professional/amateur Mariachi bands, strolling guitar players, and/or dancers. See your Yellow Pages.

Advance Preparation: Make arrangements for entertainment.
Activity: Guests are entertained by Mariachi bands and/or folk dancers.
Variation: Accomplish some of this musical atmosphere with recordings.

Piñata

Ages: 4–adult
Time: 20–30 minutes
Materials Needed: Purchase or make a piñata. You will also need a heavy cord, pulley, broom, and blindfolds.
Advance Preparation: Fill piñata with novelty items, candy, and nuts. Hang the piñata from a hook in the ceiling, a tree limb, or over a basketball hoop. A rope pulley system may also be used.
Activity: Blindfolded guests take turns whacking at the piñata with a broom trying to break it open. Each turn consists of three swings. When the piñata breaks, all dive for the treats.
Note: Simple piñatas can be made from lunch bags. Decorate bags into animal faces or flowers made of tissue paper.

Bean Toss

Ages: 3–adult
Time: 15–20 minutes
Materials Needed: Large sombrero, dry lima beans or pebbles packaged in little tissue paper bags cut from a circle.
Advance Preparation: Purchase hat and beans. Package 10 beans in a little bag—one bag per guest.
Activity: Players stand behind a throwing line which is 10 feet from the sombrero. Guests pitch their beans into the hat. The winner is the one who landed the most beans in the sombrero.
Note: Use bean bags for younger children.

Blind Bargain

Ages: 4–adult
Time: 10 minutes
Materials Needed: Small cards and a silver crayon.
Advance Preparation: Make lottery tickets. Write numbers on all the tickets and color over them with silver crayon.
Activity: Guests scrape off the crayon to see if they have the winning number. You may have more than one winning ticket.

Best Shot

Ages: 7–adult
Time: 15 minutes
Materials Needed: Wood rubber-band gun or a table-tennis ball gun and a large carnival face with an opening through which to shoot a rubber band or table-tennis ball.
Advance Preparation: Create a funny carnival face on poster board and adhere it to a large cardboard box. Purchase guns.
Activity: Players have five shots each. Winners are the players who hit all five shots or some other winning combination.

Bullfight

Ages: 7–10 years
Time: 15 minutes
Materials Needed: Red fabric pieces for the matador's cape.
Advance Preparation: Purchase fabric and cut pieces to resemble a cape sized appropriately for the guests.
Activity: Partners frolic and imitate a bullfight with one another. After a few minutes they may switch roles.

Lotería (Bingo)

Ages: 6–adult
Time: 15 minutes plus
Materials Needed: Mexican bingo game.

Advance Preparation: Purchase game.
Activity: Play Lateria.

Snake Shake

Ages: 5–adult
Time: 15 minutes
Materials Needed: Fiesta music and a disc/tape player.
Advance Preparation: None.
Activity: A leader is chosen (must be quick). Players hold one anothers' hips at the waist with the leader being the head of the snake. The object is for the leader to move and make quick turns from side to side attempting to break the snake. Those who let go are out of the game until a new game begins (the players behind someone who lets go are still part of the snake unless they, too, let go).

Carnival Games

See the Clown/Jester/Carnival, Water/Beach, and Western/Country/Chuck Wagon chapters for additional ideas.

Ring the Bull

Ages: 8–adult
Time: Spontaneous
Materials Needed: Heavy paper, 20-inch square piece of half-inch-thick piece of plywood, five metal coat rack hooks, metal rings (resembling actual rings used to pierce the noses of bulls), colored markers, and cord.
Advance Preparation: Sketch a horned cow's head on the paper and color it with markers. Attach it to plywood with the metal hooks. Attach a shower curtain ring to one end of two 30-inch pieces of cord. Tie the cords on a hook about 20 inches above the bull's head.

Activity: Play like quoits attempting to ring the hooks. Players toss from a toe line about 3 feet from the board. Each successful ring counts one point.

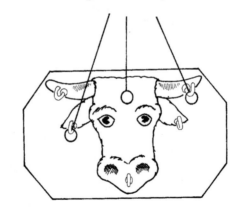

Mexican Folk Dances

"Corrido" (Mexican epic poem/ballad)
"El Jarabe Tapatio"
"Jesusita en Chihuahua" (Jessie polka)
"Caballito Blanco"
"Evangelina" (polka from northern Mexico)
"Las Chiapanecas"
"Mexican Mixer"
"Sandunga"
"Chiapanecas"
"La Llorana"
"Little Old Men"
Also try a bit of authentic flamenco music.

Mexican Folk/Mariachi Tapes

Mexican Fiesta. London Orchestra
Fiesta Mexicana. Francisco Araiza. Deutsch Gramaphone
The Soul of Mexico. Alshire International
The International Mariachi. Aavante Productions, Tucson, Arizona

BRAVO!

7: Oriental

CHINA HONG KONG TAIWAN KOREA JAPAN SINGAPORE

Not so long ago, the Orient seemed remote and strange. A journey to the Far East was mostly a dream—time and travel expense were prohibitive. Communication, trade, and international travel have changed all of this dramatically. Today we enjoy the wonderful culture of the East. Its cuisine, art, and ideas have greatly influenced the world and, even today, the rich culture of the Orient continues to reveal to the Western world more about these people.

For the Orientals, beauty and social thought are important traditions. The actress, artist, and philosopher are highly respected in these cultures. Dance, cloisonné, bonsai, and oriental proverbs are examples of the beautiful traditions that have had an impact on our Western culture.

Enjoy a voyage to the Orient without leaving your own backyard.

INVITATION

Write the invitation message on a miniature kite, fan, or in an origami figure.

JOIN US FOR TEA
Saturday, April 19, 1997
2:00 P.M.–4:00 P.M.
Togos Tea Room • 3100 South Race
Wear your kimono and write a party wish on a small, colorful piece of paper for the "wishing tree."

DECORATIONS

- Display **paper fans** and **umbrellas.** To create fans, pleat paper, punch holes, and tie with a ribbon.
- **Colorful kites/sails/tissue-paper fish** are perfect for decorating the walls and ceiling.
- **Carp windsocks** flutter on poles in late April on Boys' Festival Day. Several carp may fly from one pole—one for each son.

- **Paper lanterns** can be made or purchased. Light them with votive candles.

- Sit on **pillows** and dine on **straw mats.**
- **Karate belts** for each guests are great fun—use black crepe paper.

Cherry and **plum blossom flowers** create an exciting setting. Flowers symbolize both beauty and luxury.

Kishea tassels for guest's hair can be created with tissue paper and straws.

Post **proverbs** all about the party area. You may also have assorted proverbs printed on napkins or type proverbs on cards and display them in little picture frames.

Bells tinkling at the party entrance are delightful.

A "**tree of fortunes**" displays colorful tissue pieces with fortunes written on them in Chinese or Japanese and English (in smaller print). Decorate a small tree outside or an artificial tree inside by hanging the tissue pieces.

Remember the **Chinese gong, symbols, bamboo placemats, screens,** and **vases.**

Create and hang **colorful birds, butterflies, insects,** and **flower kites.**

Hang **red scrolls** symbolizing good luck and prosperity. Script in Chinese calligraphy and decorate border with gold tempera paint.

Burn **incense.**

Fiery dragons are traditional Chinese decorations.

TERMS

Dragon (male)	Pearl	Confucius
Bamboo	Junk	Porcelain
Silk	Origami	Cloisonné
Phoenix (female)	Kite	Ricksha
Cherry blossom	Sampan	Rice paddy
Jade	Pagoda	Kimono
Karate	Yen	Panda
Chopsticks	Genghis Khan	Geisha
Haiku	Dynasty	Coolies
Judo	Marco Polo	Tatami (straw mats)

PROVERBS

Chinese use proverbs in their everyday speech. Their proverbs seldom predict but instead act as a reminder of how people should act and prepare themselves for the future. Most importantly, proverbs carry the wisdom and authority of the past.

Deal with the faults of others as gently as your own.
Think three times, then do it.
Silence is golden.
All that glitters is not gold.
The wise man remains silent while the fool babbles on.
Words whispered on earth sound like thunder in heaven.
Birds of a feather flock together.
It is easier to catch a tiger than to ask a favor.
He who laughs last laughs best.

Don't put two saddles on a horse.
You can't have your cake and eat it too!
Long visits bring short compliments.
People who live in glass houses shouldn't throw stones.
One kind word will keep you warm for three winters.
Two wrongs don't make a right.
The highest towers begin from the ground.
A barking dog never bites.
A fool and his money are soon parted.
He who rides a tiger cannot dismount.
Every cloud has a silver lining.
One dog barks at something, and the rest bark at him.
Every ladle strikes the edge of the rice pot once in a while.
    (Disagreements happen even in the best of families.)
Everyone gives a shove to the tumbling wall.
All good things must come to an end.
A penny saved is a penny earned.
Honesty is the best policy.
Necessity is the mother of invention.
A friend in need is a friend indeed.
Absence makes the heart grow fonder.
Variety is the spice of life.
Health is better than wealth.
Brevity is the soul of wit.
A rolling stone gathers no moss.
Drawing pictures of rice cakes won't stop hunger. (If you really want something,
    you must work hard for it.)

SOME TRADITIONAL FOODS

- Fish/pork
- Lamb/poultry
- Tea
- Tempura
- Fortune cookies
- Mandarin oranges
- Stir-fry
- Hibachi cooking
- Rice

- Decorate a round layer cake with miniature parasols. Tuck parasols (some open and some closed) on top of the cake. Serve dinner on a very low table or grass mat with guests seated around on cushions. Create the table with a piece of plywood and bricks. Remember chopsticks.

FAVORS

- Chinese yo-yos
- Little fans
- Paper blows

- Chinese jump ropes
- Japanese dolls
- Toy tops

ACTIVITIES/GAMES
Hang a Wish Upon a Tree

Ages: 7–adult

Time: As guests arrive

Materials Needed: An ornamental tree in the yard or an indoor tree. Wishes written by the guests or hostess.

Advance Preparation: Write and tie the wishes on the tree.

Activity: If the guests bring wishes, they each hang a wish upon a tree and then remove their shoes before entering the party area. Sometime during the party, guests take a wish and read it aloud. This assures that the wish will come true.

Dragons

Ages: 4–teen

Time: 20–30 minutes

Materials Needed: Oriental disc/tape for background music.

Advance Preparation: Purchase recording or check it out from your library.

Activity: Ten children grasp one another's waist creating a line of children (a dragon). The object is for the front of the line to catch the dragon's tail. If successful, the front person becomes the tail and play continues.

Variation: When the tail is caught, you may have the tail. Do a little dance before falling back in line.

Japanese Shadow Tag

Ages: 4–7 years

Time: 15 minutes

Materials Needed: None

Advance Preparation: None

Activity: Guests chase each other and step on one another's shadow.

Dizzy Tops

Ages: 3–10 years

Time: 20 minutes

Materials Needed: Gaily painted Japanese tops, Oriental music, disc or tape player.

Advance Preparation: Purchase tops and discs/tapes of Oriental music. Set up a disc/tape player.

Activity: Guests spin tops while music plays in the background.

Variation: Re-enact the professional top spinners. Execute a great variety of tricks such as jumping steps, walking an inclined board, and tossing and catching spinning tops on a decorated board.

Origami

Ages: 5–adult

Time: 30–40 minutes

Materials Needed: Origami paper and origami books (check your library).

Advance Preparation: Practice paper folding or arrange for someone proficient in origami to teach guests at the party.

Activity: Fold paper into unique shapes and figures. Music may be playing in the background.

Note: This handcraft has been practiced in Japan for over ten centuries.

Juggling

Ages: 9–adult
Time: 20–40 minutes
Materials Needed: Bean bags and recordings for background music. Plenty of space, away from windows, etc.
Advance Preparation: Purchase or make two/three bean bags per guest.
Activity: Juggle!
Variation: Thrill your guests with breathtaking diabolo stunts. Once the diabolo spins on the string it will begin to hum, and it is ready to be tossed into the air and caught again with the string. It is a

fascinating spinning and flying technique, often defying the laws of gravity. The spinning diabolo needs lots of open space.

Dominoes

Ages: 8–adult
Time: 1–2 hours
Materials Needed: Set of dominoes for every five guests.
Advance Preparation: Know the rules for dominoes

well enough to explain them to guests who do not know how to play.
Activity: Play dominoes. It is great fun.
Note: Dominoes are Chinese in origin.

Flight of the Kites

Ages: 4–adult
Time: 40 minutes
Materials Needed: Kites enough for each guest (guests may bring a kite to the party) and a windy day!
Advance Preparation: Purchase kites or make them.

Locate a safe area to fly several kites at once. Keep away from power lines, utility poles, telephone lines, and trees. Respect others' property.
Activity: Fly kites remembering to keep your back to the wind!

Kite trains: Launch the first kite. When it has reached 30 feet, attach a second kite to the control line. Add kites every 20 feet. Kite trains take a lot of strength.
Ghost flight: Add lights to your kite (battery-operated miniature Christmas lights are great). You may also use luminous paper and fly at night.
Musical kites: Fly a kite using bamboo tubes—the wind whistles through them for a bit of music.
Kite demonstration: Check with a kite/toy store to find someone who would demonstrate kite flying.
Windwands: Fly well even on windless days … 50-foot nylon streamers are attached to 12-foot poles and when flown in numbers will exhilaratingly paint the sky. All ages will enjoy watching windwands flutter merrily on fiberglass flexible poles. You may improvise windwands easily with shorter poles and streamers.
Kites Day: In China, "Kites Day" is celebrated on the ninth day of the ninth moon. It often features "The Dragon Kite."

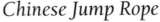

Chinese Jump Rope

Ages: 6–12 years
Time: 30 minutes
Materials Needed: Chinese jump ropes purchased at a toy store. You will need one rope for every three people. Background music.
Advance Preparation: Practice some of the jumps and be prepared to demonstrate.

Activity: Jump rope and have music playing in the background. Two children stretch the rope around their ankles 6 inches above the ground. The third guest jumps inside and outside the rope without touching the rope. Difficulty is determined by moving the legs farther apart.

Paper, Rock, Scissors (Jan, Ken, Po)

Ages: 6–teen
Time: 30 minutes
Materials Needed: None.
Advance Preparation: None.
Activity: Guests play in pairs. Each takes a turn counting one, two, three—show! On show, each extends a hand in one of three positions: fist (rock), two fingers (scissors), or flat hand (paper). Positions which win a round are: stone breaks scissors, scissors will cut paper, and paper wraps stone. If positions are the same, the round ends in a tie. One point is scored for each win. This is an old Japanese game.

Chinese Hop

Ages: 7–12 years
Time: 20 minutes
Materials Needed: One stick (12 inches long) for each guest.
Advance Preparation: Gather sticks and lay them out in rows about 18 inches apart. Keep relay teams small. Remember this as you lay out the sticks for each team.
Activity: On "Go" the first member of each relay team hops over each stick in his row, picks up the last stick, and hops back. Upon returning, he taps the second player who continues the relay. This continues until all sticks have been picked up. If a player's foot touches a stick or if both feet touch down, the player must go back to the starting stick and begin over. The first team to pick up all the sticks is declared the winner. Repeat the game.

Luck of the Dive

Ages: 8–adult
Time: 15 minutes
Materials Needed: Old screwdrivers, old oysters from a fish delicatessen (they will give them away usually), and a few imitation pearls and chains.
Advance Preparation: Collect oysters early and freeze. Purchase a few pearls and chains from a jewelry store. Tuck the pearls in some of the oysters without breaking them open. Be sure to hide the pearls well.
Activity: Each guest is given a raw oyster in a shell and a screwdriver. All open an oyster hoping to find a real pearl in it. Give a chain to those who discovered a pearl in an oyster.

Tinikling

Ages: 9–adult
Time: 30–40 minutes
Materials Needed: Several pairs of bamboo sticks, 2 x 4's that are 24 inches long (a pair for each set of bamboo sticks), a record/tape of Tinikling Dances, and a disc/tape player.
Advance Preparation: Order the recording and practice the dance. Resource: Tinikling Dance, ACC 8095, 9015C Kimbo Educational, 800-631-2187. Purchase the bamboo sticks (bamboo fishing poles) from a sporting goods store. Cut 2 x 4's into 24-inch pieces.
Activity: Demonstrate the Tinikling Dance and then let guests try the dance. It is fun and not too difficult. The disc/tape has talk- and walk-through instructions. Once you learn the basics, move on to make up steps. This dance is done in Taiwan and is a popular dance in the Philippines.

Dragon's Tail Dodge Ball

Ages: 8–adult
Time: 30–50 minutes
Materials Needed: Two or three beach balls or Nerf balls.
Advance Preparation: Purchase the balls.
Activity: Form a large circle with several dragons (two players, one grasping his partner's waist) inside the circle. The object of the game is to hit the dragon's tail (the second player). If successful, the dragon's head becomes the tail and the person throwing the ball becomes the new head. The tail goes back into the circle.
Variation: To make the game more challenging, allow only a bounced pass to hit the dragon's tail.

Giant Fire Dragon Parade (Chinese New Year Procession)

Ages: 3–8 years
Time: 20 minutes
Materials Needed: Large boxes, crepe or butcher paper, foil paper, colored paper, markers, glue, and cord or twine.
Advance Preparation: Link several big boxes together by threading a long cord through all the boxes. Cover the boxes with brightly colored crepe paper. In the first box cut a large eye opening for the leader.
Activity: Children finish decorating the dragon and then stand up under each box to form a giant walking "fire dragon" that invades the party.

Variation: The mighty, wriggling dragon dances through the streets leading a parade. Acrobats, clowns, dancers, jugglers, drummers, percussionists, and stilt walkers join the procession. Play Chinese music, "The Dragon Dance." End with the excitement of firecrackers!

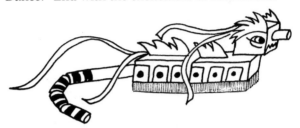

Dragon Boat Festival

Ages: 5–adult
Time: 20 minutes
Materials Needed: Oriental junks or sampans with sails and a pool.
Advance Preparation: Purchase boats or make boats (see "Regatta" in Water/Beach chapter) and fill wading pool with water.

Activity: Guests sail in a Chinese regatta. They must blow their boats across the pool. Young children sail as an activity—they need not race.
Variation: If you are near a lake have races with canoes made into Chinese-style boats.

Chopsticks Marble Pickup

Ages: 8–teen
Time: 15 minutes
Materials Needed: Bowls, marbles, and chopsticks.
Advance Preparation: Gather all the materials needed and put the marbles in bowls.
Activity: Play as a relay. The object of the game is to take a marble from one bowl and place it in another bowl with chopsticks. The first team to finish is the winner. Keep relay teams small.
Variation: Put lots of ice cubes in a tub of warm water. Guests see how many they can pluck out of the water before the cubes melt.

Ribbon Dancing

Ages: 6–adult
Time: 20 minutes
Materials Needed: Crepe paper ribbons or satin ribbons 6 inches to 8 inches in length, 3/8-inch dowels, fishing bait hooks, and music for the ribbon dancing. Attach ribbon to hook and dowel.
Advance Preparation: Make or purchase ribbons for the ribbon activities and order a recording for the dances.

Activity: Participants enjoy simple ribbon movements to music: waves, spirals, swings, circles, figure eights, and jumping over the ribbon. Guests take turns being leader.

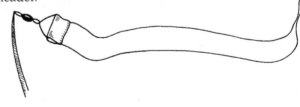

Ball, Hoop and Ribbon Activities for Young Children
(ages 4–8)
KIM 8016C Kimbo Educational, 800-631-2187.

Modern Gymnastics With Ribbons
KIM 4035M Manual
KIM 4035C Kimbo Educational, 800-631-2187.

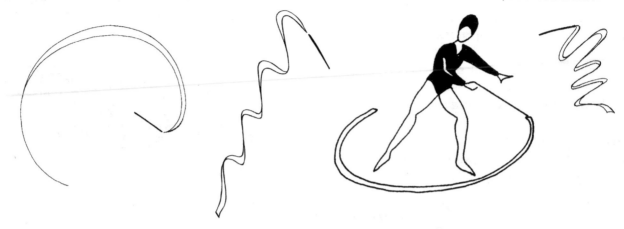

Flowering Tree Relay

Ages: 4–14 years
Time: 15 minutes
Materials Needed: Several small trees or branches and one real or silk flower for each guest.
Advance Preparation: Place trees 10 feet apart and 50 feet in front of the guests. Attach string or a Christmas ornament hook on each flower for fastening to the tree.
Activity: Guests are divided into several teams (keep small). On the signal "Go," the first guest on each team races to his/her tree, attaches a flower, runs back, tags the second team member and goes back to the end of the line. Play continues and the first team to hang all their flowers on the tree wins.
Note: Younger children should just decorate the tree with flowers and you may give them more than one flower to hang. This is a Korean festival game.

Chinese New Year (February 13)

See "Chinese 'Lucky Money'" in New Year chapter.

Doll's Day Celebration
Boy's Day Celebration

See "Catch a Goldfish" in Water/Beach chapter.

Oriental Music Recordings

All the Best from China, #CLUC-CD61. Madacy Inc.
Shakuchi Japanese Flute, #72076. Electra None Such.
Japanese Traditional Instrumental & Vocal Music, #72072. Electra None Such.
Japanese Kabuki and Other Traditional Music (puppet and theatrical opera), #72084. Electra None Such.
China Shantung Folk and Instrumental Pieces, #72051. Electra None Such.
Music of Chinese Pipa, #72085. Electra None Such.
Phases of the Moon Traditional Chinese Music, #MT36705. CBS.

SEE YOU ON THE ROAD TO SHANGRI-LA!

8: The Pacific Islands

HAWAII   ❀   SOUTH SEA ISLANDS   ❀   PHILIPPINES

Like the Orient, the Pacific Islands were remote and inaccessible to the rest of the world until the great trade routes opened in the late 1700s. Captain James Cook was probably the best known of the explorers who introduced Western ways (both good and bad) to the peoples of the Pacific, and at the same time brought news of life in "paradise" to the "civilized" world. Close behind the explorers, Christian missionaries arrived in the islands, bringing with them their religion and customs. The Polynesians, Malays, and others were great mariners themselves and, as a result, intermixed their own cultures and cuisine. It's in this balmy, beautiful tropical atmosphere that East meets West and island meets island.

Set the mood of your favorite island paradise and charm your guests with its cuisine and cultural arts. Set sail on a warm summer's evening.

INVITATION

ALOHA

Hele Mai Polynesian Luau

Date _____

Time _____

Place _____

_____

R.S.V.P. _____

Wear sandals, bright shirts, muumuus, and straw hats.

DECORATIONS

- Hostess welcomes guests with **leis** usually made of **flowers**. Leis are also made from feathers, nuts, seeds, and shells. Favorite flowers used for leis include carnations, jasmine, orchids, plumeria, tuberoses, and ginger.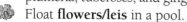
- Float **flowers/leis** in a pool.
- **Bamboo torches** create a wonderful environment for the luau.
- **Garden torches** are large candles on a stick that can be stuck in the ground. Also use **tiki** or **oil-burning lamps**.
- **Fans/shells** are popular in island decorations.
- Place a **baby orchid** or a **parasol** at each place setting.
- The **hibiscus** is the state flower of Hawaii.
- Hang colorful **kites/sock fish** about the party area.
- Remember the **gong**.
- Fill **outrigger canoe models** with nuts.
- Display **colorful birds** in the trees or on poles.
- Burn **incense**.
- Incorporate **bamboo mats** and **palm leaves**.
- Decorate with **foliage**—ti, monstera, lycopodium, dracaena, and hala leaves.
- **Rattan** or **wicker chairs** create an island look.
- Fly **flags** from the island countries.

- Adorn the party area with **garlands of flowers** and **assorted tropical flowers**.
- Create a **grass hut** using grocery bags cut like grass and layered around a card table. You may also use **bamboo mats**. Make or purchase **palm trees** and indoor **ornamental trees**. Wrap a limb with burlap or brown paper bag strips. Cut leaves from a heavy green paper.

- Display **shellfish, starfish,** etc. in a draped **badminton net**.
- **Tapa paper** and **ti leaves** are used as table coverings.
- Let **wind chimes** ring throughout the party.
- Hang colorful **lanterns**.
- Post **Hawaiian street signs**—Kapiolani Boulevard or Kalakaua Avenue.

ISLAND TERMS

Balmy	Lei Day (May 1)	Archipelago
Brilliant	Enchanting	Polynesian (many islands)
Beachcomber	Tropical paradise	Gong
Grass skirts	Exotic	Torch lighting
Enticing cuisine	Lagoon	Volcano

HAWAIIAN WORDS

Ae—yes
Ai—eat
Aloha—love; greetings; welcome; farewell
Hale—house
Hale Maui—come here
Hiamoe—sleep
Hauoli—happy
Hula—dance
Kane—man
Mahalo—thanks
Mahimahi—a delicious fish

Maikai—good or handsome
Kai—sea
Menu—bird
Mole—old chanted song
Moku—island
Moana—ocean
Muumuu—loose long dress
Nani—beautiful
Kaukau—food
Keiki—child
Ko—sugar cane
Lani—sky, heavenly

Lei—wreath or garland
Luau—feast
Poi—food from taro plant
Pua—flower

Puili—bamboo
Wahine—woman
Wai—water
Wikiwiki—hurry

FOODS

- Rice
- Fish
- Spiced chicken
- Spiced pork
- Bananas
- Papayas
- Pineapples
- Coconut

- Macadamia nuts
- Poi
- Serve tropical fruits in coconut shells.
- Kalua pig roasted in a pit is always featured at a luau. Two costumed natives carry the roasted pig on a shoulder-high platform around the pool past the tables.

FAVORS

- Leis of fresh flowers, shells, nuts, leaves, or seeds (you may order leis from your florist)
- Beachcomber hats
- Macadamia nuts

ACTIVITIES/GAMES
Hula Dance

Ages: 5–adult
Time: 30–40 minutes
Materials Needed: Hula dancers or music for hula dancing and someone who can teach some basic movements. Dancers wear grass skirts, tea leaf skirts, long dresses, and colorful cloth skirts.
Advance Preparation: Make arrangements for dancers or a hula dance teacher. Purchase or make grass skirts (fringe grocery bags or tissue paper and tape around waists).
Activity: Guests enjoy hula dancers or may participate in learning the hula. Dancing is still the most famous and popular art of the islands. Hula dancers sway their hips and wave their arms very gracefully to music. These rhythmic movements tell stories. Dancers stand with knees bent while feet remain flat on the floor. The hands gracefully tell the stories: rippling motion depicts water, arched fingertips depict the rainbow, etc. The dance ends with hands forward, palms down, and a bow. The dances are accompanied by a ukulele/Hawaiian steel guitar and a drum. Others may accompany with rhythm instruments.
Variation: Create hula puppets with brown lunch bags.

Fire Dancing

Ages: 3–adult
Time: 20 minutes
Materials Needed: A professional fire dancer.
Advance Preparation: Make arrangements for a professional fire dancer to perform at your party. See "Entertainment" in your Yellow Pages.
Activity: Guests enjoy watching a fire dancer.
Note: This dance came from Samoa.

Puili-Hawaiian Rhythm Sticks

Ages: 8–adult
Time: 30–40 minutes
Materials Needed: Puili sticks and island music. Resource: Puili-Hawaiian Rhythm Sticks ACC 7046 (10 Puili Stick 7/8 of an inch diameter), 7046C Kimbo Educational 800-631-2187.

Advance Preparation: Order music and purchase or make puili sticks. Practice enough to demonstrate the rhythm of puili sticks.
Activity: Individuals and partners do routines to island music such as "Hukilau."

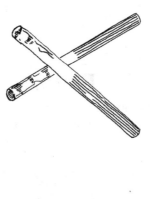

Limbo Dance

Ages: 7–adult
Time: 30 minutes
Materials Needed: Calypso music and bamboo sticks.
Advance Preparation: Purchase records/tapes of Calypso music and two or three bamboo sticks.
Activity: Each guest dances his way under a pole held up horizontally, bending backward to avoid touching the pole as it is progressively lowered.
Note: This dance in sometimes done at luau parties but it originated in the British West Indies with the African slaves.

Shell Game

Ages: 6–adult
Time: 30 minutes
Materials Needed: Several clam shells and one or more pearls. Marbles may be substituted for pearls.
Advance Preparation: Gather shells and purchase pearls.
Activity: Each group of guests gathers around a shell master with three shells. Under one shell will be a pearl. The shell master disguises the pearl under the shells by moving the shells around. Players guess under which shell lies the pearl. The winner keeps the pearl.
Variation: This may be played with chips and guests may gamble on each game—guessing where they will find the pearl.

Outrigger Racing

Ages: 7–adult
Time: 30–40 minutes
Materials Needed: Small toy canoes, plastic banana split bowls, pencils, straws, rubber bands, waterproof glue (hot glue gun), and wading pools.
Advance Preparation: Fill pools with water and make a sample outrigger.

Activity: Race the boats. Younger children play as an activity.
Variation: Construct outriggers from cucumbers or plastic banana dishes.

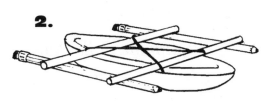

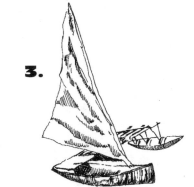

Kite Flying

See "Flight of the Kites" in the Oriental chapter.

Poi Dancing

Ages: 8–adult
Time: 30 minutes
Materials Needed: Poi balls and soft Maori music (chant). Colorful ribbons and free-flowing skirts. Dancers wear ribbons around their foreheads.
Advance Preparation: Purchase or make poi balls: tennis balls wrapped in fabric and attached with a 9-inch cord.
Activity: Guests enjoy watching a group of graceful dancers or participating in this graceful folk dance. They form a line with someone at the head of the line who calls out the dance movements. The poi ball movements are similar to the yo-yo—arcs, around the world, over the shoulder, over the head, around the ankles and knees, underhand, forward and backward, and always in unison and perfect rhythm. The dance movements imitate the flight of butterflies, swimming fish, gliding birds, etc.
Note: This dance came from the Maori people in New Zealand.

Hawaiian Songs

"Hawaiian Wedding Song"
"Hawaii Beyond the Reef"
"Sweet Leilani"
"Aloha Oe"
"Hawaii Ponoi" (state song)
"Song of the Islands"
"Like No a Like"—"Remembrance"
"Don Ho"
"Sing Me a Song of the Islands"
"Blue Hawaii"
"Drifting and Dreaming"
"Song of Old Hawaii"
"Across the Sea"

Island Recordings

Moonlight Time in Old Hawaii. Vault Records.
Blue Hawaii. Peters International.
Calimbo Steel Band #62 (includes the limbo). GNP.

Filipino Songs

"Lulay" ("Serenade")
"Nan Soboy" ("We Pray")

Philippine Folk Dances

"Apat Apat"
"Carenosa"
"Chotis DeNegros"
"Liki"
"Palay Dance"
"Pandango Sallaw"
"Rigodon"

ALOHA!

9: Pirate/Nautical/Shipwreck/Calypso

The subject of piracy continues to excite imaginations and pique curiosity in spite of its ambiguousness and historic distortions. Piracy is the legacy of a crueler age when the world was wild and lawless, "might was right," and independence was guarded fiercely. The pirates themselves were often fleeing from the miseries of poverty, unemployment, indentured servitude, or slavery.

Piracy has flourished through the ages in many parts of the world. Earliest Mediterranean civilizations plundered each other's vessels. Vikings pillaged the European coasts; Barbary corsairs of Northern Africa robbed ships in the Mediterranean; Europeans (the Dutch, French, and mainly the British) plundered the Caribbean and the Americas. As the world grew smaller and more civilized, piracy faded. Today only rumors of buried treasure and swashbuckling legends remain.

The terms "pirate" and "privateer" are often confused. A pirate is one who robs ships on the high seas while a privateer commands a privately owned ship commissioned by sovereignty to capture "enemy" ships. It's easy to see how one country's privateer could be another's pirate. For example, Sir Frances Drake was an English hero and a villain to the Spanish. And, while the English called John Paul Jones a pirate, he was an American hero! Samuel Clemens, commenting on his Elizabethan pirate ancestors, explained it well: "But this is no discredit to them for so were Drake and Hawkins and others. It was a respectable trade then and monarchies were partners in it."

INVITATION

On brown wrapping paper, create a treasure map. Char the edges, roll, and tie with twine. Place invitations in old bottles and hand deliver.

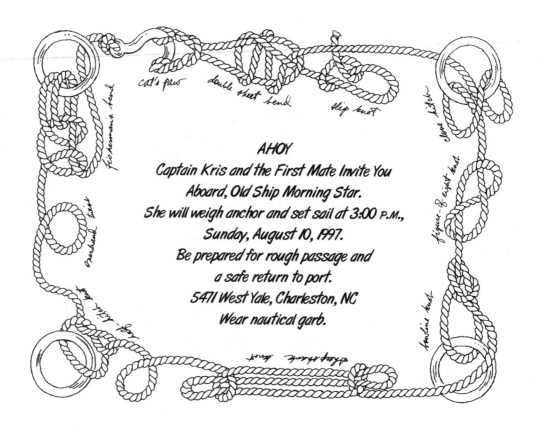

AHOY
Captain Kris and the First Mate Invite You
Aboard, Old Ship Morning Star.
She will weigh anchor and set sail at 3:00 P.M.,
Sunday, August 10, 1997.
Be prepared for rough passage and
a safe return to port.
5471 West Yale, Charleston, NC
Wear nautical garb.

Pirate Costume

Earrings, red kerchief tied over head, patch over an eye, unshaven stubble (use eyebrow pencil), calico-cotton shorts, sash, thongs, rubber sword, hook for hand, tricorn hat, and a pirate's hat are a few ideas for a pirate's costume.

Signing on the Crew

As guests arrive to board the ship, the captain has them sign a parchment scroll with a quill pen and says, "Make your mark!" Then he says, "On board!"

DECORATIONS

⚓ Remember **nautical flags** and the **red flag.**

⚓ Hang a large **treasure map** on the front door.

⚓ Mark party location with a **skull and crossbones flag** (black and white cloth).

⚓ Display **stuffed birds** about the party area. If you have a parakeet, let it become a part of the party atmosphere.

⚓ Use any nautical paraphernalia such as **anchors, fish, shells, ship's wheel, nets, glass floats,** and **flags.**

⚓ Fill an old trunk with **treasures** (old jewelry, etc.).

⚓ Burn **torches** and build a **bonfire.**

⚓ Drape and coil **old ropes.**

⚓ Hang **ball and chains** by an old **pirate ship** created out of cardboard. Add a **cannon** or two!

⚓ Get out your **Halloween skeletons!**

⚓ Light **old candles** placed in the top of rum bottles.

⚓ Light **old lanterns** and place them around the party area.

⚓ Find an **old ship's telescope** or make them with gold foil paper or brass paper from a craft store.

⚓ Fill a small **treasure chest** with "gold." Attach each piece with fishing line and run it to each guest's place setting. Each guest pulls a line for a piece of gold.

⚓ Make **signs** with wood or cardboard using pirate lingo.

⚓ Place a **gangplank** at the party entrance.

⚓ Decorate the serving table with **bright shiny pennies** (brighten with 3 T. salt and ½ cup vinegar).

⚓ Fabricate a **pirates' den/cave** from a large box or card table. Drape with a tarpaulin or brown cloth.

⚓ Cover tables with **burlap cloths.**

⚓ Let a **parrot** preside over the table!

⚓ Add pirates' paraphernalia to the den: **old kegs, chains, skeletons, old pieces of wood, rum bottles, mugs, Jolly Roger flag, barrels, playing cards,** and **nets** (badminton).

⚓ Nestle a **crocodile** and **ticking clock** in a corner.

⚓ Transform the backyard treehouse into Robinson Crusoe's island house.

NAUTICAL/PIRATE TERMS

Galley
"No-prey, no-pay"
Maroon
Brotherhood
"Man the quarter-deck"
Prize
Grog
"Give us a jug"
Booty
Porthole
"Yo ho ho and a bottle of rum"
Gold
Swashbucklers
Bounty
Cargo
Buried treasure
"Hit the deck"
Castaway
Seaworthy lad
"Man overboard!"

Mutiny
Fetch
"Ye fools"
Pillage
Saint's blood
"Man the lifeboats"
Knots
Plunder
Cutlass/sword/dagger
Ahoy
Pirates' den
Swarthy ruffian
High seas
"Thar she blows!"
Walking the plank
Scuttlebutt (gossip)
Peg leg
One-legged Jolly Roger (flag)
Admiral
Starboard/port

Leeward/windward
Steward
Bow/stern
Disembark
Traitor
Dastardly
Full measure
Crafty
Hark-ye
Merry life
Fierce
Numskulls
Seamen
Rascals
Fair shares
Flogged
Curses
Lusty lad
Bowels of pity
Galleons

CREW

Captain
Sailing Master
Musicians
First Mate

Quartermaster
Boatswain
Head Steward
Surgeon

Gunner
Navigators
Purser
Carpenter

KINDS OF PIRATES

Freebooters—pirates or plunderers.
Buccaneers—English, French, or Dutch freebooters who preyed on Spanish ships and colonies along the Spanish coasts of America in the 1600s.
Privateers—an armed private ship commissioned to cruise against the commerce or warships of an enemy.
Corsairs—a privateer of the Barbary Coast who had an official assignment from a sovereign state to harass enemy ships.
Mutineers—someone who refused to obey constituted authority (especially military or naval authority).

Sea Hawks
Sea Dogs
Sea Wolves

Sea Rovers
River Pirates
Noble Rovers

Marauders
Cutthroats
Seagoing Villains

FAMOUS PIRATES/SEAFARERS

Blackbeard
Peter Pan

Barbarossa (Red Beard)
Captain Blood

Ben Gunn
Khair-ed-Din (Barbarossa)

Black Bart
Captain Hook
Sir Frances Drake
Blue Beard
Captain Kidd
Captain Greaves
Fletcher Christian
Captain Cook
Sir Henry Morgan
Robinson Crusoe

Ale Pichinin
Jean Laffite
Bartholomew
Roberts
Long Ben
Captain Pete
Long John Silver
Mary Read
Sir John Hawkins
Calico Jack

Rackham
Captain Blood
Anne Bonny
Captain Thomas
Tew
Eric Bloodaxe
Ching Yih
Captain Chang
Paow
Captain Bellamy

Pirate Ships

Tiger
Morning Star
Black Angel
Prophet Daniel
Buck

Happy Delivery
Blessings
Peace
Revenge

Amity
Golden Hind
Sugar
Whidaw

Piracy Articles

When a man joined a pirate crew, he had to sign the pirate's articles (rules) and swear over a Bible or ax that he would follow them.

I   Every man shall obey civil command and have an equal vote in the affairs of the moment.

II   If a man defrauds the company, he shall be marooned with one bottle of powder, one bottle of water, and one small arm and shot.

III   If any man rob another he shall have his nose and ears slit and be put ashore where he shall encounter hardship.

IV   If anyone shall game for money with either cards or dice or be blasphemous, he shall be flogged or marooned.

V   The candles should be put out at eight at night…if any man desire to drink after that hour, he shall sit upon the deck in darkness.

VI   Each man shall keep his cutlass and pistol clean. …fit for engagement at all times or shall be cut off from his share of the prize and suffer other punishment.

VII   If a man deserts in time of battle, he shall be punished by death or marooned.

VIII   If any man shall lose a limb or become crippled he shall have 800 Pieces of Eight from the common stock. For lesser hurts proportionately.

IX   The captain and quartermaster shall each receive three shares of a prize. The master gunner and the boatswain two shares, all other officers one and one half and private gentlemen one share.

X   If any man meets a prudent woman and offers to meddle with her without her consent, he shall suffer death.

REFRESHMENTS

⚓ Drinks served in mugs or coconut shells.

⚓ Treat guests to fresh fruits, fish, salted meat, and biscuits. Biscuits and salt beef were the daily diet of pirates.

⚓ Salmagundi (grand pirate salad) is made with marinated meat tossed with pickled vegetables, eggs, and anchovies; seasoned with garlic, salt, pepper, vinegar, and oil.

⚓ Rum, beer, gin, grog, and sherry were popular pirate drinks.

FAVORS

⚓ Gold party rings
⚓ Toy pistols
⚓ Eye patches
⚓ Jewelry
⚓ Chocolate coins
⚓ Telescope
⚓ Rubber swords/knives
⚓ Bandannas
⚓ Sea stories

⚓ Scarves
⚓ Play money
⚓ *Treasure Island*
⚓ Recording of *Pirates of the Caribbean*
⚓ Compass
⚓ Pirate hat
⚓ Foil bubble-gum coins
⚓ Dice
⚓ Deck of playing cards

ACTIVITIES/GAMES
Crocodile Search

Ages: 3–9 years
Time: 15 minutes
Materials Needed: Inflatable crocodile.
Advance Preparation: Inflate and hide the crocodile. If by a lake, hide it partially in the water.

Activity: Guests hunt for the giant crocodile. The first to discover the crocodile is the winner. Do this at the beginning of the party so children may play with crocodile in the pool or lake.
Variation: Make a tape of "swamp sounds" and play near the crocodile.

Pirate Treasure Hunt

Ages: 8–adult
Time: 20–30 minutes
Materials Needed: Treasure maps and treasures. A compass is optional for guests 10 years and older.
Advance Preparation: Create the maps using visual signs and clear directions ("take five steps to the flower box," etc.). Keep difficulty appropriate for the age of the pirates. Hide treasures in various locations. Pirates may search individually or in small groups.
Activity: Pirates or groups of pirates are each given a map and begin the search for treasure. Activity ends when each group of pirates has found its treasure.

Variation: With older pirates, create an orienteering map and put a flag at each destination. The flags will help keep the groups of pirates on course. Boy or Girl Scout compasses are easy for young treasure hunters to use.

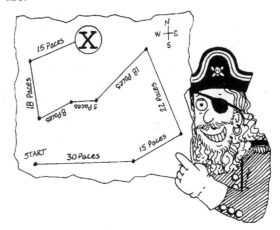

Pieces of Eight

Ages: 8–adult
Time: 10 minutes
Materials Needed: Treasure chest, surprise packages wrapped in metallic gold paper.

Advance Preparation: Wrap favors in metallic gold paper and place them in an old trunk.
Activity: When guests leave, each takes a party treasure favor.

Go for the Gold

Ages: 8–adult
Time: 10–15 minutes
Materials Needed: A treasure chest and a key that will open the chest. Additional keys that look like the "golden key" and treasure.
Advance Preparation: Put treasures in the chest and gather enough keys for each pirate. You may use a combination lock and different combinations.

Activity: Each guest attempts to open the chest with his key. Try to arrange guests so that the person with the golden key is near the end of the line to open the chest. You may have several keys that open the chest and several treasures.
Variation: Sing or play the song, "Yo Ho Blow the Man Down," when playing this game.

Magic Treasure

Ages: 8–teen
Time: 15–20 minutes
Materials Needed: Sack of coins for each guest pirate and several treasure chests.
Advance Preparation: Bag assorted coins for each guest. Each bag should have the same number of coins. Decorate several treasure chests.
Activity: Give each pirate a bag of coins. Three or four guests stand 6 feet behind a treasure chest and toss their coins into the chest. Pirates may keep all the coins

that land in their own treasure chest. The activity ends when all pirates have tossed their coins.

Sailor's Escape

Ages: 4–9 years
Time: 10 minutes
Materials Needed: Bandannas and sailor hats.
Advance Preparation: Purchase enough bandannas and hats for each guest.

Activity: Tie bandannas around the heads of half the guests (pirates). Put sailor hats on the remaining half of the guests (sailors). All the sailors hide. If the pirates find all the sailors in less than 5 minutes, they win a treasure chest full of treasures! Repeat the game and have all the guests exchange hats.

Pirate's Ship Caravan

Ages: 8–12 years
Time: 10–15 minutes
Materials Needed: Wading pool, large tub from a hardware store or tank from a farm store, and toy sailing ships.

Advance Preparation: Purchase the ships and fill the tub with water.
Activity: Blow the ships across the pool. The first ships to reach the other side are the winners. This may also be done in a relay.

Charades of the Sea

Ages: 10–adult
Time: 30–40 minutes
Materials Needed: Paper and pencils.

Advance Preparation: Make a lists of nautical terms.
Activity: Play charades using sea terms or ship parts.

Saint's Blood

Ages: 8–12 years
Time: 10–15 minutes
Materials Needed: Caran D'ache water-soluble crayons, wet sponge, fake blood, mirrors, and paper towels.

Advance Preparation: Gather all materials and set them out on a table.
Activity: Pirates paint themselves with scars and slashes.

Calypso Limbo Dance

Ages: 7–adult
Time: 30 minutes
Materials Needed: Calypso music and bamboo sticks.
Advance Preparation: Purchase discs/tapes of Calypso music and one or two bamboo sticks.

Activity: Each guest dances his way under a rod held up horizontally, bending backward to avoid touching the rod as it is progressively lowered.
Note: Reggae music may be used for this dance.

Calypso Folk Music

Ages: 8–adult
Time: 30 minutes–1 hour
Materials Needed: Discs/tapes of Calypso music and disc/tape players. Hire a Calypso group.
Advance Preparation: Purchase the music or make arrangements for a professional group.
Activity: Guests enjoy Calypso and dances such as the tango, rumba, cha-cha-cha, and mambo.

Note: Calypso is a folk music that originated in the British West Indies among the African slaves who worked the plantations on the island of Trinidad. The improvised words of a calypso song are very important—more than the music. Spontaneously making up clever words and rhymes about some matter of current interest marked a good calypso singer. Calypso became very popular and spread throughout the Caribbean and other parts of the world.

Dig for the Treasure

Ages: 4–12 years
Time: 10–15 minutes
Materials Needed: Wading pool/box/trunk, sand or Styrofoam packing, and treasures to hide in the sand.
Advance Preparation: Fill the pool, box, or trunk with choice of filler and hide favors in it.

Activity: The pirates search for the treasure. Determine the number of treasures each may find and keep.
Variation: Hide pennies in the sand. To brighten the pennies, soak them in 3 T. salt and 1/2 cup vinegar.

Shipwreck

Ages: 5–10 years
Time: 10 minutes
Materials Needed: An old stuffed chair, coffee table, etc.
Advance Preparation: Locate all articles needed.
Activity: One guest is designated the "Captain." The Captain calls out "shipwreck" and names a place where the sailors can go for safety—front step, a picnic table, etc. The sailors all climb on the object squeezing together. Those who cannot get on fall off and are out of the game. The Captain continues calling out "shipwreck" and names objects upon which the sailors may climb. The trick is that more and more sailors fall off because the captain names smaller and smaller places. Repeat play. Be careful not to put guests in dangerous places.

Variation: Captain calls out orders for the crew. "On board and mates in galley"… line up and assign pirate names; "Roll call"… line up and call pirate names; "Life boats"… sit three guests behind one another (toboggan style) and sing "Row, Row, Row Your Boat"; "Man overboard"… jump into the pool; "Mates in galley"… all hold hands; "Hit the deck"… lie on floor; "Scrub the deck"… all on hands and knees scrubbing; "Crow's nest"… kneel on one knee and look out with a spyglass; "Shipwreck"… freeze; "Pirate Attack"… man the torpedoes (run to a tree): "In the brig"… make arrest and put a pirate in jail! Go over commands and actions before starting the game. Use cones/frisbees to mark the bow, stern, starboard, and port sides of the boat.

Pirate Poem

"Where are the days that have been, and the seasons that we have seen, when we might sing, swear, drink, drab and kill men as freely as your cake-makers do flies … when the whole sea was our Empire, where we robbed at will, and the world but our garden where we walked for sport?"

—*Captain John Ward, Pirate*

Nautical Songs

"Sailing Sailing"
"The Road to Mandalay"
"Anchors Aweigh"
"Barnacle Bill the Sailor"
"Three Little Fishies"
"Asleep in the Deep"
"Bells of the Sea"
"Red Sails in the Sunset"
"Sailor's Hornpipe"
"Row, Row, Row Your Boat"
"Michael, Row the Boat Ashore"
"Blow, Winds, Blow" (A pirate song)

Sea Chantey Songs

Sea chanteys were folk songs of seafaring men. A popular version of these songs was the call-response form. Chanteymen with a talent for singing sang the solo lines and the responses were sung by the crew as they worked, pulling and hoisting the jibs and sails.

"Blow the Man Down" ("Blow" meant "Knock")
"Haul on the Bowline"
"Rio Grande"
"Blow, Boys, Blow"
"Reuben Ranzo"
"Hul Away, Joe"
"Paddy Doyle's Boots"
"Rolling Home"
"Good Bye Fare-Ye-Well"
"Drunken Sailor"
"The Codfish Shanty"
"Bottle O!"
"Shenandoah"

Calypso Songs

"Mary Ann"
"Banana Boat Song"
"Calypso Holiday"

Nautical/Island Recordings

Northeast Winds Ireland by Sail, #6S230. Folk Era.
Northeast Winds Songs from Ireland and the Sea. Folk Era.
The Boarding Party Tis Our Sailor Time, C97. Folk-Legacy Records, Inc.
All Along the Merrimac. Folk Era.
The Boarding Party Fair Winds and a Following Sea, C-109. Folk-Legacy Records, Inc.
The Heart of Trinidad. GNP.
Calimbo Steel Band (includes the Limbo), #62. GNP.
Calypso 1912–1937. Rounder.
Peter Pan. RCA.
Pirates of the Caribbean. Disney.

SHARE A BIT OF THE PRIZE!

10: Safari Party

Join a caravan and journey to Kenya and Tanzania in the wilds of eastern Africa. There, game-rich plains and woodlands have long attracted hunters in search of exotic wildlife. Today, however, the adventure consists of hunting the big game with cameras rather than guns. Outfit the hunters and climb aboard a Land Cruiser for a very special safari expedition. With the sun just peeking over the horizon and a hunting guide ready, prepare to enjoy the spectacular history and tribal lore of the African bush. By day's end, you are ready to sit by an evening campfire in the wilderness and listen to a storyteller sharing tales of Africa.

INVITATION

GRAB A VINE AND
SWING OVER TO A SAFARI PARTY
Saturday, May 31, 1997
3:00 P.M.
Dayton's Hinterlands
3100 South Chase
Dress for an African Safari
R.S.V.P. 555-9100

Note: Include little sponge animal capsules in the invitations for children. Seal with a safari animal sticker and write "hand cancel" on the envelope.

DECORATIONS

🦒 Place **stuffed animals** around the party room. Hide in trees, bushes, fences—a monkey climbing a rope, etc.

🦒 Create a **backyard jungle.** Hang a rope from a tree to resemble a vine from which guests may swing.

🦒 Make or find **animal skin drums.**

🦒 Hang **posters**—roaring lion, snarling tiger, African children, African shields, safari hunts, etc. Check with a travel agent for old books with beautiful pictures.

🦒 **African wood carvings** of assorted animals make delightful table decorations.

🦒 Create a large **grass hut**—use a card table or box as a base. Cut grocery bags to resemble grass and wrap around the card table or box. Grass mats, found at an import store, also work well to create a grass hut.

- Cover the tables with **leopard fabric**.
- Cluster **coconuts, banana bunches,** and **animals** on the serving table.
- Hang **inflated plastic safari animals** all around the party area—in trees, etc.
- Create large **life-sized animals** cut out of cardboard or Styrofoam sheets. Paint and set them out in the game preserve.
- Recycle **safari expedition posters.** Travel agents often have outdated posters and travel books. Better yet, generate expedition posters on your computer.

- Drape or hang **mosquito netting/cheesecloth.** Fabricate a tent over a picnic table using poles in the center and at the corners. Purchase netting at camping stores.

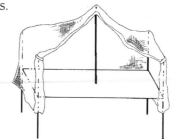

SAFARI TERMS

Tom-toms
Loincloths
Jungle gear
Pith helmets
Witch doctor
Gazelle
Hunter
Herds
Giraffes
Vine
Elephants
Wild boar
Stalking
Monkey/apes
Antelope
Natives

Tiger
Leopard
Tarzan and Jane
Lion
Hippopotamus
Grass huts
Zebra
Rhinoceros
Quicksand
African veldt
Wildebeest
Jackals
Pink flamingos
Baboons
Alligator

Cats
Storks
Game preserve
Bwana
Snakes
Prowl
Cheetahs
Slither
Land Rover
Majestic
Lion's den
Explorer
Adventure
Watering hole
Grazing/grasslands

REFRESHMENTS

- Box of animal crackers may be used at every place setting.
- Fresh fruits, especially coconuts and bananas.
- Cake decorated with animal crackers (also use as candle holders).

- Jungle juice.
- Make animal-shaped sugar cookies.
- Bake a snake in miniature bread pans. Carve the head round and slice in half. Decorate with clusters of tiny jelly beans and a red licorice piece for the tongue.

FAVORS

- Safari hats
- African animal wood carvings
- Toy snakes
- Plastic inflatable animals

- Plastic animals
- Bird whistles
- Bug boxes
- Butterfly nets

ACTIVITIES/GAMES
Baby Elephant Walk/March

Ages: 3–6 years
Time: 10–15 minutes
Materials Needed: "Baby Elephant Walk" recording or sheet music purchased at a music store and a disc/tape player.
Advance Preparation: Check equipment and music. Be familiar with the tumbling stunt and elephant walk.
Activity: Demonstrate the elephant walk. Guests pretend they are elephants and do the elephant walk to the music, "Baby Elephant Walk," from the Paramount Picture, *Hatari.*

Variation: Add commands.
   "Halt"—Elephants stop!
   "Left Face"—Elephants turn left!
   "Right Face"—Elephants turn right!
   "About Face"—Elephants turn around!
   "Attention"—Elephants salute!
Directions: Children bend over keeping legs and arms straight. Place hands flat on the floor and walk with heavy elephant steps.

Wild Animal Balloon Sculptures

Ages: 3–10 years
Time: Spontaneous toward the end of the party
Materials Needed: A person who creates balloon sculptures.

Advance Preparation: Hire someone who does balloon sculptures. See "Balloons" in your Yellow Pages.
Activity: Guests receive a balloon sculpture.

Safari Expedition

Ages: 3–12 years
Time: Spontaneous throughout the party
Materials Needed: Tents.
Advance Preparation: Set up tents or lean-to's created with tarpaulins.

Activity: Guests enjoy storytelling or other activities in the tent or under a lean-to.
Variation: Older guests would enjoy an overnight in the wilds under a tent or lean-to.

African Storyteller

Ages: All ages
Time: 30 minutes
Materials Needed: Actor/dramatist.
Advance Preparation: Hire or seek out a friend to be an African storyteller. Check out African folk tales from your library.
Activity: Guests enjoy African folk tales told by a storyteller. Keep in mind that the African storyteller often combines the art of acting and drama as he tells a story. He alters his voice and uses mime to act the parts of

each character. African proverbs and riddles are also popular among storytellers.
Variation: Animal tricksters are important in African folklore. In the United States, "Bre'r Rabbit" is a popular trickster. The Hare and Tortoise are primary tricksters in Nigeria and East Africa. Also, station storyteller assistants in different parts of the jungle. As the story unfolds, strange sounds come from various places in the jungle!

African Dancers

Ages: All ages
Time: 15–25 minutes
Materials Needed: Professional African Dancers.

Advance Preparation: Check the Yellow Pages for an African Dance Group or a college dance group. Arrange to have them perform for your party.
Activity: Dancers entertain safari guests.

Taboo

Ages: 7–adult
Time: Throughout the party
Materials Needed: One small bag of beans for each guest.
Advance Preparation: Fill each bag with the same number of beans—about 30.
Activity: The words "yes" and "no" are taboo. Guests may

not use these words throughout the party. Each time a guest catches another using the taboo words, the culprit must forfeit a bean. Guests with the most beans win.
Note: Taboos are quite popular in Africa. They may be put on a snack, extra food, objects, or something harmful.

African Farm Tea

Ages: adult
Time: 2 hours
Materials Needed: Wicker or canvas porch furniture, pith helmets, wooden serving pieces, and English stoneware.
Advance Preparation: Bring out the linens, stoneware,

and farm-fresh foods (grapes, pineapple fritters, crullers, mulberry jam, dark bread, and custard-based pies). Place a hydrangea plant in a helmet for the centerpiece.
Activity: Take tea with some friends on the porch, gazebo, or patio in a setting of jungle greens and grasslands. Remember a pink flamingo.

Bag a Lion

Ages: 3–7 years
Time: 15 minutes
Materials Needed: Large box, yellow tag board, black magic marker, and bean bags.
Advance Preparation: Create a lion's head from tag board. Attach it to the box. Cut out a large open mouth. Make or buy bean bags. For a bit of dimension add yarn to the mane.

Activity: Hunters toss bean bags into the lion's mouth. Each guest has three to five tosses. Keep score only with the older children.

On a Safari

Ages: 3–10 years
Time: 25 minutes
Materials Needed: See the Backyard Sports Fest chapter for obstacle course directions. In addition you will need large boxes, rubber snakes, and large stuffed safari animals or plastic inflatable animals from a novelty store. Hanging vines (ropes), swimming pool (river), and people costumed as a gorilla, lion, elephant, etc.

Advance Preparation: Create a jungle maze (obstacle course) through which hunters must climb, jump, or crawl. Hang a good climbing rope on which guests may swing. Knots in the rope will make it easier to hang on.
Activity: Hunters go on a safari through the wilds of Africa. They walk cautiously, avoiding dangerous jungle animals. The activity may be timed or additional physical limitations may be placed on the hunters.

Monkey Sling

Ages: 3–12 years
Time: 15–20 minutes
Materials Needed: Plastic inflatable monkey or a stuffed monkey covered with a plastic bag. Inexpensive sponges and a pail of water.

Advance Preparation: Hang the monkey high in a tree.
Activity: Guests throw wet sponges attempting to knock the monkey out of the tree. You may keep score for the older children. Small children throw as an activity.

Catch a Monkey's Tail

Ages: 3–8 years
Time: 15–20 minutes
Materials Needed: Brown fabric strips (2 inches by 12 inches).
Advance Preparation: Make 6 fabric monkey tails.
Activity: Guests are monkeys and hunters (²/₃ hunters and ¹/₃ monkeys). The game begins with the monkeys putting a tail in a back pocket and running out into the jungle. The hunters line up along a fence and on a given signal, the hunters disperse into the jungle and try to catch a monkey's tail. As soon as a hunter nabs a tail he goes back to the hut and prepares to be a monkey for the next hunt. The hunt ends when all the tails are nabbed. A new hunt then begins with new monkeys.
Note: Hunters may not hold a monkey or be rough with a monkey when nabbing a tail. For small children, you may simplify the rules further.

Campfire

Ages: 6–adult
Time: 30–60 minutes
Materials Needed: Firewood, fire pit, and songs or stories for the entertainment around the campfire.
Advance Preparation: Prepare fire pit in an open area for the campfire. Purchase or cut firewood. Arrange for the entertainment.
Activity: Sit around the campfire and prepare your evening meal, sing songs, or tell stories.

Please Feed the Elephants

Ages: 3–10 years
Time: 10 minutes
Materials Needed: Several coffee cans, cellophane tape, markers, peanuts, and construction paper.
Advance Preparation: Decorate each can and put a number on it. These are elephant feeding bowls.
Activity: Guests are given five to ten peanuts each which they must use to feed the elephants. From a designated spot, guests throw nuts into the bowls. The guest with the highest score wins. Keep score with older children only.
Variation: Have certain numbers written down ahead of time. The scores closest to the numbers written win!

Ring an Elephant's Trunk

Ages: 4–12 years
Time: 10 minutes
Materials Needed: Gray tag board (3 sheets), strong tape, strong paper plates, and markers.
Advance Preparation: Make an elephant's head with posterboard. Create a 3-inch-diameter trunk out of poster board. Cut little slits in a circle above the elephant's mouth and push the trunk through the slits. Tape the trunk on the back side. Cut centers from the paper plates to create rings. Make six to nine rings.

Activity: Hunters ring the elephant's trunk. Each hunter has five tries. Each ring scores two points. Smaller children play as an activity and do not keep score.

Elegant Elephant Soccer

See "Crazy Soccer" in Special Birthdays chapter.

Safari Stationery

Ages: 4–12 years
Time: 20 minutes
Materials Needed: Packets of plain, inexpensive stationery or stationery tablets, washable ink pads, and fine-point markers.
Advance Preparation: Prepare sample stationery using thumbprint animals on the stationery.

Activity: Guests create safari animal stationery. Have practice paper and an ink pad for each guest. Make thumbprints and draw in the animal features on each piece of stationery. Small guests create fewer pieces of stationery.

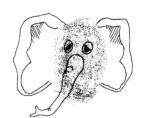

An Adventure

Ages: Teen–adult
Time: 1 hour
Materials Needed: The documentary film *Headhunters of Borneo* or hire an explorer (hunter) who has a story to tell!
Advance Preparation: Arrange for the film or an explorer to come to your party.

Activity: Guests will enjoy the documentary film or a safari presentation given by an explorer (hunter).
Variation: Bring the game preserve to your party. Hire an animal trainer and a few of her animals from the zoo. Be sure to check references.

Jungle Puppet Show

Ages: 3–10 years
Time: 15–20 minutes
Materials Needed: Puppet stage (blanket fastened across a doorway, a tipped card table, a bush or large box), and jungle animal puppets.
Advance Preparation: Set up a stage and have guests bring puppets or gather puppets yourself. Practice giving directions for an impromptu puppet show.
Activity: Explain to the guests that they are going to perform an impromptu puppet show.

1. Select two characters at a time.
2. Let the characters practice for a short time.
3. Remind the participants to be natural, speaking and acting just as the characters would.
4. Sample characters—two jungle explorers, two jungle animals, or a hunter and a monkey hiding in a tree.

Note: Youngest guests can either watch older children put on an impromptu puppet show or they can parade their animals across the puppet stage with a simple message or animal sound. Add music!

Bug Hunt

Ages: 4–9 years
Time: 15 minutes
Materials Needed: Butterfly nets and bug boxes.
Advance Preparation: Purchase nets and boxes.

Activity: At the close of the party give each child a butterfly net and a bug box. Let them catch bugs until they are ready to leave.

Elephant Feast

Ages: 3–7 years
Time: 10–15 minutes
Materials Needed: Cardboard box (medium size), paint or markers, peanuts in the shell, and a serrated knife.
Advance Preparation: Paint or draw a large elephant face on front of box. Cut a hole for the mouth (larger mouth for younger children).

Activity: Children throw peanuts in the elephant's mouth. This may become a relay for older children. A relay will necessitate two or more boxes. Teams of three or four will make the activity move quickly.

Spear a Little Fruit
(Tropical Bird Shoot)

Ages: 6–teen
Time: 20 minutes
Materials Needed: Balloons, chopsticks, pencils, dowels, or blow guns.
Advance Preparation: Blow up several balloons and place them loosely among branches in a tree or throughout the jungle.

Activity: Natives attempt to jar the fruit (balloons) out of the tree by throwing the spears. Activity ends when all the fruit has been speared out of the tree.
Variation: Use African blow guns to jar the balloons. Create balloon birds by adding feathers and eyes (seals or draw with markers). Bag a few birds with blow guns. Feathers of tropical birds were highly prized!

Jungle Party

Ages: 7–adult
Time: 10–15 minutes
Materials Needed: Wicker paper-plate holders, assorted fruits (limes, oranges, bananas, packaged dried fruit).
Advance Preparation: Just before the party begins, hide fruit all around the party area (jungle).
Activity: The guests (natives) are preparing for a big jungle celebration and must search the jungle for fruit. Natives go into the jungle and pick the hidden fruit.

The winner is the guest with the most pieces of fruit. After the search for fruit is over, have the natives place their fruit in a bag. Next, the guests line up and balance wicker plates on their heads. On a given signal, they walk toward the village (designated line) balancing the wicker plates. Should the plates fall off, guests must stop and balance them before they can proceed again toward the village. The guest who reaches the village first becomes the village chief.

Rolling Hoop Target

Ages: 8–teen
Time: 15 minutes
Materials Needed: Hula Hoop and bean bags or crumpled soda cans.

Advance Preparation: Locate materials needed.
Activity: The object of this game is to see how many bags or cans pass through the hoop at one time. Participants, each with a bag or can in hand, stand in a

line or semicircle. A hoop is rolled in front of the group and on a given signal guests throw their bags through the moving hoop simultaneously. The degree of difficulty is determined by the size and speed of the hoop's roll.

Variation: Throw the hoop through the air at varying speeds.

Lion Tamer

Ages: 5–10 years
Time: 10–15 minutes
Materials Needed: Large boxes, serrated knife, a whistle, cord or heavy string, and props for lion tamer.
Advance Preparation: Make five cages out of large boxes or mark cages with cord on the ground. Collect costume props for the lion tamer (keep it simple). Cages can be made by cutting bars on the face sides of the large boxes. You may also paint the boxes if you have extra time. To make the game go smoothly the lion tamer should use a whistle attached to a lanyard.

Activity: Choose a lion tamer to catch lions. Children (lions) crawl back and forth between two safety zones trying to escape a tag by the lion tamer. At the blow of a whistle, lions continue to leave the safety zones. When lions are tagged they must go directly to a cage. As the cages fill up, the lions rotate back into the game. An adult should supervise the cage rotation. Rotate the position of lion tamer often. Stop play when children are still enjoying the game.

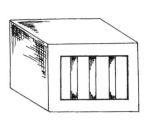 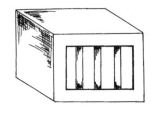 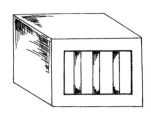

Jungle Story

Ages: 3–9 years
Time: 15–30 minutes
Materials Needed: Story and costume props for story characters. Puppets or stuffed jungle animals.
Advance Preparation: Choose a story appropriate for the age of guests. Practice reading or telling the story.
Activity: Read or tell the story. Use puppets or stuffed animals to give it more life. Guests may act out the parts or dress like the story characters with simple costumes.

Variation: Storyteller assistants create animal sounds from behind bushes in the backyard during designated parts of the story.

Lasso a Giraffe

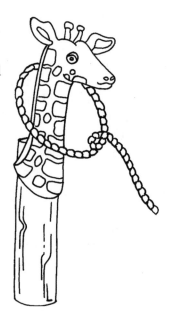

Ages: 7–10 years
Time: 15 minutes
Materials Needed: Three sheets of yellow tag board, brown construction paper, tape, scissors, lasso rope (for directions, see "Rope-Spinning Tricks" in Western/Country/Chuck Wagon chapter) or Hula Hoop.
Advance Preparation: Cut a giraffe head and decorate it. Attach the giraffe head to a post or make a neck with rolled poster board pieces stacked in a column. Make two or three lasso ropes and practice.

Activity: Guests lasso a giraffe with a lasso rope or Hula Hoop. They may have three tries to catch the giraffe. Older guests may keep score.

Wild Gorilla

Ages: 8–adult
Time: 10–20 minutes
Materials Needed: A gorilla suit rented from a costume rental company. If the costume is not available locally, arrange for rental by mail. Be sure to reserve the costume well in advance.
Advance Preparation: Rent a gorilla suit.
Activity: As guests arrive, the gorilla greets them with a big hug!

Top Spinning

Ages: 6–adult
Time: 20 minutes
Materials Needed: Coconut shells and enough tops for every guest.
Advance Preparation: Collect shells and purchase tops.
Activity: Line up lots of coconut shells which will be the targets. One player after another spins the top attempting to hit a coconut shell with the spinning tops. If a shell is hit, the player claims it and keeps it. The player with the most shells is the winner.
Variation: Spin and pass giant tops through goal posts (cone with sticks).

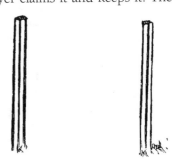

Elephant Train

Ages: 3–8 years
Time: 15 minutes
Materials Needed: Several boxes, cord, gray felt, gray spray paint, "The Baby Elephant Walk" song and a disc/tape player.
Advance Preparation: Cut a hole in the bottom of each box for the child's head, paint boxes gray, add large elephant ears and a trunk. Connect the train by threading a cord through all the boxes.
Activity: Children form a giant elephant train. The train moves about to the music, "The Baby Elephant Walk."

Comet or Bolo Throw

Ages: 9–adult
Time: 20–30 minutes
Materials Needed: Rocks, golf balls, leather or cloth pouches, streamers, and string.
Advance Preparation: Make comets by encasing a golf ball or rocks in a leather or cloth pouch. Insert streamers and wrap with string.
Activity: Toss at a target as a carnival game. Supervise this activity well.
Note: African boys are very adept at throwing javelins, sticks, and rocks when hunting. Darts are also a favorite contest. These activities are very similar to some of the Native American games found in the Thanksgiving/Native American Indian chapter.

Singu (Juggling)

Ages: 10–adult
Time: 20–30 minutes
Materials Needed: Small pieces of coconut shell and kukuinu nuts. You may substitute seashells and golf balls for shells and nuts.
Advance Preparation: Gather shells and nuts—one shell and two nuts for each guest.
Activity: Nestle the coconut shell in the palm of the left hand as fingers are bent. To begin juggling, players hold the shell in the left hand with the palm facing up. Place one nut on top of the shell and hold the second nut in the right hand. Throw the right nut into the air and catch it in the left hand clicking on the shell as it lands. While the right nut is in the air, quickly grab the left nut with your right hand. You are in a starting position once again. Now toss the left nut up in the air and while it is suspended in the air, quickly bring the right hand and nut over and tap the shell in the left hand to make a click. Catch the left nut in the left hand making a click. This completes a simple juggling pattern. Repeat several times. If everyone becomes good enough, form two lines with partners facing one another. Instead of throwing the nut straight up into the air, throw it across to your partner. All jugglers start at the same time and repeat the pattern several times.

Safari Music Recordings
Tropical Jungle.
The Nature Company.

Saving the Wildlife,
Mannheim Steamroller.
American Gramaphone Records,
Inc.

PROWL OVER AND EXPLORE THE WILDS OF AFRICA!

II: Space Mission

People have traveled into space for a long time, but our first journeys were imaginary—in science fiction. For example, in 1865, Jules Verne, the author of *Twenty Thousand Leagues Under the Sea,* also wrote a story about a trip to the moon, titled *From the Earth to the Moon.* This story and others like it were simply fantastic and quite impossible. However, on October 4, 1957, these stories suddenly became reality. *Sputnik I* was launched by the U.S.S.R. marking the beginning of the Space Age. Since then, hundreds of craft have been launched into space. Take your Martians and Earthlings on a journey into space orbiting the planets for a special mission featuring unidentified flying objects and ice-cream cone space capsules.

INVITATION

Address guests on the envelopes as Astronaut _____. Younger children may wish to dress as astronauts with moon boots, etc. You will need to indicate this on the invitation.

MISSION: JUSTIN'S BIRTHDAY PARTY
BLASTOFF: Saturday, December 20, 1997
COMMAND BASE: 3305 Pierce Place
Denver, Colorado
United States
North American Continent
Planet Earth

SCHEDULE
TIME—ACTIVITY
1700—Arrival
1715—Preflight Dinner
1800—Briefing (space video)
2030—Astronaut's Snack
2045—Mission Assignments (space games)
2130—Mission Complete (departure)
For permanent assignment on the spaceship,
call Justin at 555-2292.

ARRIVAL

When guests arrive give them name tags with space assignments—commander, flight director, launch director, mission director, medical director, pilot, payload specialist, and recovery director. For small children, draw spaceships or characters on their name tags.

Greet guests with a remote-control robot—all ages will enjoy it! Purchase robots at a novelty or electronics store.

Play "space music" as guests arrive giving them an "unearthly" feeling. "Kitaro in Person" from Canyon Records and "Fresh Aire V," a Mannheim Steamroller tape from American Gramaphone Records, are excellent for background music. Synthesizer albums called "Music from the Hearts of Space" are also very good.

DECORATIONS

- Cover table with **dark blue tablecloths.**
- Place **blue votive candles** on a mirror or foil to decorate the party table.
- **Space toys** and **characters** make excellent centerpieces.
- **Glitter paper** is excellent for festive space decorations.
- Fabricate a **large paper spaceship** for the front door.
- Build a large **three-dimensional spaceship** from gray tag board and place it outside the front door or by the mailbox.
- Hang foil-covered **moons** and **stars.**
- Brighten the room with **self-sticking luminous stars.**
- String **white blinking Christmas lights.**
- Suspend **large Styrofoam balls** that have been covered with foil, tissue paper, or **blue** and **white** balloons.

- Sprinkle **sparkling confetti** on the party table.
- Tie **helium-filled balloons** on the chairs, etc.
- Create a dark room. Hang **black landscape plastic** on the party room walls and adhere luminous stars.
- Drape **dark blue** and **gray crepe paper streamers** or **foil serpentine.**
- Fly **sky sculptures.** Attach kite strings to bunches of helium-filled balloons. Trail crepe paper strands from the balloon bunches.
- Create **planets** with round balloons and **rockets** with long balloons. For larger planets use giant-sized balloons.

SPACE TERMS

Asteroid	Jettison	Meteorite
Robot	Laser	Lunar
Star	Rocket fuel	Reentry
Atmosphere	Satellite	Thrust
Galaxy	Space probes	Blastoff
Nova	Galactic	Solar system
Rocket	Launch pad	Control panel
Spaceship	Docking orbiters	Trek
Compute	Mission control	Aliens
Rendezvous	UFO	Liftoff
Booster	Ozone	Meteor
Planet	Tracking	Beam
Moon dust/rocks	Capsule	Moon
Eclipse	Sun spots	Extraterrestrials
Clone	Command module	Teleporter
Space dust	Stardust	Comet
Martian	Milky Way	Starlight adventures
Command center	On target	Cosmic journey
Mission successful	Countdown	Orbit

SOME FAMOUS SPACECRAFT

- Sputnik I & II (Russian satellites)
- Explorer I (First American satellite)
- Vostok I (Russian Yuri Gagarin orbited the Earth)
- Freedom 7 (Alan Shepard Jr., first American to enter space)
- Liberty Bell 7 (Virgil Grissom)
- Friendship 7 (John Glenn, first American to orbit Earth)
- Faith 7 (Gordon Cooper orbited Earth)
- Molly Brown (Virgil Grissom, John Young orbited Earth)
- Gemini 4–11 (two-man flights preparing for space exploration)
- Eagle (lunar module)
- Mariner 10
- Apollo 7–10 (preliminary moon flights)
- Apollo 11 (Neil Armstrong and Ed Aldrin moon walk)
- Skylab II (first orbiting space station)
- Voyager I (sent to Jupiter and Saturn)
- Voyager II (grand tour of outer solar system)
- Atlantis (space shuttle)
- Discovery (launching military satellites)

"That's one small step for a man, one giant leap for mankind."
—*Neil Armstrong, on taking the first human steps on the moon*

PLANET SYMBOLS

☿ Mercury   ♄ Saturn

♀ Venus   ♅ Uranus

⊕ Earth   ♆ Neptune

♂ Mars   ♇ Pluto

♃ Jupiter

REFRESHMENTS

- Serve space food (dried fruit, nuts, beef jerky, etc.).
- Create a "power pack" menu using space terminology ("booster burgers," "moon dogs," "liquid fuel," "Milky Way candy," etc.).
- Make a rocket cake by inserting a toy rocket into the center of an angel food cake. Surround it with trick candles.
- Serve juice in cartons (astronauts must drink from sealed containers).
- Ice-cream cone space capsules are great for the space party. Fill cones with soft ice cream and freeze. Pipe a country name on each cone with a decorator tube from the grocery store. Serve inverted cone (capsule) on a flattened foil muffin cup.

FAVORS

- Rockets filled with space treats (use a paper towel tube and glitter paper)
- Space books or science fiction paperback books
- Power pack bags filled with space paraphernalia
- Space characters
- "Space Dust" candy
- Toy rockets/hand helicopters/gliders

ACTIVITIES/GAMES
Jump the Planet

Ages: 7–12 years
Time: 10 minutes
Materials Needed: A ball, rope, and large bag.
Advance Preparation: Put a volleyball or a playground ball into a bag. Tie a long rope to the bag.
Activity: Players form a large circle. One player is in the center and swings the rope with the ball (planet) on the end. The object of the game is to jump the planet as it moves around the circle. If a player is touched by the planet, she must go out of the game until another player is touched, then she can rotate back into the circle. Only one player is out at a time.

Rocket Launch

Ages: 3–6 years
Time: 40 minutes
Materials Needed: Large boxes or tubes, cardboard/poster board (for fins, guages, switches), clear plastic yard goods, strapping tape, twine, paint, markers, paper cups, handles or knobs (spools), and any paraphernalia for space instruments. Silver spray paint.
Advance Preparation: Create spaceships. Spray paint the boxes silver and construct one or more spaceships. Create a control panel for each spaceship. Some of the instruments may be drawn on the control panel. Let guests help construct the control panels by gluing knobs, spools, etc. Construct the control panels as part of the party activity—must be well organized and should only take 15 minutes of the party time.
Activity: Guests pretend they are astronauts and pilot the ship through space.
Variation: Prerecord a narration of a ride through space. Below are some ideas to get you started:

"This is your pilot speaking."
"We are ready for liftoff."
"Check your equipment."
"The countdown and blastoff!"
"We are moving into interplanetary space … the Earth is becoming very small."
"Look out—meteoroids ahead."
"We are entering the Milky Way Galaxy, etc."
"Buckle up—we're entering a cosmic dust storm."
"We are back in our galaxy … Earth is in view."
"Fire the retro-rockets."
"May Day! Coming in for a hot landing!"
"Splashdown and mission accomplished!"
"Astronauts disembark."

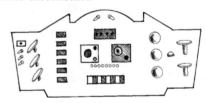

Shuttle Launch

Ages: 7–12 years
Time: 15–20 minutes
Materials Needed: Hula Hoops, wire hangers, gold/silver foil paper, string, paper clips, tacks, tape, and scissors.
Advance Preparation: Hang Hula Hoops where shuttles can be flown without interruption. Make two sample shuttles.

Activity: Children construct paper rockets and sail them through the hoops. Determine a boundary line (launch pad) from which the "shuttles" are launched. To make the launch more difficult, slowly turn the hoops.
Variation: Set up a long course outside. Fly for distance.

Paper Space Shuttle

1. Fold an 8 ½ x 11 inch sheet of foil paper in half.

2. Fold the corners at one end to the center fold line.

3. Now fold these corners over again to center fold.

4. Fold up the sides.

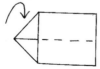
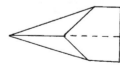

5. Fold both sides back creating wings. Make a narrow body.

6. Tape/staple nose together.

7. Add paper clips to front of the wings and tape back together.

8. For stability, add a 1-inch section of paper tubing to the back. Attach with paper clips. You are ready to launch!

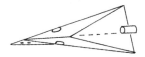

Flight Into Space (Relay)

Ages: 7–12 years
Time: 10–15 minutes
Materials Needed: Paper space shuttles, card tables, Hula Hoops, wire coat hangers, foil paper, paper clips, tape, tacks, toilet paper tubes, and scissors.
Advance Preparation: Make a sample space shuttle and set up a space obstacle course.

1. Landing pad: shuttle must land on a table from 12 feet away.
2. Cosmic dust storm: shuttle must pass through a doorway, a Hula Hoop, and wire hangers which are bent open.
3. Bad weather: shuttle must fly over a chair.

Activity: Astronauts are divided into several relay teams. Each team may be given a name—Saturn, Martians, etc. At liftoff, each team begins flight. Tell astronauts that a serious cosmic dust storm is occurring and there are many obstacles in space. Watch out for the meteoroids! Team members must fly through and around the obstacles to reach the space stations. The first team to have all members finish the course is the winner. Keep teams small—about four on a team.
Variation: Glue and staple tart-sized pie pans together forming flying saucers. Fly the saucers through the hoops.

Parachute Launch

Ages: 7–teen
Time: 15 minutes
Materials Needed: Vinegar, soda, 1-quart soda or wine bottles, paper towels, corks, plastic bags, string, quick-drying glue, large carpet tacks, and tape.
Advance Preparation: Cut plastic bags into 14-inch square pieces, enough for each guest to have one piece. Cut strings into 14-inch lengths (4 for each parachute). Prepare a sample parachute and be able to demonstrate how to roll up the parachute before each launch. Make a launch pad on the patio or wherever the launches will take place.

Activity: Launch parachutes from a 1-quart soda or wine bottle. The astronauts fill their bottles with ½ cup water and ½ cup vinegar. Put 1 tsp. soda in a small piece of paper towel, roll it up and wrap the ends. To prepare for launch, astronauts place the soda in the bottle, positioned on the launch pad. They quickly insert the cork, step back and watch the launch! Guests may also launch their parachutes from a tree, a second-story window, or deck without using the soda-vinegar mixture.

Directions for Parachute Construction

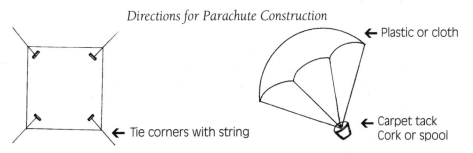

← Plastic or cloth

← Tie corners with string

← Carpet tack
Cork or spool

Variation: Tie a space character to the parachute or purchase novelty parachutists. Guests throw the parachutes high into the air attempting to land them in a (1-foot circle) target area. The target area should be larger for younger children.

Moon Rock Pickup

Ages: 3–adult
Time: 20 minutes
Materials Needed: Old pieces of paper crumpled to form moon rocks or real rocks, toy robot claw hand or barbecue tongs.
Advance Preparation: Gather or make moon rocks. Purchase toy robot claw hands or borrow tongs.
Activity: Astronauts are divided into several teams (four members on a team). To begin the relay, the first astro-naut in each team leaves his spaceship (toe line) at a starting signal, walks out on the moon (about 30 feet from their space ship), picks up a moon rock, and returns it to his team's ship (large box). Repeat space walks until all the moon rocks are picked up. The team picking up all their rocks first is the winning team. Young children should play this as an activity. Each should have a claw to pick up moon rocks.

Adventure Into Space

Ages: 4–10 years
Time: 15 minutes
Materials Needed: Aluminum foil and a space bag.
Advance Preparation: Make little meteoroids (marble sized) from the aluminum foil. Hide them in space (party area).
Activity: Astronauts navigate in space searching for meteoroids. They collect meteoroids and place them in their space bag. At the end of the search, astronauts go to the space store and exchange the meteoroids for a prize. The prizes may have different values and the larger meteoroids may be worth more.
Variation: Make meteoroid paths leading to various planets. Paths begin at the launch pad and each astro-naut follows her path to a planet. A prize may await each participant at the end of the path.

Zodiac Signs

Ages: 7–adult
Time: 10 minutes
Materials Needed: Birth date of all the guests, zodiac signs and astrological information (check your library), and note cards (that will work for place cards).
Advance Preparation: Draw the zodiac sign and write the astrological information for each guest on the cards.
Activity: Guests enjoy a kind of fortune-telling called astrology.

Space Rendezvous

Ages: 2–6 years
Time: 10–15 minutes
Materials Needed: Giant balls or balloons, balloon sticks, markers, space probe surprises (moon dust, etc.), American flag stickers, masking tape, and the audio-tape, "Journey into Space." Resource: "Journey into Space," KIM 9108, Kimbo Educational, 800-631-2187.
Advance Preparation: Blow up balloons and attach to a balloon stick to stabilize. Space them around the party area. If balls or balloons are not available, create giant planets with poster board. Decorate and hang or stabi-lize with a box. Tape space probe surprises to the last planet. Purchase audiotape.
Activity: Children pretend they are astronauts and take a journey into space to visit the planets. Give each as-tronaut an American flag. Let the guest of honor be the captain and lead the young astronauts through space. As they journey and visit each planet, the captain leads them in a hop, jump, skip, run, or moon walk from planet to planet. When they reach the first planet, one astronaut places a flag sticker on the planet and gives it a name. The activity ends when all the planets have been visited, flags placed by each planet, and the last planet probed for a space surprise.
Note: There should be one planet for each astronaut. Each may take home a flag as a party favor. You may also wish to provide space music for this activity.

Moon Crater Walk

Ages: 3–6 years
Time: 10 minutes
Materials Needed: Deep-dish paper plates and space music.
Advance Preparation: Place the craters (plates) about the party area.
Activity: Little astronauts walk carefully on the craters pretending to be on the moon. Play music during the walk. You may give each child a toy robot claw hand.
Variation: Create moon craters with pillows or cushions laid out in a small area. Cover with a blanket or king-sized spread. Darken room with a black light and astronauts jump from one crater to another. Add a bit of fun by hiding stars (pennies covered with luminous tape) in the crevices.

Robot Walk

Ages: 3–6 years
Time: 10 minutes
Materials Needed: Disc/tape player, space music with a march tempo.
Advance Preparation: Check equipment and music.
Activity: All guests pretend to be robots and walk stiffly. One guest is the leader (captain) and leads the other robots around the space platform area. Play space music.

Navigate Your Space Lifeline

Ages: 4–adult
Time: 15–20 minutes
Materials Needed: Several old skeins of yarn (each guest having a different color) and a space prize for each guest.
Advance Preparation: Intertwine 300-foot yarn pieces about the yard or party area. Determine a starting place (spaceship) where each astronaut will pick up his lifeline.
Activity: Guests follow their lifelines to the end of the journey into space where they will discover a space surprise.
Note: The lifeline should be shorter for small children—about 80 feet. The astronauts wind up the yarn as they journey through space toward their destination.

Balloon Rocket Flight

Ages: 6–teen
Time: 20 minutes
Materials Needed: Plastic straws, long balloons, rubber bands, and recipe cards.
Advance Preparation: Make a sample rocket and cut the recipe cards to the appropriate size.
Activity: Guests blow up the balloons through the attached straws and then release them flying through the air.

Moon Ball

Ages: 7–adult
Time: 30–40 minutes
Materials Needed: Beach ball, glow-in-the-dark spray paint, and a volleyball net. Black light may be used indoors.
Advance Preparation: Paint beach ball with luminous paint and set up a volleyball net.
Activity: Play volleyball in the dark with a moon ball.
Variation: Players stand in a circle and keep the moon aloft as long as possible.

Mission Impossible

Ages: 6–12 years
Time: 20 minutes
Materials Needed: Glow-in-the-dark spray paint or chalk, flashlight, space paraphernalia, and old file folders with "important" documents.
Advance Preparation: Spray-paint paraphernalia and file folders filled with important documents. Hide in space.
Activity: In a darkened room, Earthlings search the planets for hidden papers (secrets with global significance) and space paraphernalia. The object of the mission is to locate the objects and return them back to Earth (base) without being caught.

Laser Tag

Ages: 7–adult
Time: 30 minutes
Materials Needed: Two flashlights and large boxes.
Advance Preparation: Purchase flashlight and batteries. Fabricate a space station with boxes.
Activity: In a darkened room or backyard, players hide in space as the Space Patrol counts to 50. The Patrol guards the space station with a laser gun (flashlight). The object of the game is for all the invaders to reach the space station without being caught in the laser's beam. The first invader to be frozen with the laser's beam is the next Space Patrol. Begin a new game when all players have been frozen or have returned safely to the space station.

Satellite in Orbit

Ages: 6–12 years
Time: 15 minutes
Materials Needed: Blankets enough for each team and several beach balls (satellites). Music if desired.
Advance Preparation: Collect all materials needed.
Activity: Guests are divided into two or more teams. Each team holds a blanket. One beach ball is passed from one blanket to another. Pass back and forth until one team misses. The other team/teams then earn a score. Play continues for a certain length of time or until a certain score is reached.
Variation: Place three or four balls in each blanket. The object of the game is to keep all the balls in orbit. The team keeping their satellites in orbit longest is the winner.

ALL SYSTEMS GO!

12: Tom Sawyer Adventure

The real genius of Samuel Clemens, better known as Mark Twain, was his ability to make people laugh. With a twinkle in his eye, he told tales on the Mississippi River steamboats and later around miners' campfires in the Southwest. Many of these funny stories echoed his mischievous and spirited boyhood in Hannibal, Missouri, and his experiences as a riverboat pilot. When he began to write down these stories, he acquired his pen name "Mark Twain." It was one of the signals Sam heard used in his days on the Mississippi River. When the water was 2 fathoms (or 12 feet) deep and safe for navigation, the bowman, who measured its depth with a knotted rope, would yell, "Mark Twain."

INVITATION

Make a mini origami frog and glue it on a note card. Directions for origami can be found at your library.

DECORATIONS

🐸 Fabricate a **Tom Sawyer hideout** with slingshots, corncob pipes, straw hats, bags of treasure, fishing poles made of limbs, old maps/papers, and wicker fishing baskets.

🐸 Display **nautical paraphernalia**—flags, ship's wheel, ropes, compass, chronometer, simple navigation charts or maps drawn on old paper sacks, fog signals (bells, whistles, and sirens), logbook, and buoys.

🐸 Remember **Becky Thatcher paraphernalia**—parasols, bonnets, etc. Exhibit **old boat replicas** or **pictures** of **old riverboats** and **rafts**.

🐸 Build a **large raft** from small logs lashed together ... remember the sail. Light a hideout with **old lanterns** and a **bonfire**.

🐸 Fabricate a **cemetery** with **gravestones** made of Styrofoam insulation or pieces of poster board.

TOM'S TERMS

Adventures	Charm	Fishing
Gang	Island	Pickins'
Raft	Sandbar	Trouble
Aim	Corncob pipes	Freckles
Graveyard	Dreaded	Critters
Reckon	Stroll	Pirates
Bare feet	Crawdads	Tricked
Hollering	Lazy	Frog jumping
Respectable	Scalawag	Jubilee
Bats	Explore	Prowling
Whooping	Loot	Whitewash
Reform	T'aint	Steamboat a'comin
Bribe	Fetch	"Get on board"
Hideout	Mischievous	Mark Twain
Ribiter (frog)	Swimin' hole	Lurking
Cave	Foolin' around	Pilot house
Hooky	Mississippi mud	Anchors aweigh
Riverboat	Treasure	

STORY CHARACTERS

Tom Sawyer	Huckleberry Finn	Muff Potter
Becky Thatcher	Big Jim	The cat
Aunt Polly	Ben	Injun Joe
Sid		

REFRESHMENTS

- Cake
- Lemonade served in pint jars
- Watermelon
- Red checkered tablecloth
- Mint julep tea
- "Slumgullion" (a meat stew)
- Create a cave with sugar cubes and frosting on top of the birthday cake.
- Surround the cave with a raft, gold treasure coins, rope, etc. Use cinnamon sticks or tongue depressors for the raft.

FAVORS

- Water guns
- Corncob pipes. (Order from Mark Twain Book and Gift Shop, 213 Hill, Hannibal, MO 63401, 314-221-2140.)
- Bandannas (put prizes in bandannas).
- Mark Twain books, especially the short story, "The Celebrated Jumping Frog of Calaveras County."
- Flashlights/pen lights
- Candy cigarettes or bubble gum cigars

ACTIVITIES/GAMES
Cave Meanderings

Ages: 4–14 years
Time: 15–20 minutes
Materials Needed: Kite string and bags of treasure.
Advance Preparation: Run the kite string (one for each guest) throughout the party area. Run it under bushes, around obstacles, and behind trees, etc. At the end of each string is a treasure.

Activity: Guests pretend they are lost in the cave as

were Tom Sawyer and Becky Thatcher. Guests follow their kite string to keep from becoming lost as they search the cave for the treasure.

Variation: This may also be done in a dark room or at night outside. Use flashlights to assist you in the dark. You may wish to do this activity first and have the bubble gum cigars, corncob pipes, etc. in the bags of treasure.

Torch Tag

Ages: 8–14 years
Time: 30–60 minutes
Materials Needed: One flashlight for each guest.
Advance Preparation: Collect flashlights and check batteries.

Activity: Tom Sawyer loved to play detective games. In a darkened room or outdoors at night, guests play hide-and-seek with flashlights. You are "It" if you are the first one spotted with the flashlight.

Tom Sawyer and Becky Thatcher Look-Alike Contest

Ages: 4–14 years
Time: 15 minutes
Materials Needed: Straw hats, suspenders, long skirts, bonnets, parasols, fishing pole, bandannas, and rope belts.

Advance Preparation: Indicate this activity on the invitation and include ideas for costumes.
Activity: Select the guests who most resemble Tom and Becky. You may want to have more than one set of winners or take pictures of all the guests.

Whitewash the Fence

Ages: 4–14 years
Time: 15 minutes
Materials Needed: Whitewash, brushes, paper towels, soap, and water. Use large or small boards and vary the size of the paintbrushes accordingly. Paint shirts and drop cloths. Whitewash can be made by mixing water-based paint and water.
Advance Preparation: Find boards and materials

needed for this activity. Test brush size with board sizes to keep activity in the time frame allotted.
Activity: Guests whitewash the fence. Prizes given for the fence best covered in the fastest time.
Variation: For older guests, play this as a relay. Each guest takes two turns painting two old boards. Teams should have only three or four members so turns come up quickly.

"On Board"

Ages: 4–14 years
Time: 10 minutes at the beginning of the party and 15 minutes at the end of the party.
Materials Needed: Small limbs or tongue depressors, saw, scissors, heavy paper for sails, permanent marker, waterproof glue, swimming pool, straws, steam whistle, and an electric fan.
Advance Preparation: Make a sample raft or paddle boat. Fill a swimming pool with water and set up an electric fan, keeping fan and cord away from the water.

Activity: At the beginning of the party guests glue a raft together. After rafts are dry, crew members race them in a swimming pool (lazy river). Younger crew float rafts as an activity. A fan can create a wind or guests may blow rafts with straws. While the crews are busy, release some thundering blasts from a steam whistle!
Variation: If you have access to a lake and logs, build real rafts in advance of the party and take raft rides. Watch out! Real snags and sandbars still lurk in the treacherous Mississippi. Remember to wear life jackets.

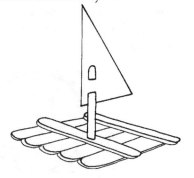

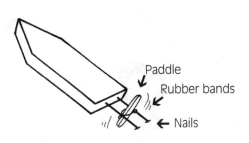

Paddle
Rubber bands
← Nails

Island Campfire

Ages: 4–adult
Time: 30 minutes
Materials Needed: Logs, kindling, matches, and water; or small logs with a flashlight and yellow tissue paper.

Advance Preparation: Dig a fire hole and check location for open fire regulations.
Activity: Sit around the campfire telling pirate stories or eating a snack.

Freckles, Freckles, Freckles

Ages: 4–10 years
Time: 15 minutes
Materials Needed: Caran D'ache water soluble crayons/eyebrow pencils, mirrors, wet sponges, and paper towels.
Advance Preparation: Set up a table or makeup center.

Activity: Guests create freckle faces. Give ribbons to the biggest freckle, cutest, funniest, cleverest, and the most freckles.

River Pirates

Ages: 4–12 years
Time: 20 minutes
Materials Needed: Refrigerator crates or large boxes, twine, scissors, foil-covered chocolate coins or real coins, Styrofoam bead packing or sawdust.
Advance Preparation: Put together boxes to create a cave. For a more detailed explanation, see "Gold Mine" in Western/Country/Chuck Wagon chapter.
Activity: Guests/pirates search the cave for the treasure.
Variation: Hide treasure behind trees or in the graveyard.

Frog-Jumping Jubilee

Ages: 3–adult
Time: 20 minutes
Materials Needed: Containers of water, large plastic tarpaulin, frog stable (large tub filled with mud, moss, and covered with a screen), plastic ice-cream bucket, squirt guns, 6 to 9 frogs, large nails or stakes to stabilize the launch pad. Worms from a sporting goods store. Three straw hats, permanent markers, ribbons, and paper.
Advance Preparation: Draw concentric circles on a large launch pad (vinyl tarpaulin or concrete driveway). Catch or buy bullfrogs or 4-inch grass frogs. If you are catching frogs, it is best to catch them at night. Use a flashlight and fish net. Point the light at the frog's eyes while you slowly approach and then catch the frog from behind. To order frogs, check "Biology Products" in your Yellow Pages, or order from: Blue Spruce Biological Supply, Castle Rock, CO 80104, 303-688-3396. Award ribbons that have silly captions stapled to the top: "giant leap," "fantastic spring," "jittery jump," "vigorous vault," "sprightly skip," "laborious leap," "lively leap," "lazy leap," "slippery skip," "marvelous move," and "super spring." Name the frogs: Hopper, Goliath, Fred, Jumpin' Jack, Murky Mac, Leapin' Lena, Slimy Sal, Hoppin' Harry, Jeremiah, and Slippery Sam.

Note: Treat the frogs with extreme care. When you are finished with the frog jumping, return the frogs to their natural surroundings—a pond or lake.
Activity: Guests in groups of three don a straw hat and choose a frog. Begin the race in the center circle. Place the frogs in a plastic tub without a bottom and cover with a lid or board. The race starter lifts the tub and the race begins. Contestants squirt the frogs with water guns encouraging their frogs out of the large circle. The first frog out of the large circle is the winner. Children will often want to repeat their turns—let all have a turn first before repeating.

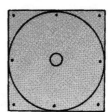

Launch Pad
Diameter: 12 feet

Water Balloon Throw

Ages: 6–adult
Time: 20 minutes
Materials Needed: Sturdy water balloons, chalk, and a street or long driveway or sidewalk.

Advance Preparation: Fill water balloons.
Activity: Guests throw water balloons for distance. Mark the point where the water balloon stops with each contestant's initials. The farthest throws win.

Watermelon Seed Spitting

Ages: 5–adult
Time: 15 minutes
Materials Needed: Watermelon pieces, the back side of the frog-jumping tarpaulin or driveway marked for scoring, small paper cups, and napkins.
Advance Preparation: Purchase watermelons and cut into pieces. Mark lines with a permanent marker on the back of the frog-jumping tarpaulin. Lines can be in intervals of 5 feet.
Activity: Guests spit several practice seeds and then five seeds for the longest distance. Longest distances win. Award ribbons with crazy captions stapled to the top: "sure spit," "spit fire," etc.

Gunny Sack Race

Ages: 6–adult
Time: 15 minutes
Materials Needed: Several gunny sacks.
Advance Preparation: Mark a starting and finish line. Collect several potato sacks from a feed store or a burlap bag company (see your Yellow Pages).

Activity: Guests line up, pull a sack up over their feet and legs, and run or hop. The guest who crosses the finish line first is the winner.

Bubble Gum Cigar Blow

Ages: 7–adult
Time: 15 minutes
Materials Needed: Bubble gum cigars, ribbons with funny captions: "bubble face," "awesome," "rubber lips," etc.
Advance Preparation: Purchase bubble gum cigars and make ribbons with captions typed and attached to the top of the ribbon.

Activity: Guests "warm up" their chew and then have five attempts to create the largest bubble. Award ribbons for appropriate bubble results—for example the guest with gum all over her face receives the ribbon with the caption "bubble face."
Note: Pass out bubble gum cigars one event prior to doing this activity. This will shorten the time it takes for the gum to be ready for the big blow!

Corncob Bubbles

Ages: 3–12 years
Time: 15 minutes
Materials Needed: Corncob pipes (purchase from the Mark Twain Museum in Hannibal, MO, or from a toy store). Bubble soap or Ivory liquid detergent.

Advance Preparation: Purchase corncob pipes early. If you cannot find them, order by mail.
Activity: Guests blow bubbles with their corncob pipes.

Goin' Fishin'

Ages: 3–9 years
Time: 15 minutes
Materials Needed: Fishing poles with magnets attached to the end of a string, plastic fish (dimensional or flat with metal washer glued to the fish), small wading pool, and prizes.

Advance Preparation: Gather materials needed and fill the wading pool.
Activity: Guests go fishing. Each fish color corresponds to a particular prize. Small children fish as an activity. Give them a prize for each catch.

Maze of the Caves

Ages: 6–teen
Time: 20 minutes
Materials Needed: Several (12–16) large cardboard boxes. Appliance stores will save refrigerator, washer, and dryer boxes for you if you ask them in advance. Twine or strong string, serrated knives, strapping tape, and a flashlight.
Advance Preparation: Diagram on paper a maze with dead ends, several turns, and a detour of some kind. Build the cave, putting the open ends of the boxes down so you can create narrow doors, round doors, and dead ends. Tie and tape boxes together. They must be secure or the cave maze will allow light inside.
Activity: Guests find a way through the cave, one "Free Spirit" at a time!

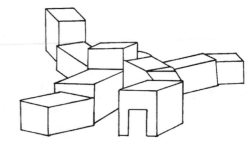

Showboat

Go a steamboatin'! The floating theater or showboat was especially popular on the Ohio and Mississippi Rivers at the time of Sam Clemens. Jerome Kern's popular operetta, *Show Boat*, reenacts the excitement in river towns with these performances. Serenade guests with a calliope concert. Let gangways become the "stage" and bring a little showboat to your party. End with the sounds of the belching riverboat stacks and "Toot, Toot, Tootsie! Good Bye."

Show Boat *Songs*

"Ol' Man River"
"Waiting for the Robert E. Lee"
"Here Comes the Show Boat"
"Dixie"
"Bye Bye Blackbird"
"Side by Side"
"Meet Me in St. Louis"

CATCH A BIT OF TOM SAWYER'S FREE SPIRIT!—DON'T PLAY HOOKY!

13: Water/Beach

Whether it's an ocean, lake, river, or babbling brook, water has always held a special fascination for humankind. For many, it has a calming effect—a source of peace and a place for thought and reflection. Its almost universal appeal makes it a natural focus for rituals, games, and sports. Water play of all kinds—from swimming and diving to water polo—is enjoyed by cultures around the world. Waterside activities like sunbathing, shell collecting, or just walking along a beach are other pleasant pastimes. Children as well as adults are intrigued by water. Running through a sprinkler or splashing in a mud puddle are among the best-loved and simplest joys of childhood.

It's little wonder that in many countries certain bodies of water are considered sacred—the Nile, the Ganges, and a scorpion-shaped lake in Tibet are examples. Spectacular waterfalls around the world are awesome in their beauty and power. In whatever form or location, water is an endless inspiration for stories, poems, and paintings as well as providing the world's best-loved playgrounds.

INVITATION

Draw a large drop of water. Write the party invitation on the "water drop" and then cover it with cellophane. If swimsuits and towels are needed, remember to indicate this on the invitation. Other water animals such as an octopus, stingray, starfish, seahorse, etc. may be used for the invitations.

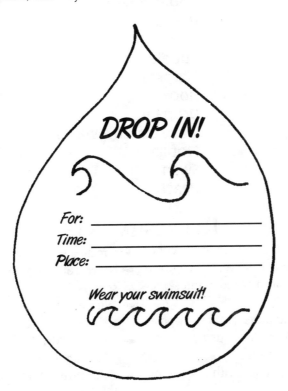

DECORATIONS

- Sprinkle **white glitter** on **dark blue paper table-cloths.**
- Hang **dark blue balloons** throughout the party area.
- Create a nautical feeling with **paddles, flippers, goggles, nets, glass floats, inflatable boats, buoys, life jackets, nautical flags, rope ladders, ship wheels, nets, seashells,** and **coral.**
- In the front yard, tie a **large inflatable whale** between two trees. Make it spout with a watering hose.

- Make or purchase **sand castle candles.**
- Lay out a **beach towel** with **umbrella** and **radio.**
- Place **tissue fish,** etc. in a net.
- Hang **water sports posters** around the party area.
- Float **assorted candles** in the swimming pool.
- Elevate a **doll's chair** and place a **lifeguard doll** in it.
- Create **large waves** with blue butcher paper—use as a background. With a paintbrush, spatter white paint for a splashing effect.

TERMS

Water drop	Aqua	Yachtsmen
Trudgen	Frog kick	Sailboat
Coral	Shark	Sprinkle
Frog	Splash bash	Snorkel
Flutter	Dog paddle	Port/starboard
Ship	Harbor	Water derby
Dolphin	Cast	Lifeguard
Hoppity	Puddle	Set sail
Crawl	Flippers	Ring buoy
Canoe	Hook	LifeSavers
Dinghy	Drop in!	Regatta
Sinker	Wave (catch a wave)	Triple dip
Pad	Flotilla	Swim-n-slide
Fins	Swan	Reef
Flying fish	Beach	

REFRESHMENTS

- Freeze fruit juice or punch in ice cube trays. When ready to serve, crush cubes in food processor or blender and serve snow cones.
- Freeze juices and pureed fruit in disposable cups (add a little sugar). Thaw slightly before serving.
- Serve cantaloupe filled with a scoop of vanilla ice cream.

- Create a sand castle birthday cake.
- Serve refreshments in beach toys—scoops, buckets, etc.
- With a hot glue gun, attach tiny shells to hors d'oeuvres picks.
- Serve soft drinks from a canoe, dinghy, or inflatable boat loaded with ice.
- Decorate a birthday cake with LifeSavers.

FAVORS

- Bubbles
- Baskets
- Goldfish
- Plastic watering can
- Water guns
- Canvas tote
- Beach towels
- Small goldfish bowl (brandy snifters)
- Beach pails
- Water toys
- Sunglasses
- Seahorse combs
- Rings made of seashells
- Sun visors (glue on shells)
- Shell necklaces
- Plastic pinwheels
- LifeSavers
- Temporary tattoos

ACTIVITIES/GAMES
Water Play

Ages: 2–5 years
Time: 15–20 minutes
Materials Needed: Two or more wading pools or a beach; sprinkler and interesting water toys.
Advance Preparation: Fill the wading pools well ahead of the party allowing water to warm up. Have towels ready and determine a drying off place for the little "fish."
Activity: Guests play and splash in the wading pool and under the sprinkler.

Quicksand

Ages: 3–12 years
Time: 10–15 minutes
Materials Needed: Wading pool, fine sand, water, and pennies or small rubber balls.
Advance Preparation: Fill the pool with sand (purchase from a hardware store) about 4 inches deep. Flood with water and hide pennies or balls in the sand.
Activity: Guests may play in the "quicksand" and after playing a while have them find the pennies or balls with their toes.
Note: If there are more than four guests, fill two pools or use a large wading pool.

LifeSavers Relay

Ages: 8–adult
Time: 20 minutes
Materials Needed: LifeSavers candy (with holes) and large cocktail picks.
Advance Preparation: Purchase candy and picks.
Activity: Divide guests into small relay groups. Holding the picks in hand, pass the LifeSavers with picks to the next person in the relay. The first team to finish passing the candy is the winner.

Tugboats and Bridges

Ages: 3–6 years
Time: 10 minutes
Materials Needed: Nautical background music such as "Anchors Aweigh," etc. Disc/tape player.
Advance Preparation: If playing background music, have all necessary equipment ready.
Activity: Half of the children become bridges by arching their bodies into bridge shapes. The remainder of the children are tugboats traveling on their hands and knees or crawling on their tummies through the bridges. Scatter bridges around the edges of the party area allowing plenty of space for the tugboats to travel. "Chug, chug, chug—what good navigators you are."
Variation: If you are at a beach, children may play in very shallow water.

Sardines

Ages: 7–14 years
Time: 20 minutes
Materials Needed: Plenty of good hiding places indoors or outdoors.
Advance Preparation: Remind players that the hiding place must be large enough to accommodate all the sardines.
Activity: Children pretend they are fishermen and hunt for a sardine. One guest is chosen as the sardine. All the fishermen leave the party area and count to 50 while the sardine hides. The fishermen begin "fishing" for the sardine. The first child to find the sardine hides with the sardine very quickly and quietly. The next fisherman to discover the two sardines hides with the sardines. Now there are three sardines. Play continues until the last fisherman finds all the sardines hiding together. The fun in this game is the ingenuity of the first sardine in finding a good hiding place for all the sardines. It is also important not to giggle or make a noise as all the sardines pile into the hiding place.

Frog Jumping

See "Frog-Jumping Jubilee" in Tom Sawyer Adventure chapter.

Bubble-Blowing Contest

Ages: 4–adult
Time: 15 minutes
Materials Needed: Plastic bubbles (older children), regular bubbles, and large or small plastic bubble hoops.
Advance Preparation: In 10 cups of water, mix one cup of Joy soap with ¼ cup liquid glycerine for a great bubble mixture.

Activity: Blow small- to giant-sized bubbles using varying sizes of hoops. Wave through the air to create all kinds of bubbles.
Variation: For giant bubbles fill a plastic swimming pool with water and add 2 cups of soap and 1 cup glycerin. Use small Hula Hoops as bubble wands. Wire coat hangers will also act as giant bubble wands.

Water Ring Toss

Ages: 5–12 years
Time: 20 minutes
Materials Needed: Styrofoam rings (8 inches in diameter), Ping Pong balls, and large tub or swimming pool.

Advance Preparation: Fill pool and float rings. Fill a sand pail with Ping Pong balls.
Activity: Guests throw Ping Pong balls into the rings. Guest with the most hits inside the rings is the winner.

Water Gun Target Shooting

Ages: 3–adult
Time: 15–20 minutes
Materials Needed: An old white bedsheet, 4 water guns or squirt bottles, permanent markers, food coloring, and thumbtacks.
Advance Preparation: Draw a large target on the sheet with permanent markers. Attach to a fence. Fill squirt guns with colored water (each gun should have a different color).

Activity: Each guest shoots at the target three times. If there are more than four guests, mark the shots to identify the contestant.
Variation: Hang sheets and create color designs with water guns or spray bottles. Children enjoy just squirting the different colors on the sheets. You may also attach plastic pinwheels to the fence and guests make the pinwheels spin with the water's spray.

Tub of Bubbles

Ages: 3–12 years
Time: 15–20 minutes
Materials Needed: Large wading pool, very sudsy soap, and coins or small rubber balls.
Advance Preparation: Just before this activity begins, spray water under high pressure into the wading pool. The liquid soap will transform into a mound of bubbles.
Activity: Guests search through the bubbles to find coins or balls. You may wish to keep throwing favors back into the suds to extend the activity.

Water Obstacle Course

Ages: 3–teen
Time: 15–20 minutes
Materials Needed: Flippers and goggles (2 or more sets), water guns, boxes, candles, bottles, matches, inner tubes, water balloons, milk cartons, large plastic sheet (slide), 2 stopwatches, bricks, balloons, plastic knives, shaving cream, and wading pools.

Advance Preparation: Set up the water obstacle course and make some trial runs with your own children.
Activity: Time each child's run through the obstacle course. To move this activity along, have more than one stopwatch. After one guest is well into the course another guest may begin. Supervise well.

START	Put on the flippers and goggles and run to a designated line and back. Take off the flippers and goggles and proceed to the next part of the obstacle course.
FIRST	Run through several inner tubes with a mist of water spraying over the tubes.
SECOND	Break one water balloon that has been tied to the fence or stored in a large container.
THIRD	Slide down a giant water slide. Stabilize a large plastic sheet (12 feet x 30 feet) with sand-filled milk cartons. A mist of water must spray over the plastic to make it slippery. Place the sprinkler in a safe location away from line of traffic.
FOURTH	Jump into a small wading pool and hold breath under water for a count of 10 seconds.
FIFTH	Shoot out a lighted candle with a water gun.
SIXTH	Walk a plank that has been laid over the top of a wading pool (not too high) filled with water. Reinforce plank at each end with bricks.
SEVENTH	With a plastic knife, each participant must shave a balloon covered with shaving cream.
EIGHTH	Water dogs take a seal position (lie on ground and use straight arms) to drag their bodies around the shore. Set up cones around which the seals travel!

Swim Cap Water Brigade

Ages: All ages
Time: 15–20 minutes
Materials Needed: Swim caps (one for each team) a permanent marker, and buckets (one small and one large for each team).
Advance Preparation: Fill large buckets with water and place a rubber swim cap by each water bucket. Place small empty buckets at the end of the yard and mark a fill line on each.

Activity: Teams line up for a relay. The first person in line fills the cap with water, runs with the water-filled cap to the empty bucket, and empties the cap of water into the bucket then returns to the next teammate. The first team to fill its bucket to the fill line wins the relay. Younger children just fill the bucket as an activity.

Flipper Relay

Ages: 7–teen
Time: 20 minutes
Materials Needed: Flippers and goggles (one pair for each team) and a bucket of water.
Advance Preparation: Have all equipment ready and have your children make a trial run. Dipping the flippers and feet in buckets of water makes it easier for team members to slip on the flippers. You may also want to have a few varying sizes of flippers to accommodate different foot sizes.

Activity: Teams (four on team) begin the flipper relay. The first person in each team puts on flippers and goggles, runs to a designated line and back, then removes the equipment and gives it to the next teammate. Play continues until the first team finishes the relay.
Variation: If you have access to a pool, you may do this relay in the pool and swim a lap rather than running with the flippers.

Regatta

Ages: 3–12 years
Time: 15 minutes
Materials Needed: Small sailboats (purchase or make), lumber, a plastic liner (purchase at a hardware store or use a plastic tablecloth), nails, hammer, electric fan, and an extension cord.

Advance Preparation: Build dual water channels in which to race the sailboats. Decorate the channels with flags or balloons. Line with plastic and fill with water. Place or hold the fan about 5 feet behind the dual water channels.

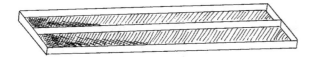

3 pieces (1″ x 4″ x 8′)
1 piece (1″ x 8″ x 8′)
2 pieces (1″ x 4″ x 8″)

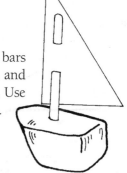

Activity: Children sail their boats in the wind created by the fan. Children 7 years and older can pretend they are in a regatta and race their boats. Smaller children just sail their boats as an activity with no competition. You may use a wading pool for smaller children since they will not be racing one another.

Variation: Carve Ivory soap bars into little boats. Add a sail and blow them across the water. Use a large plastic wading pond.

Water War

Ages: 12–teen
Time: 30–40 minutes
Materials Needed: Sponges, plastic buckets, spray bottles, squirt guns, water balloons, two large buckets for water reserves, and a "safe zone" sign. Guests should bring swimsuits and towels.
Advance Preparation: Fill water balloons and buckets. Gather water paraphernalia and attach "safe zone" sign to a tree or fence.
Activity: Guests engage in a water war. Warriors may enter safe zone to dry off or rest. When more than two enter the safe zone, the first one in the zone must rotate back into the water war. Allow for 5-minute breaks to prepare weapons, especially water balloons.

Watermelon Keep Away

Ages: 7–adult
Time: 30 minutes
Materials Needed: Lake or beach, cooking oil, and watermelons.
Advance Preparation: Purchase watermelons and grease with liquid cooking oil, if desired.
Activity: Guests divide into three or four teams and wade into water about chest high. Play begins by passing a watermelon under the water from one team member to another. The watermelon will sometimes pop up out of the water and fly through the air.
Note: Follow this activity with a watermelon feast.

Water Balloon Volleyball

Ages: 8–adult
Time: 30–40 minutes
Materials Needed: Pool or lake, water balloons, net or string.
Advance Preparation: Fill 30 water balloons and put up volleyball net or string.
Activity: Play volleyball using a water balloon instead of a volleyball. Play by tossing and catching balloons rather than bumping and hitting. When a balloon bursts, the team on the other side of the net scores a point.
Note: For added thrills, play with two or three water balloons at a time. Build excitement by filling the balloon with varying amounts of water and varying the balloon sizes.

Sprinkler Volleyball

Ages: 10–adult
Time: 30–40 minutes
Materials Needed: Volleyball or giant beach ball, net, and a sprinkler.
Advance Preparation: Set up the volleyball net with a sprinkler spraying over the net and courts. Fasten sprinkler head to the top of the volleyball standard.
Activity: Play volleyball under the sprinkler.
Variation: Set up a volleyball net in a sand or dirt court. Soon mud will appear!
Note: Be considerate of courts used for this activity. Some may not allow for this kind of court disruption!

Jump the River

Ages: 7–12 years
Time: 15 minutes
Materials Needed: Sticks, shovels, and beach buckets.
Advance Preparation: Create a make-believe river with sticks or lines drawn in the sand. For more realism, dig a trench and let water flow in your river. The river should be 15 inches wide to begin the jumping.
Activity: Guests jump over the river. All can jump at once if it's a long river. After each turn, draw or mark lines to widen the channel. The winner is the guest who can jump the widest river.

Sand Sculpture

Ages: All ages
Time: 30 minutes–1½ hours
Materials Needed: Pails, bowls, paper cups, funnels, milk cartons, cans, plastic containers, pans, sticks, big plastic spoons, scoops, water buckets, and old rulers to act as cutting edges.
Advance Preparation: Gather all water paraphernalia.
Activity: Build sand sculptures. Pack the wet sand into a mold. Carefully turn the mold upside down and lift it off. Create spaceships, cities, castles, sea creatures, etc.

Giant Water Slide

Ages: 5–adult
Time: 30 minutes
Materials Needed: Large plastic sheet (12 feet x 30 feet), large bags of sand, and a lawn sprinkler.
Advance Preparation: Fill large bags with sand to stabilize the plastic slide. Place the sprinkler by a tree out of the line of traffic. Do not keep the plastic on the grass too long—it will burn the grass (2 hours maximum).
Activity: Guests glide down the giant slide.

Hopscotch on the Beach

Ages: 8–12 years
Time: 30 minutes
Materials Needed: Beach, sticks, and shells.
Advance Preparation: Draw hopscotch squares in the sand with a stick and write the number at the side of each square.
Activity: Play hopscotch. The object of the game is to advance your token (shell) to square 10 and hop back out. The first person to do this is the winner. Remember, players must jump over any square that has a token in it. Example of the first turn: jump over square 1 and through the remainder of the course up and back. If you do not miss, throw your token into square 2. Now you must jump over square 1 and 2. If your token lands in a wrong square or if you hop on a line, you must move your token back one square and it becomes the next player's turn.

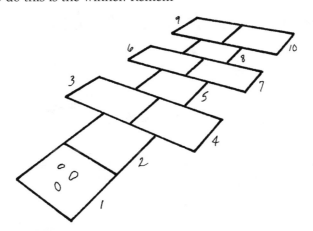

Origami Frogs

Ages: 9–14
Time: 15 minutes
Materials Needed: Origami paper and someone to demonstrate how to make jumping origami frogs. Also check the library for origami books.

Advance Preparation: Make a sample frog.
Activity: Guests make origami frogs.

Catch a Goldfish

Ages: 3–teen
Time: 10–15 minutes
Materials Needed: Wading pool, plastic bags and ties from a pet store, feeder goldfish, and a chemical to remove chlorine from the water.
Advance Preparation: A day or two before the party, fill a wading pool with water. This will naturally re-move the chlorine. Order fish from a pet store and pick them up the day of the party. Put the fish in the pool filled with water free of chlorine.

Activity: Just before the guests leave, they catch (with their hands) a goldfish and take it home in a plastic bag filled with pool water. You may have two fish for each guest.

Whimsical Boat Regatta

Ages: 7–adult
Time: 20 minutes
Materials Needed: Swimming pool, lake, or child's pool.
Advance Preparation: In the invitation, ask guests to make and bring a whimsical boat made out of a boot, box, cooler, bottle, Styrofoam, etc. If at night, create lighted boats. Send invitation about a month ahead allowing time to plan and create the whimsical boats.

Activity: Hoist nautical flags and begin the floating of whimsical boats. Race boats if you wish. Part of the fun and excitement can be the bribing of the judges. Award ribbons with funny captions or names for the boats. You may wish to award a sweepstakes winner.

Beach Ball Volleyball

Ages: 6–adult
Time: 30–50 minutes
Materials Needed: Large beach balls.
Advanced Preparation: Purchase beach balls.
Activity: Play beach volleyball without a net. Players toss the ball into the air and must keep it up with volleyball hits. Players may not hit the ball twice in a row. The most hits without touching the ground wins or play to 15 hits. Adjust scoring for age appropriateness.

CATCH A WAVE AND HAVE A WHALE OF A DAY!

14: Western/Country/Chuck Wagon

Did you know that the cowboy era lasted only about 25 years? It peaked in the early 1880s. After the Civil War many soldiers began drifting to Texas in search of adventure, land, and work. At the same time, Texas had become overrun with wild, tough longhorn cattle originally brought into northern Mexico by early Spanish settlers. Soon enterprising men began to buy up surplus cattle and hire crews of cowboys to drive them to railheads in Missouri and Kansas. These drives involved thousands of cattle and horses and took weeks to complete. Many cowboy songs and tales originated on these long cattle drives along the western trails. Cowboys also worked on ranches in Montana and other western states where they rounded up and branded cattle. The life of a Western hero was far from glamorous and exciting. It was risky, dusty, monotonous, and demanding, but the young men loved the freedom the range offered them. The cowboy era ended with the building of fences and the outbreak of range wars between farmers (nesters) and ranchers.

INVITATION

"Wanted" posters, Western paraphernalia, bandannas, or a poem utilizing Western lingo can make fun invitations. Address envelopes "Wanted" and seal with Western stickers.

> **ROUND UP SOME FUN**
> Rustle up your trusty hat
> Put on your boots
> Slip on your spurs
> Saddle up
> Stake a claim
> Saturday, August 16, 1997
> Forenoon to Dusk
> Blaze a trail up Mill Creek Canyon. Meet the cookie slingin' grub at the Circle H Ranch. Sarsaparilla and eatin' gear will be provided.
> R.S.V.P. 555-4789

DECORATIONS

- Light and hang **old lanterns.**
- Guests will enjoy sitting on **straw bales.** Put boards on top of straw bales for even more sitting space.
- Display old **wash pans, jugs,** and **kitchen paraphernalia.**
- Serve sarsaparilla or coffee from a **chuck wagon.**
- Make **sawhorses** into horses with **saddles,** etc.
- Call cowpokes to supper with a **large triangle gong.**
- Cover tables with **red gingham-checked paper** or **red vinyl.**
- Decorate with **red, white,** and **blue bunting.**
- Use **red gingham-checked bandannas, napkins,** and **plates.**
- Insert bud vases in **children's cowboy boots** and arrange **daisies** or **dry wildflowers** in the vases for centerpieces. Check secondhand stores for boots.
- Hang personalized **"Wanted" posters.**
- **Livestock sale posters** are also fun.
- Keep cold drinks on ice in **whiskey barrels** and **old metal tubs.**
- Create a **dummy** sitting in an **old washtub**—stuff pants and shirt and lay a hat across his face.
- Arrange napkins in a **metal** or **wooden stirrup.**
- Serve drinks in **clean tin cans** or **Mason jars.** Stack in the chuck wagon.

- Set up a **life-sized teepee.**
- Make a **corral** with **hobby horses** tied to **hitching posts.**
- Hang **old clothes** or **underwear** from tree limbs.
- Set **cactus** around the corral.
- Spread **straw** all about the corral.
- Fabricate a **western saloon front** as in Dodge City or Abilene, Kansas. Use butcher paper and tempera paint.

- On a United States map outline the **Old Western trails.** Check the library for trail information.
- Display **old mining tools** by the gold mine. (Check your Yellow Pages for supplies.)
- Identify rest rooms as **"Fillies," "Steers,"** or **"Outhouse."**
- Fabricate a **Boot Hill** with wood slab pieces and black permanent markers.

BRANDS

As guests arrive give them a brand using a rubber stamp or marker.

∧	Open A	▬	Bar
/	Slash	☐	Box
◇	Diamond	⊔	Lazy
Ⅎ	Connected	(	Quarter circle
⅄	Reverse		

WESTERN SLANG/LINGO

Cowpokes	Cookie (cook)	Pistol/six-shooter
Stampede (herd of cattle out of control)	Wagonmaster	Chuck wagon (food wagon)
Tenderfoot (novice)	Grub/chow/eats (prepared food)	Chaps

Sarsaparilla (carbonated drink flavored with dried sarsaparilla roots)
Santa Fe Trail
Lasso, rope, or lariat
Fiddle/guitar
Cow pies
Corncob pipes
"Woman" (wife)
Boot Hill (graveyard)
Bandanna (scarf for dust)
Snake oil (questionable medicine)
Cactus juice
Corral
Longhorns (fierce cattle)
"Ride 'em, cowboy"
Rodeo (cowboy's circus)
"Howdy partner"
Westward ho

Roundup
Plumb loco (crazy)
Happy trails
Posse
Buckaroos
Doggie (motherless calf)
Pokey (jail)
"Pitchfork" fondue
Rustle/rustler
Empress Mine Co.
Hoedown (party)
Hangover Mine Co.
Lost Dutchman Mine
Explosives
Enter at your own risk
No firearms allowed
Sagebrush Gulch Mine
Danger

Draw (gulch or gully)
Trading Post
Hoedown
Rawhide
Blaze a trail
Wild West
Yahoo!!
Wrangler
Bunkhouse (barracks for ranch hands)
Marshal/sheriff
Spurs
"Spooked" herd
Cinch, saddle
Watering hole
Last chance
O.K. Corral
Dry Gulch Saloon
Adios (good bye)
Mosey over
Showdown

BUDDY BEST FASTEST GUN IN THE WEST!

ROSY DIED OF THE JITTERS!

JAKE BITTEN BY A SNAKE! NOW UNDERGROUND WITH ALL THE CRITTERS!

HERE LIES AN HONEST LAWYER.

FAMOUS WESTERN FIGURES

Wild Bill Hickok
Wyatt Earp
Kit Carson
William G. Fargo
Buffalo Bill Cody
Judge Roy Bean

Annie Oakley
Deadwood Dick
Calamity Jane
Jessie and Frank James
Sam Colt
Pistol Pete

John Stetson
Billy the Kid
Will Rogers
The Dalton Boys
The Lone Ranger
Cisco Kid

WANTED POSTERS

For lots of good humor, display personalized "Wanted" posters. Below are some ideas you may use to develop posters for each guest—use your imagination!

Words for Wanted Posters

Slim Sam	Salty Sal	Wins gold medal
Dead-eye Dick	Marksman	Bandits
Dusty Dick	Gentleman Sam	Surpassing marks-
Blazing	Cattle Kate	manship
Pistol Pete	Rodeo star	Rough rider
Pony Pete	Wild bull rider	Unflinching courage
Hurricane	Dynamite	Buckskin king
Alkali Ike	Range rider	Swift in course
One confused cowpoke	Superhuman	Dangerfield Burr
Flo	ability	Tornado

Drunken desperado
Lover/fighter
Gold Pocket City
Wild/daring
Dead shot
Dude
Humble cabin

Old scout
Pistol packin'
Amazin' Annie
Lariat Lil
Haunted hills
Wild Nell
Border ruffian

Tarnation
Sharpshooter
Border belle
Crack shot
Renegade queen
Highfalutin' terms
Best in the West

Phrases for Wanted Posters

Stopped a stagecoach and cowed the driver
Sends scoundrel to the doctor
Not content to rest on her laurels
Amazing proficiency with horses
Most impressive horsewoman
Riding at top speed, leaping sluices and other obstacles
Strange sense of adventure
Ride, rope, and wrangle
Unravaged by wind, weather, or hard work
On the range instead of in the kitchen
Positively No Profanity
Range Ridin', cattle ropin' Rita
Unsaddled cayuse, bronco, mustang
Ride any horse … catch any crook
Riding the unbreakable bronc
Snaring the uncatchable steer
This rodeo queen, who teaches third grade in the off season, can out-jump and out-lasso any dude on the playground circuit!
Dynamite Duane buys old mine: Gets shaft!

Wins $200,000 in poker game
Hansi Oakley grabs her students and holds them hostage until they read hundreds of books and learn their library skills
Loses husband in poker game
Mounting the metal horse (motorcycle)
Marksman Morton outshoots Billy the Kid
Pistol Packin' Pam can out-shoot, out-lasso, and out-yell any man who crosses her path
Singin'/dancin' Jeanne turns down opera contract to ride, rope, and wrangle
Lands in jail and eats beans
Gets loaded and loses it!
Can ride any horse and catch any crook!
Caught in gambling raid!
Hurricane Sal wanted for her herculean strength and monumental savvy
Loses Visa card
Elopes with "Cookie" and the marriage crumbles

COOKHOUSE SPECIALS

- Coleslaw
- Barbecue or "grub steak"
- Hot dogs
- Hamburgers
- Biscuits
- Apples
- Fish/wild game
- Baked beans

- Cake
- Fresh or dried fruit
- Cookie jar
- Jerky
- Chocolate chip cookies (Cow chips)
- Serve food in aluminum pie tins and drinks in tin cans.

FAVORS

- Brass house tokens
- Bandannas
- Sheriff's badges
- Plastic canteens
- Play money

- Gold nuggets in a pouch
- Personalized "Wanted" posters
- Lariat ropes
- Water guns
- Cap guns

ACTIVITIES/GAMES
Animal Roundup

Ages: 5–adult
Time: 20 minutes
Materials Needed: Peanuts, brown lunch bags, and prizes.
Advance Preparation: Hide peanuts all around the ranch.
Activity: Guests (ranch hands) are divided into several groups. Each group selects a ranch animal and a ranch foreman. All the ranch hands begin their roundup of peanuts. When someone finds a peanut he/she may not touch it—instead the ranch hand must stand beside the nut and make the sound of the group's animal. When the foreman of that animal group hears his animal sound, he goes directly to his ranch hand and collects the peanut for his team. Remember, in this treasure hunt only the foreman can pick up the treasure. Play continues until all peanuts are found. The animal team with the most peanuts wins! Suggestions for ranch animals: Cows, horses, sheep, pigs, chickens, dogs, or ducks.

Gold Rush

Ages: 3–adult
Time: Spontaneously
Materials Needed: Small rocks (³/₄ inch), metallic gold spray paint, and mining pans.
Advance Preparation: Spray-paint the small rocks gold. Hide the "nuggets" under rocks along a stream.
Activity: Miners rush for gold along the stream. They may use their gold nuggets to put someone in jail or to buy a drink.

Variation: For younger children, fill a swimming pool or large tub with sand and gold nuggets. Purchase sand from your hardware store or lumberyard.

Chuck Wagon

Ages: All ages
Time: Spontaneous throughout party
Materials Needed: Locate a real chuck wagon or make one from large cardboard boxes, electrical conduit, old sheets or canvas, markers, serrated knife, twine, strapping tape. Metal cans for drinks.
Advance Preparation: Build a chuck wagon and have it ready for serving. Collect fruit and vegetable cans.
Activity: A chuck wagon is very decorative. In addition, if constructed from wood, it's great for serving drinks. Children love climbing in and out of the wagon.

Gold Mine

Ages: All ages
Time: Spontaneous throughout party
Materials Needed: Large boxes, brown or gray paint, brushes, strapping tape, straw/sand or sawdust, gold spray paint, small rocks (nuggets), twine, mining pans, serrated knife, and a flashlight.
Advance Preparation: Create a gold mine shaft by taping or tying large refrigerator boxes together to form the shaft. At the end of the shaft, hide lots of gold nuggets in sawdust/straw/sand. It is best to fill a shallow box with the sawdust/sand/straw and place it at the end of the mine shaft. To make nuggets, spray small rocks with gold metallic paint. For added excitement, sew small pouches of leather-look fabric for guests to carry their nuggets.
Activity: Guests pan for gold nuggets. They can use the nuggets to purchase drinks at the party, pay the sheriff to put someone in jail, buy a party favor, etc.

Pony Express

Ages: 7–10 years
Time: 15 minutes
Materials Needed: Two stick horses and backpacks.
Advance Preparation: Purchase or make stick horses.
Activity: Make a large loop for the Pony Express route. Divide the guests into two teams and station them at the various Express stations. For easy identification, have one team wear blue scarves and one team wear red scarves. On "Go," the riders at the first station begin riding their horses to the second Pony Express sta-

Fancy riding (high steps)
Four horses in a trot
Two horses race in gallop
Barrel race
Trick riding

tion. When the first rider arrives, she gives the horse and backpack to the next rider. The second rider continues on to the third station. The ride continues until the final rider reaches the end of the Pony Express loop. Put up signs with names of Western towns at each station.

Variation: Make stick horses for all the cowpokes. Use cotton socks and dowels. Award gold nuggets for the best rides in the following rodeo events:

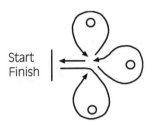

Jail

Ages: All ages
Time: Spontaneous throughout the party
Materials Needed: Large boxes or fir strips, paint, dowels for window bars if using box, sheriff's badge, toy gun and holster, hinges and nails if using fir strips, paintbrushes or spray gun, and twine to tie jail sides together.
Advance Preparation: Construct and paint jail.
Activity: Sheriff arrests guests (on phony charges). Guests mine for gold nuggets and pay the sheriff a couple of nuggets to arrest someone of their choice. You will need a jailer to attend the jail while the sheriff is making arrests. Cowpokes must sing a song to get out of jail.

Jail Construction (box): Cut jail window from a large refrigerator box. Cut door in back of box. Insert dowels in window.

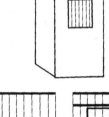

Jail Construction (wood):
Fir strips—42
1" x 4" x 8'—4
1" x 4" x 10'—1
Construct 3

Construct 1

Holdup

Ages: All ages
Time: 5–10 minutes
Materials Needed: Holdup paraphernalia
Advance Preparation: Work out details of the holdup

with the person who will be playing the part of the robber.
Activity: Stage the holdup, steal nuggets, take hostages—use your imagination!

Horse Rides

Ages: All ages
Time: Throughout the party
Materials Needed: Horse (rent from ranch or stable). With the owner, work out details on caring for the horse.

Advance Preparation: Have horse familiar with property.
Activity: Guests may ride the horse. An adult or teenager should lead the horse when children are riding.

Cow Chip Throw

Ages: All ages
Time: 15–20 minutes
Materials Needed: Paper plates, straw, glue.
Advance Preparation: Glue two paper plates together

(right sides together) to form saucer shape, paint brown, and glue straw on the painted "cow chip."
Activity: Throw chips for distance.

Horseshoes

Ages: 10–adult
Time: Spontaneous throughout the party
Materials Needed: Horseshoe game and cones/flags.
Advance Preparation: Set stakes and mark horseshoe area with cones/flags. Go over playing and safety rules with guests. Post the rules near the play area.

Activity: Pitch horseshoes.

Round the Campfire Sing-Along

Ages: All ages
Time: Spontaneous throughout the party
Materials Needed: Singing cowboy or fiddler, bonfire, pit, logs, straw bales, and music (words) for sing-along. If this is a large party you may want to use a microphone and loudspeakers. Remember a fire extinguisher.

Advance Preparation: Make all necessary music arrangements. Dig fire pit and gather firewood. Use logs or straw bales for seating around the fire. Check local fire and burning regulations.
Activity: Sing around the campfire.
Variation: Use a taped collection of Western music.

Clogging

Ages: All ages
Time: 20–60 minutes
Materials Needed: Clogging music, disc/tape player, and exhibition dance group/clogging instructor.
Advance Preparation: Investigate clogging in your community by checking the Yellow Pages under square dancing, bluegrass society, adult education classes, and

your parks and recreation department. Arrange for an exhibition with an instructor.
Activity: Clogging exhibition. You may wish to have guests participate with a few simple clogging steps.
Note: Clogging is country-and-western but its steps are derived from Irish, German, Scottish, English, and African folk dances.

Hayride

Ages: All ages
Time: Spontaneous throughout the party
Materials Needed: Wagon, straw, and a vehicle.
Advance Preparation: Make all necessary arrangements.

Activity: Hayrides throughout the party. It is important for children to understand the safety rules of riding in a moving wagon.

Rope-Spinning Tricks/Snagging a Nag

Ages: 7–adult
Time: 30 minutes
Materials Needed: 10- to 12-foot ropes between 1/4-

and 3/8-inch in diameter. The rope should be braided (sash cord) and is usually available at a hardware store.
Advance Preparation: Make lariats.

1. Work out rope stiffness. Tie a slipknot at one end of the rope. Snip off tail.

2. Feed the other end of the rope through the slipknot and pull the slipknot tight.

3. Tie a simple knot at the end of the rope (spoke).

4. Lariat with noose (Like a wheel)

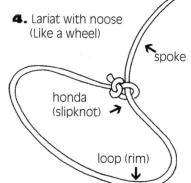

spoke

honda (slipknot)

loop (rim)

The spinning hand is like the hub of a wheel. The easiest spin is the "flat loop." Your feet should be slightly apart and your body should lean slightly forward at the waist. Hold the rope at the slipknot in your left hand. Place the knotted end of the rope between the second and third fingers of your right hand. Bring the loop over to your right hand. The rope should lie loosely across the right-hand fingers. You are ready to spin. Practice spinning—don't try to make the rope spin too fast. Practice tricks and lassoing a post, etc.

Activity: Guests practice rope spinning and lassoing a post/hobby horse. Go over safety rules—lasso objects and not people.

Variation: Hire a professional rope spinner or fill a wading pool with water and lasso little plastic ducks with heavy string lariats!

Square Dancing

Ages: 8–adult
Time: Up to several hours
Materials Needed: Self-calling recordings, disc/tape player, and amplification. You may wish to hire a professional caller. If using self-calling discs/tapes, inquire about the difficulty of the dance (it should be appro-priate for your party guests). Resource: Square Dancing the American Way, Kim 4061C, Kimbo Educational, 800-631-2187.

Advance Preparation: Purchase self-calling discs/tapes or arrange for a professional caller.
Activity: Square Dancing

Melodrama

Ages: 7–adult
Time: 30 minutes
Materials Needed: Young people or adults who would write or find a short melodrama and present a play for the party guests. "Booing" and "hissing" signs.

Advance Preparation: Locate a local drama group that will put on a short melodrama for your party.
Activity: Guests enjoy a short melodrama. "Booing" and "hissing" signs can add a lot of fun to the play. If you are outdoors or in another appropriate setting, throw popcorn.

Posse Hunt

Ages: 3–10 years
Time: 20 minutes
Materials Needed: Stolen loot (chocolate coins) or play money in loot bags enough for each guest. Combining small loot bags into one large loot bag is optional.
Advance Preparation: Hide the loot.
Activity: Posse hunts for the loot and rustlers. Guests may go out on their own to discover individual loot bags or a storyteller (sheriff) can lead a young group on the posse hunt. As the posse makes its way through the woods, the sheriff warns them of impending dangers,

discovers Indian lore, or finds clues left by the rustlers. Below is a list of dangers, clues, and lore to be discovered by the posse.

Old mine shaft and cabin
Old campfire site
Indian symbols on rocks (see Thanksgiving/Native American Indian chapter)
Broken piece of Indian pottery
An arrowhead (purchase arrowheads and hide them)
Buffalo or buffalo chips
Band of Indians on the warpath ... light a smoke bomb for a smoke signal or pour water on dry ice.

Frontier Flicks

Ages: All ages
Time: Length of movies
Materials Needed: Television, VCR, Western movie, and an "old movie house."

Advance Preparation: Set up movie and generate a computer sign "Frontier Flicks."
Activity: Watch old frontier flicks!

Ye Old West Photos

Ages: All ages
Time: Throughout the party
Materials Needed: Cameras, film, and Western attire.

Advance Preparation: Gather attire and camera equipment.
Activity: Take pictures of cowpokes and wranglers.

Cowboys and Rustlers

Ages: 7–12
Time: 30 minutes
Materials Needed: Large box (bank), markers, bank notes, spud guns or wooden toy rubber-band guns, handcuffs, and masks.
Advance Preparation: Paint box with a large "Bank" sign. Gather paraphernalia.

Activity: Set up a bank with a bank president. Rustlers hold up the bank and run with the loot. Rustlers hide out until the sheriff has gone. Rustlers strike again robbing another bank. The sheriff and her posse chase the rustlers. Game continues until the sheriff finds the rustlers and makes an arrest. When the rustlers are caught, they go to jail. Play again.

Shoot-Out!

Ages: 4–adult

Time: Spontaneously throughout the party

Materials Needed: Backdrop for wind protection (large box), candles, matches, water guns, bucket of water, and a table.

Advance Preparation: Set up candles on the table with a backdrop behind for wind protection. Have matches, water guns, and water ready. Practice and have presentation ready for guests.

Activity: Guests practice their draw and try to put out all the candles. Award certificates!

Option: Use Ping Pong balls on whiskey bottles for targets instead of candles—easier to use. Paper cups placed along the edge of the table/stump are also easy targets to knock off with water guns.

Shoot-Out Certificate

I,_____

Now know that my draw was slow and I was all show, and no go!

Trick Horse or Professional Rope Twirler

Hire someone who rides a trick horse or is a rope twirler. Check your Yellow Pages!

Live Ranch Animals

Borrow or rent live calves, lambs, goats, and ducks. Children will love petting these lovable animals. Make a corral with straw bales. Have plenty of water and feed for your ranch guests!

Western Songs

"Whoopee-Ti-yi-Aye Git Along Little Doggies"
"The Streets of Laredo"
"Bury Me Not on the Lone Prairie"
"The Poor Lonesome Cowboy"
"Home on the Range"
"The Old Chisholm Trail"
"Red River Valley"
"The Texas Rangers"
"Oh Suzannah"
"The Dreary, Dreary Life"
"The Colorado Trail"
"Buffalo Gals"
"Clementine"
"Sweet Betsey from Pike"
"Boots and Saddle"
"Big Rock Candy Mountain"
"There's a Tavern in the Town"
"Happy Trails to You"

ALL TRAILS ARE LEADING TO A GOOD TIME!

15: Wheels, Wheels, Wheels

TOY CARS	SCOOTERS	BICYCLES	TRAINS
RIDING TOYS	SKATEBOARDS	ROLLER BLADES	WAGONS

Of all humankind's inventions, one of the first remains one of the most important. The wheel probably appeared around 3500 B.C. and must have resembled a crude solid stone or wooden cylinder. Whatever its appearance, it revolutionized society for all time, making many daily tasks easier and faster. The first awkward wheels were used for transportation. Later, lighter and more versatile wheels were constructed with spokes and rims. The uses of the wheel today are innumerable, ranging from microscopic components of high-tech instruments to huge, powerful machinery.

Among great wheel inventions, the railroad played a key role in the development of our nation. The majesty and power of the "iron horse" captured imaginations and became the subject of countless stories, paintings, and songs that remain popular long after the railroad era has faded into nostalgia. Wheels—big or tiny, powerful or delicate—are an integral part of our work and play.

INVITATION

Create the invitation using any wheel theme, road signs, or a map. Write a poem using lingo relating to the "wheels" you choose.

GET IN GEAR
Warm Up Your Engines
For a Road Rally
Sally's House
3204 Ranch Drive
Race Starts at 2 P.M.,
Saturday, May 10, 1997
Yield to a Great Time!

DECORATIONS

- **Checkered flags** are great for the race car scheme.
- Assorted **road maps** or **trail maps** can be used in many ways.
- Make a large **gas pump** for fill-ups.
- Place giant "YIELD," "CURVE," etc. **signs** around the front yard. (Use poster board and paint-stirring sticks.)
- **Toy cars** (antique, etc.) add a festive touch.
- Incorporate **train sets** or **race car tracks** in the party setting.
- Hang a "Stop" or "Yield" sign on the front door.
- Create a **mini village** with small cars for a centerpiece.
- Hang **posters** of cars, bicycles, 18-wheelers, skateboards, etc.
- **Helmets, pads,** and other **cycling paraphernalia** are fun and easy to use as decorating items.
- **Old license plates** (collection) create a fun atmosphere.
- Hang colorful **flags/pennants**.
- Use **name tags** with license plate numbers.
- Make up **personalized license plates** ... watch for clever personalized plates.

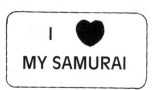

- Hang a **neon sign** that reads "Eats."
- Display **railway station signs** ... New York Central Station, etc.
- Bring out **antique lanterns**, especially old railroad lanterns.

TERMS IN MOTION

Exit	Blazing	Phone is ringing
Pedal power	CB radio	Tank car
BMX	Caboose	Cruise
Engineer	Speed limit	Trails
Yield	4 x 4	Hazard
Truck stop	Ten-four	Hopper
Quarter pipe	Flatcar	Gas/fuel
Conductor	25 mph	Traffic
Stop	Zone	Accelerate
Zoom	Good buddy	Toot/clang
Doughnut	Diner	Wheelie
Porter	Passing	Bike-a-Thon
R.R. crossing	Ignition	Dispatcher
Squad car	Handle	Choo choo
Glass pack	Coach	Burn rubber
Brakeman	Merge	Rally
Slippery	Radar	"Iron horse"
Pony Express	Smokey	Blast
Mechanic	Boxcar	Rumble
All aboard	Gear	Cargo
Slow	Autobahn	"Pufferbellies"
Cycle	Ears on	Puffing
Service	Stock car	Express
Whistle-stop	Burnout	Turbocharged
Curve	Cop	

Railroad Companies

Pennsylvania
Southern Pacific
Chicago & Northwestern
Santa Fe
Union Pacific

Missouri Pacific
New York Central
Central Pacific
Burlington Northern

REFRESHMENTS

- Rent a dining car at a railroad museum and have a dinner party catered.
- Popcorn and soda.
- Cake/cookies in the shape of road signs—YIELD, STOP, R.R.
- Create license plate or road map place mats and cover with clear contact paper.
- Serve cookies in a toy dump truck or bread sticks in a log truck.

- Turn hot dogs into race cars by adding wheels (pickles).
- Serve refreshments on a race track paper tablecloth or a checkered cloth.
- Whistle your train crew to work.
- Set up an electric train as the focal point on the serving table. Dispense food morsels to the hungry conductors.

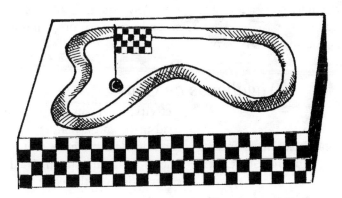

FAVORS

- Cycling paraphernalia—horns, etc.
- Maps
- Mini cars, trucks, trains, etc.
- Flashlights
- Travel posters from a travel agency

- Play helmets
- Tickets to a roller rink or car rally
- Goggles
- Construction/firefighter/engineer hats
- Bandannas

ACTIVITIES/GAMES

Construction

Ages: 2–7 years
Time: 1 hour
Materials Needed: Scrap lumber pieces, toy construction helmets, toy loaders (sit-on style), trucks, rocks, toy plastic hammers, and a large sandbox.
Advance Preparation: Collect all equipment needed for the construction site.

Activity: Construction workers work hard in the construction site.
Optional: While little guests are busy constructing, an adult can be giving rides (one little guest at a time) on a rented dump truck.

Traffic Sound Effects Tape

Ages: 4–9 years
Time: Play at various times throughout the party
Materials Needed: Tapes, tape recorder, and sources for sounds—trains at a crossing, cars starting up at a busy intersection, and sirens. Songs that relate to cars, cycles, etc. ("Granny On Her Motorcycle" or "The Real McCalls" by Bill Fries and Chip Davis from American Gramophone Records.)

Advance Preparation: Tape sounds. Find and purchase songs relating to cars, cycles, etc.
Activity: Play sounds/music as guests arrive and during the party. Keep the volume in a pleasant range.

Village Play

Age: 4–8 years
Time: 45 minutes
Materials Needed: Assorted boxes/containers, triangular-shaped blocks for hills, blocks, markers, tape, spools, straws, clay, poster board, dowels, mini cars, tissue tubes, and wide masking tape for roads.
Advance Preparation: Prepare large play area for the village. Collect all the materials for the project. Make up a list of ideas for the village or tell a story about it to generate ideas. Use an entire room!
Activity: Guests create a village using materials provided. Remember bus stops, a fire station, places of employment, shopping mall/shops, etc. Create tunnels, bridges, roads, etc.

Variations: Create the village in a sandbox or build a farm complete with animals. On a piece of cardboard, draw a simple village road system. Place each corner on a stack of books. From under the village, drag a magnet (with a small metal car on top) around the village. Any time the car goes off the road, deduct a 10-second penalty. Young children play as an activity.

Vagabonds on Course

Ages: 7–12 years
Time: 15 minutes
Materials Needed: Identical state road maps enough for each pair of guests, markers, and a list of identical towns for each pair.
Advance Preparation: Make a list of towns. The towns, when plotted and connected with a line, should form an outline of a car, train engine, etc.

Activity: Each pair of guests receives a list of towns, a road map, and a marker. Guests plot the towns and carefully determine the picture created by connecting lines from town to town. The first pair of guests to discover hidden outline (car, etc.) wins.

Cycles on Parade

Ages: 5–12 years
Time: 30–50 minutes
Materials Needed: Streamers, coiled paper, pinwheels, flags, balloons, Mylar strips, foil paper, scissors, twist ties, and tape.
Advance Preparation: Gather materials needed.

Activity: Decorate and parade bicycles. Give each guest a ribbon—most creative, most awesome, prettiest, best design, most colorful, most outrageous, funniest, etc.
Variation: Use wagons, scooters, or little riding toys. Guest may also come to the party with cycles already decorated.

Little Engines

Ages: 3–6 years
Time: 20 minutes
Materials Needed: The story, "The Little Engine That Could," tape player, toy whistles, engineer hats, and bandanna scarves.
Advance Preparation: Gather all materials needed and familiarize yourself with "The Little Engine That Could." Indicate on the invitation to dress as engineers.

Activity: Guests listen to the story and, when the little engine begins to climb the mountain, guests stand and make a train by grabbing waists. They take little steps, toot whistles, and climb the mountain. Be careful not to let the train break apart.

Remember Spare Parts

Ages: 4–12 years
Time: 10–15 minutes
Materials Needed: A large tray with an assortment of used car parts (from a repair shop) and accessories, a timer, paper, and pencil.
Advance Preparation: Select objects for the tray. For younger children, keep objects simple. Place them on the tray and cover with a cloth.

Activity: Guests view and feel the objects on the tray for 2 minutes. Cover and set aside. Younger children are asked what they saw and felt on the tray—they give answers orally. Older guests write down all the objects they remember and the winners are those who have written down the most correct answers.

Weary Wheels

Ages: 7–teen
Time: 30 minutes
Materials Needed: Old wheels or Styrofoam craft circles. Chalk is needed for marking lines.
Advance Preparation: Mark a toe line and a finish line.
Activity: Guests roll wheels in various competitions.
  1. Roll wheel the farthest.
  2. Roll over the finish line first.
  3. Roll the slowest.

Variation: Create a giant board game with assorted boxes and numbers. Each participant rolls 3 wheels or cars and accumulates points designated on the board. Repeat play several times.

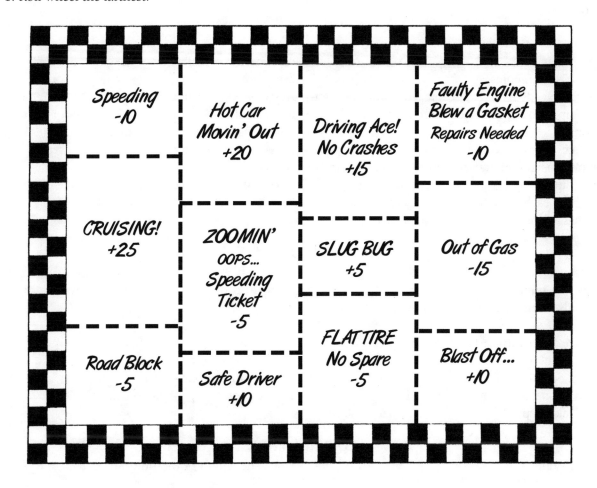

"Slug Bug"

Ages: 4–10 years
Time: 15 minutes
Materials Needed: Marbles, walnut shell halves, and a race track on which the "Slug Bugs" run. The track can be a 6-foot-long board about 12 inches wide. Edges can be made with wood quarter-round. You need two outside edges and a center lane. Paint and brushes for decorating "Bugs." Plenty of paper towels.
Advance Preparation: Collect all materials needed and build the race track. Put one end of the track on a stool or chair to create an incline.

Activity: Guests put a walnut shell over a marble and run a "Slug Bug" down the track. The marble acts as a wheel under the shell. Before the race, guests may paint their "Slug Bug" (walnut shell). Younger children play as an activity—they will not be interested in racing the "Bugs."

Obstacles for the Remote Car

Ages: 6–teen
Time: 30 minutes
Materials Needed: Several remote-control vehicles, small cones, cardboard boxes, and other obstacles.
Advance Preparation: Create an obstacle course for the remote-control vehicles. Make the course simpler for younger guests.

Activity: Guests take remote cars through the obstacle course. Older guests may enjoy timing the journey through the obstacle course.

Pony Express

Ages: 7–teen
Time: 20–30 minutes
Materials Needed: Bicycles/scooters/roller blades, computer paper boxes, assorted colored paper, cord, and scissors.
Advance Preparation: Tie boxes to mailbox posts within the neighborhood (remember to ask for permission). Cut colored paper into envelope-size pieces enough for each guest to have 6 to 12 envelopes. Each guest has a different color. Put colored envelopes in the cardboard box mailboxes—one color for each guest in every box.

Activity: Riders run the course with cycles and collect the mail. The object is to ride and pick up the mail as quickly as possible. You may time the older riders. Riders go one at a time (one cycle may be used by all the participants).
Variation: If you are using scooters, create a tail and head on the scooter.

Magic Touch

Ages: 8–teen
Time: 15 minutes
Materials Needed: Snap-type clothespins and 5 buckets.
Advance Preparation: Paint clothespins various colors—one color for each guest, or write guests' names on pins. Set out buckets 20 to 30 feet apart.
Activity: Guests ride bicycles along a designated path with buckets spaced beside the path. Before starting, riders clip 5 clothespins on their shirts. As riders cycle along the path, they drop the clothespins in the buckets. Scoring is as follows:

    5 accurate drops—WOW
    4 accurate drops—Hot Shot
    3 accurate drops—Super
    2 accurate drops—Great
    1 accurate drop—Soft Touch

Grand Crawl

Ages: 8–adult
Time: 15 minutes
Materials Needed: Masking tape and bicycles for each guest.
Advance Preparation: Mark four racing lanes about 1 1/2 feet wide with a buffer lane 1 1/2 feet between each lane. The length of the ride can be 15 feet to 40 feet depending upon the skill level of the participants.
Activity: Cyclist ride to reach the finish line last. Feet may not touch the ground and riders must stay in their own lane.

Coast Along

Ages: 8–adult
Time: 15 minutes
Materials Needed: Masking tape for starting and coasting lines.

Advance Preparation: Mark a starting line and a coasting line about 50 feet from the starting line.
Activity: Guests see how far they can coast. Mark distance when they put a foot down on the ground.

Start   50 feet   Coast

Auto Race

Ages: 4–12 years
Time: 15 minutes
Materials Needed: Pictures of cars, bicycles, etc., poster board, glue, envelopes, and scissors.
Advance Preparation: Glue pictures on poster board

and cut into puzzle parts. Place each picture puzzle in an envelope.
Activity: Guests put puzzles together. The first guest to assemble a puzzle is the winner. Younger guests do as an activity without a winner.

Rail Nomads

Ages: 4–7 years
Time: 15 minutes
Materials Needed: Many large boxes decorated like train cars and engines. Cord and serrated knife. Glue and tie together a shallow and a tall box for the engines.
Advance Preparation: Cut out a door in the front and

back of each box (cars and engines). Tie boxes together in a circle.
Activity: Hobos climb in boxes and move from one car to another as the music plays. They must stop when the music stops. Hobos may also jump in and out of the boxes (re-enacting the hobo's jumps on and off trains long ago).

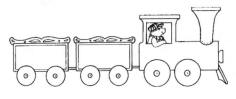

Obstacle Course

A course for riding toys, skate boards, scooters, bicycles, or roller skates.
Ages: 7–adult
Time: 20 minutes
Materials Needed: Cones, 2 planks 1 inch x 10 inches x 12 feet, large cans, one dozen lattice strips, nails, wood for ramps, and ropes for starting and finishing lines (masking tape may be used on hard surfaces). Chalk may be used to mark course directions.
Advance Preparation: Set up obstacle course.
Activity: Ride through the obstacle course. Timing each guest's ride is optional.

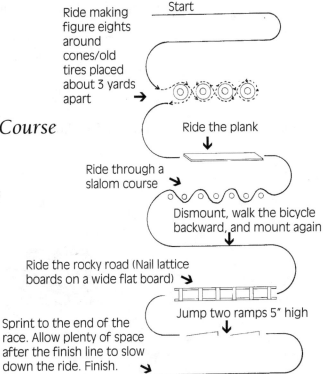

Ride making figure eights around cones/old tires placed about 3 yards apart

Start

Ride the plank

Ride through a slalom course

Dismount, walk the bicycle backward, and mount again

Ride the rocky road (Nail lattice boards on a wide flat board)

Jump two ramps 5" high

Sprint to the end of the race. Allow plenty of space after the finish line to slow down the ride. Finish.

Cycle Road Rally

Ages: 7–adult
Time: 1 hour
Materials Needed: Deck(s) of cards and a bicycle road rally course with five checkpoints.
Advance Preparation: Set up a rally course of several miles. Determine miles by the riders' skill.
Activity: Guests cycle though the road rally course and stop at each checkpoint where they pick up one card of a poker hand. The best five-card poker hand wins the road rally.
Variation: For added skill, you may also time each rider. Riders must go through each checkpoint in a specific amount of time—no more or less. The time is written down at each checkpoint.

Double-Decker Bus

Rent and give young guests a ride in a British double-decker bus. They will love it!

Songs of the Rail

The job of laying rail was hard and tedious. While men moved the heavy rails, they were led in song by "chanters." Many of the songs reflected the rhythm of their work.

"Drill, Ye Tarriers, Drill"
"Casey Jones"
"I've Been Workin' on the Railroad"
"The Gandy Dancers' Ball"
"John Henry"
"Paddy Works on the Railway"

Additional songs of the rail can be found on tapes from Jimmy Rodgers, "A Country Legacy" and others from RCA.

ALL ABOARD!

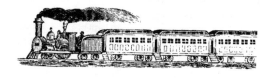

16: Winter Festival

Clean, crisp snow beckons us to the out-of-doors. Like the other seasons, winter is the source of many myths and celebrations centering around seasonal changes. Harsh cold and long nights characterized winter in the closest areas to the poles. Games and sports played in ice and snow are numerous. For instance, Native Americans threw spears on it while Europeans developed skiing. Simple games such as building snow creatures or sledding have been enjoyed by countless generations of children and adults in colder climates. No matter how bitter the elements, people manage to invent games and fun to bring pleasure to their lives.

While children in colder climates eagerly await the first snow of the season, those who live in the third of the earth too warm for the fluffy white stuff may grow up without ever seeing snow. If you are fortunate enough to live in a part of the planet where shimmering ice crystals fall from the sky, make the most of the situation with a simple winter festival in your backyard or woods.

INVITATION

Write on aluminum foil with permanent markers to create an ice pond invitation. Snowflakes or doilies are also pretty.

Slide Over to Michele's
FOR A WINTER FEST
Saturday, January 11
2:00–5:00 P.M.
10 Bradbury Lane
R.S.V.P. 555-7500
Bring a warm hat, mittens,
snowpants, and a sled.

DECORATIONS

❋ **Snowflakes** created from rectangular doilies make great place mats.

❋ **Ice candles** are made by filling large plastic buckets (5 quart) with water to about ¾-inch from the top. Place the buckets outside to freeze—about 5 hours in near zero temperatures. Take the ice candle out of the bucket before it freezes completely (it may split the bucket if left too long). When you place the ice candle in the snow upside down you will notice a small well in the bottom in which to place a votive candle. Snuggle the candles in the snow along the front porch, front walk, driveway, etc.

❄ **Snow sculptures** may greet your guests as they enter your front walkway. Decorate the snow sculptures with scarfs, hats, limbs, cones, etc.

❄ **Snowman bird feeder** decorated with limbs (arms), cranberry belt, carrot nose, pine cone covered with peanut butter and dipped in bird seed, hat sprinkled with bird seeds, assorted fruits, etc. It is delightful to watch the birds enjoy the goodies!

❄ Use a large mirror with cotton batting to simulate an **ice pond.**

❄ **Lanterns, torches,** and **large candles** are very festive in a winter parade of lights.

❄ **Hang clear cellophane straws** with fishing line to simulate icicles.

TERMS

Follies	Sledding	Frosty
Sliding	Skiing	Igloo
Olympics	Brrrrrr	Shimmering
Schussing	Cold	Ice crystal
"Snowdown"	Freezing	Snowflakes
Frolics	Mush	Snowdrifts
Flurries	Snowplow	Sparkling
Frivolity	Slip and slide	Brilliant
Icicle	Chill	Glittering
Skating	Icy	Crisp
Mogul	Eskimo	Blizzard
Slalom	Dogsled derby	Abominable
Frigid	Husky pull	Snowman

REFRESHMENTS

❄ Cocoa flavored with peppermint sticks.

❄ Hot cider, fresh hot cinnamon rolls, doughnuts, loose meat sandwiches, cheese and crackers, chili, fresh fruits and vegetables with dip.

❄ Roast hot dogs over an open fire or in the fireplace.

❄ Swiss Fondue.

❄ Ice-cream snowballs created by rolling scoops of ice cream in slightly browned coconut flakes.

FAVORS

❄ Water guns
❄ Ski posters

❄ Kaleidoscopes

ACTIVITIES/GAMES
Ice Skating

Ages: 4–adult

Time: 1–2 hours

Materials Needed: Guests bring their own ice skates. Radio/tape player with speakers, tapes, wood for a bonfire, and large plastic liner and railroad ties for ice pond if you need to build one.

Advance Preparation: Build and flood pond. Build a bonfire (check local fire codes).

Activity: Skate freely to music.

Mitten Scramble

Ages: 4–9 years
Time: 15 minutes
Materials Needed: None.
Advance Preparation: During the snack, gather all the guests' mittens and put them in a large pile. Mix them up well.

Activity: First guest to find his/her own pair of mittens wins.
Note: Parents should put each child's name in mittens.

Mini Snowman Parade

Ages: 5–12 years
Time: 40 minutes
Materials Needed: Buttons, branches, cones, rocks, scarfs, etc.
Advance Preparation: Gather paraphernalia for decorating the snowmen.

Activity: Guests create mini snowmen about 20 inches tall. Award ribbons to the funniest, fattest, cutest, sweetest, most creative, most handsome, etc.

Sledding

Ages: 3–adult
Time: 1–2 hours
Materials Needed: Guests bring their own sleds.
Advance Preparation: Select a safe sledding area.
Activity: Sledding. Be sure to go over safety rules.

Note: Be creative with your sledding gear. Use plastic bags, beach floats, inner tubes, large plastic tubs, etc. Have a contest of most original "sled"—suitcase, trash can lid, etc.

Snowshoe

Ages: 7–adult
Time: Several hours
Materials Needed: Guests bring their own snowshoes.

Advance Preparation: Select area for snowshoeing.
Activity: Snowshoe to that very special place! Build a bonfire when you arrive, tell stories, and serve s'mores.

Prints in the Snow

Ages: 4–12 years
Time: 20 minutes
Materials Needed: Warm clothes and a large area of new snow.
Advance Preparation: Ideas for prints—angel, space shuttle, snake, octopus, centipede, etc.

Activity: Guests create a print by lying in the snow and moving their arms and legs. Let guests guess what the snow prints are.

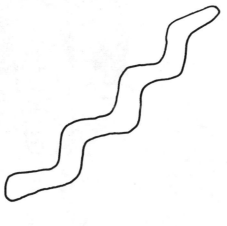
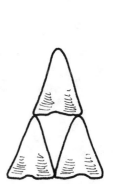

William Tell Snowball Archers

Ages: 5–teen
Time: 15 minutes
Materials Needed: Several snowmen with stocking caps perched lightly on their heads, and sticks or dowels.
Advance Preparation: Make snowmen, stabilizing the head with a dowel or stick stuck into the body. For additional head strength, spray the snowmen with water and let them freeze. Place stocking caps on the snowmen. Make several—one for each team. Determine a line from which guests may throw snowballs. Twenty-four feet is a good distance for teenagers.
Activity: For young children, the activity would consist of throwing snowballs at a snowman and trying to knock off his cap. For older children and youth, this can be done in a relay. Play more than once and keep relay teams small.

Arctic Artists (Snow Sculptures)

Ages: 4–teen
Time: 1 hour
Materials Needed: Large area of new snow warm enough to stick and mound into a ball, cans, stones, limbs, pieces of coal, ropes, skis, balloons, foil, hats, and assorted crepe paper colors.
Advance Preparation: To stimulate ideas for creatures at the party, have some suggestions ready—sharks, robot, dinosaurs, horses, snakes, bears, cats, snowcastles, etc.
Activity: Guests sculpt snow creatures. It is best to have two or three guests work on one creature. When finished, have creators tell about their work of art!
Note: Fill spray bottles or water guns with colored water and spray the creatures for special effects. Dip crepe paper (folded into rolls to resemble paint brushes) into water. Daub it over snow creatures.

Precision Snowballs

Ages: 5–teen
Time: 20 minutes
Materials Needed: Clothesline, old blanket, clothespins, scissors, and a permanent marker.
Advance Preparation: Cut several holes in the blanket. The holes should be about 8 to 15 inches in diameter. Give smaller holes a larger value and larger holes a lesser value. Keep numbers simple—5, 10, 15. Hang blanket on the line with clothespins and determine a line from which the guests throw their snowballs (vary the line).
Activity: Guests make a large pile of snowballs and then begin throwing them through the holes in the blanket. Sharpshooters throw five times and then tally their scores. The one with the most points wins the round. Play several rounds. Younger guests simply throw snowballs through the holes; do not keep track of their scores.
Variation: Suspend a plastic bat (icicle) from a tree limb—take aim! Also, throw snowballs for distance or through Hula Hoops placed in the snow.

Archaeological Dig

Ages: 4–teen
Time: 20 minutes
Materials Needed: Small plastic containers, clues, shovels, and spoons. You may wish to hide little novelty items with the clues for added excitement.
Advance Preparation: Develop clues and gather novelty items. Place them in the small containers and hide them in a large mound of snow. To vary the dig, put items out before a snowfall. Keep track of where the items were hidden.
Activity: Guests (archaeologists) dig with spoons into the mound of snow searching for clues. Which clue will lead them to discover a special prize?
Variation: Hide plastic dinosaurs. Keep track of the hiding spots and the number of objects hidden.

Search and Rescue

Ages: 5–12 years
Time: 10–15 minutes
Materials Needed: Plastic bags, small teddy bears or party favors.
Advance Preparation: Place small teddy bears/party favors individually in plastic bags and seal. Hide the bears/favors in the snow about the party area. Make sure they are visible.
Activity: Guests ("St. Bernard dogs") are part of a winter rescue team. The St. Bernards search for bears/favors until each has rescued one. Guests may keep the bears/favors.
Note: Hide an extra favor in case one is not found.

Broom Hockey

Ages: 10–adult
Time: 30–45 minutes
Materials Needed: Straw brooms, a puck (knotted cloth), and eight orange marking cones. A referee and whistle are optional.
Advance Preparation: Set up a hockey court on the ice (30 x 50 feet). Mark two goals with the orange cones. Remind guests to bring a new straw broom each. Make a puck with knotted cloth.
Activity: Guests play broom hockey using ice hockey rules. Follow the safety rule regarding "high sticking." It is very important that players keep the broom striking end below the waist at all times. A penalty results if this rule is violated. If the group of guests is quite large, it is best to have more than one hockey court. Six players on a team is recommended.
Variation: Play with ice creepers (shoes with nonskid treads). Strike for goals and score from a baseline.

Snow Obstacle Course

Ages: 6–teen
Time: 30 minutes
Materials Needed: Shovels, plastic buckets, boards, small hill, plastic grocery bags, plastic Ping Pong guns, 2 pairs of snowshoes, and a large box with a hole in the center.
Advance Preparation: Make an obstacle course with snow. Create tunnels, slides, targets, snowshoe course, ledges, etc.
Activity: Guests slip on snowshoes and go through the obstacle course as quickly as possible. See the "Obstacle Course" in the Backyard Sports Fest chapter for additional ideas. Time each guest.

Dogsled Relay

Ages: 7–adult

Time: 25 minutes

Materials Needed: Sleds, preferably with runners.

Advance Preparations: Create identical short dogsled courses for two or more relay teams.

Activity: Divide guests into teams of six. The first two members of each relay team begin the race—one pulls the sled and the other rides in the sled. They race through the course as quickly as possible. The team to finish first is the winner. Play a second time and reverse riding and pulling the sled.

WINTER FUN
COMES IN FLURRIES!

Section Two

HOLIDAYS

17: New Year

The beginning of a new year is a time of celebration for people around the world. It marks the start of the annual cycle of the seasons, a time to say good-bye to the past and look optimistically into the future. The cycle itself varies. Ancient civilizations thought the year began with the first green of spring. Earliest calendars were ten months, with the first day on March 1. It was not until Julius Caesar introduced his first calendar in 46 B.C. that the months January and February came into being.

In all the New Year's celebrations, ancient to present, there is the common notion of shedding the old and bringing in the new, starting with a clean slate—a kind of purification. Merrymaking, ringing bells, cheering, noisemaking, and sounding party horns are all old customs used by celebrants in ancient times to scare evil spirits. Today such bell ringing and hooting simply rings out the old and rings in the new.

Gift giving was also a custom in many past New Year's festivities but is now popularly associated with Christmas. The term "pin money" comes from an old English custom—husbands gave their wives money enough on New Year's Day to buy pins for the whole year. The welcoming of a new year remains one of the greatest annual festivals.

INVITATION

Sprinkle confetti in the invitation. If you are having a Casino Night, enclose a fake $10,000 bill for each guest.

TIME TO CELEBRATE
RING IN THE NEW YEAR WITH DINNER
Date _____
Time _____
Place _____

_____

Bring your favorite ethnic dish and bells
to ring in the New Year!
R.S.V.P.

DECORATIONS

- 🥂 Tie **ribbons** and **bells** to clusters of **helium balloons**.
- 🥂 Drape **streamers** galore.
- 🥂 Invite guests to bring **old photos, yearbooks,** and **old scrapbooks** for display.
- 🥂 Create a **black-and-white theme** with a touch of red or silver.
- 🥂 Post **proverbs** all around the party room. Find a book of proverbs and quotations from your library.
- 🥂 Christmas **twinkle lights** will add a festive touch.
- 🥂 Hanging **garlands** adds gaiety to any party atmosphere.
- 🥂 **Casino dealers** in **costume** create an instant Las Vegas.
- 🥂 Make **giant dice** from boxes covered with white crepe paper.

LOOT

- 🥂 Create a **Father Time** with a nylon stocking face and an old coat. Remember an **old clock!**
- 🥂 Display an **hourglass, clock,** or **watch collection.**
- 🥂 Tuck **horns** and **whistles** in a floral centerpiece.
- 🥂 Ring in the New Year with **bells,** all shapes and sizes.
- 🥂 Drape festive gold or silver **serpentine.**
- 🥂 Set **alarm clocks** around the room (alarms ring every half hour).
- 🥂 Use **confetti** liberally!
- 🥂 Make a giant **fortune wheel!**
- 🥂 Decorate the wheel with assorted **fortunes** for the New Year. With a brass paper fastener, attach a cardboard spinner to the wheel.

TERMS

Midnight madness	Wealth	Gaiety
Good luck	Magical	Resolutions
Father Time	Glad bells	Jollity
Blast	Fond wishes	Usher in
Cheers	Naughty	Toast
Timely chimes	Happy	Charm
Health	Future	Glimmering
Spirit	Prosperity	Shimmering
Hourglass	Glad tidings	Sparkling

FOODS

- 🥂 Serve ethnic foods and wear ethnic costumes.
- 🥂 Highlight the feast with a dessert.
- 🥂 Consider other elegant, traditional foods.

FAVORS

- 🥂 Noisemakers
- 🥂 Cymbals
- 🥂 Large bells
- 🥂 Hats
- 🥂 Gongs
- 🥂 Toy watches
- 🥂 Date books
- 🥂 Calendars
- 🥂 Bells

ACTIVITIES/GAMES
Noble Fairy

Ages: 4–adult
Time: Spontaneously throughout the evening
Materials Needed: Hire an actress to act the part of a "Noble Fairy" or arrange for a friend with a dramatic flair to come as a Noble Fairy with her glittering wand and silver dust.

Advance Preparation: Make arrangements for the magical guest to attend your party.
Activity: The Fairy mingles among the guests casting magical spells upon them. Using fairy-tale lingo, she waves her wand and sheds a bit of silver dust upon each guest.

Casino Night

Ages: 10–adult
Time: 3–4 hours
Materials Needed: Blackjack cloth, roulette wheel, craps cloth, dice, bingo, plenty of tables, chips, fake money, costumes/vests for dealers, and money bags or large gambling cups.
Advance Preparation: Know how to play all the games or invite a few guests who could act as dealers. Put together money packages of equal amounts for each guest. Have plenty of chips at each table. Rent or purchase games.

Activity: Guests move from game to game gambling their fake money.

Dinner and Dancing

Ages: 10–adult
Time: 2–3 hours
Materials Needed: A band or your favorite recordings for dancing, a dance floor, and a disc/tape player.
Advance Preparation: Make all arrangements needed for dinner and dancing. Indicate dress on the invitation—black tie or masquerade.

Activity: Guests enjoy an elegant dinner and dancing. If this is a family affair, adults may have dinner upstairs and the children and friends may have dinner downstairs. They then come together for dancing.
Note: Take Polaroid pictures of guests as they arrive.

Pentathlon of Table Games

Ages: 8–adult
Time: 2–3 hours
Materials Needed: Checkers, decks of cards, a trivia game, skittles, a word game, "Boggle," and another board game. Games should last about 30 minutes each.
Advance Preparation: Choose five games and set them up in the family room. Choose games appropriate to age.

Activity: Guests move about participating in the pentathlon of games. Winners of each game receive 5 points. Keep a running tally of scores as in bridge. You may set up more than five games but guests play only five.
Variation: If you have some very young children involved, play "Husker-Du." You may also play skittles.

Wishing Tree

Ages: 6–adult
Time: 15–20 minutes
Materials Needed: Walnuts in shells, fortunes/predictions typed on small slips of paper, and a hot glue gun.
Advance Preparation: Pry open nuts, remove the meat, and replace it with a fortune/prediction. Use a dictionary of quotations and proverbs for ideas. For children, you may wish to use a trinket such as a coin for wealth, a heart for marriage, candy for a sweet year, or a map piece for a long trip. Glue walnut halves together with a piece of 8-inch ribbon for a hanger. Hang them on the Christmas tree and differentiate walnuts intended for children and adults by ribbon color. Remove a few Christmas ornaments to make room for the walnuts.

Activity: Shortly before midnight, guests remove a walnut from the tree and read their fortunes aloud.
Variation: Write a prophecy of the fulfillment of some "dearest wish" tailored for each guest. Use miniature cards and envelopes. Glue a ribbon on each envelope, write the guest's name and hang it on the tree.

Looking for Lost Time

Ages: 5–adult
Time: 15 minutes
Materials Needed: Miniature hourglasses/toy watches.
Advance Preparation: On each hourglass or watch write an amount of time—e.g., 20 hours, 45 minutes, and 13 seconds. Hide the hourglasses/watches.
Activity: Divide guests into teams. Guests search for lost time. The team accumulating the most time is the winner.

Confetti Clock Piñatas

Ages: 6–adult
Time: 15 minutes
Materials Needed: Piñata (may be a clock piñata).
Advance Preparation: Write a fortune for each guest on a small card. Cut colorful ribbons into 2-foot lengths (one for each guest). Attach a jingle bell to each ribbon. Cut a hole in the bottom of the piñata and fill with confetti, small treasures/coins, and fortunes. Punch holes, one for each ribbon, in a double layer of tissue sized a little bigger than the hole in the piñata. Thread the ribbons through the holes and glue the tissue over the opening of the piñata. Hang the piñata from a chandelier or doorway within reach of the guests.
Activity: At midnight each guest pulls one of the bells hanging from the piñata. A gentle pull will release the treasures, the New Year's prophecies, and confetti. Read the fortunes aloud.
Variation: Attach the piñata to a pole.

Mimes/Magicians/Jugglers

Ages: All ages
Time: 15–20 minutes
Materials Needed: Professional or amateur (family member) mime, magician, or juggler.
Advance Preparation: Make arrangements for entertainment.
Activity: Guests are entertained by a mime, magician, or a juggler.

Chinese "Lucky Money"

Ages: 4–12 years
Time: 10 minutes
Materials Needed: Coins wrapped in red paper.
Advance Preparation: Hide wrapped coins under the bed pillows.
Activity: Children discover the "lucky money" on New Year's morning.

Family Blessings

Ages: 2–adult
Time: 10 minutes
Materials Needed: Paper and pencil optional.
Advance Preparation: Prepare thoughtful blessings for family members (identify special talents and strengths).
Activity: At the New Year's feast, the parents bestow blessings upon each family member.

Instant New Year's Harmony

Ages: 3–adult
Time: 15–30 minutes
Materials Needed: Toy instruments—tambourines, bells, horns, violins, xylophones, harmonicas, drums, sticks, etc.
Advance Preparation: Wrap orchestral instruments in gaily colored paper.
Activity: Guest may draw for prizes or select a present (instrument). As each present is opened the instrument will be revealed. Be intuitively aware of the guests and decide how best to orchestrate them—guests may want to parade with the instruments at midnight. Some guests may wish to play a short selection or guests may be divided into small ensembles to practice and perform at midnight.

Balloon Drop

Ages: 3–adult
Time: 10 minutes
Materials Needed: Large balloon net filled with balloons.
Advance Preparation: Fill balloons with prize slips, money, or resolutions. Put all the balloons in a giant net drop bag and suspend it from the ceiling. Purchase drop bag from a balloon store.

Activity: At midnight pull a string that drops all the balloons out of the bag. Each guest gathers one balloon, breaks it, and discovers a prize or resolution.
Variation: Tie long ribbons on helium-filled balloons. Insert prizes or resolutions while filling the balloons. Balloons will rise to the ceiling. At midnight guests grab a ribbon, break the balloon, and their prizes are revealed.

Favorite New Year's Songs

At midnight bring in the wassail bowl filled with hot spiced apple and cranberry juice. While singing your favorite wassail songs, dance (with tankards in hand) around the fire, table, friends, etc.

"Auld Lang Syne"
"Gloucestershire Wassail"
"Sweet Adeline"
"Gower Wassail"
"Apple Tree Wassail"
"Kentucky Wassail"
"Cornish Wassail"
"Somerset Wassail"
"Glory to the Mountain"
"Go, Tell it on the Mountain"
"Chicken Foot"
"Children, Go Where I Send Thee"

WELCOME IN A GREAT NEW YEAR!

HAND OUT SOME "MAD MONEY" FOR THE NEW YEAR!

18: Valentine's Day

February 14, a festival day of love and romance, is celebrated throughout much of the Western world. Friends and relatives exchange special greetings and presents expressing a sentimental thought or a simple message of affection. The name Valentine comes from a Christian martyr. According to legend, Bishop Valentine was a kindly man loved by the children in his town. Later, when he was jailed for his religious beliefs, children felt sad. They missed him so much they wrote loving letters to him and slipped them through the bars of his cell. Other aspects of the Valentine's Day celebration probably originate from an ancient Roman festival, Lupercalia, dedicated to young lovers. It honored Juno, the Roman goddess of women and marriage, and Pan, the god of nature. Still another source of Valentine tradition may be the medieval legend that birds meet on February 14 to choose mates. Symbols of love from ancient times are still important today. Cupid (a Greek god of love), flowers, the heart (necessary for life), candy, and lace express special affection on Valentine's Day. Share a little love with someone today!

INVITATION

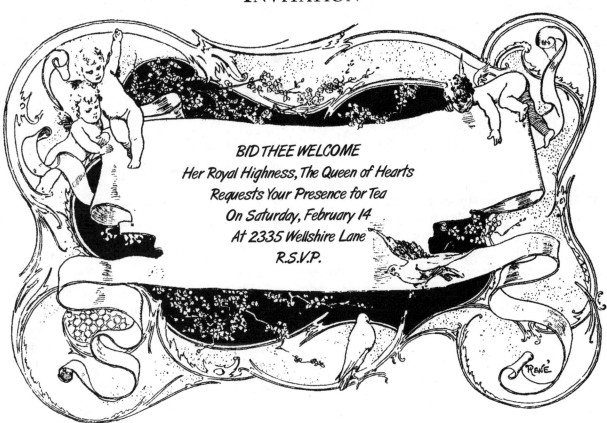

BID THEE WELCOME
Her Royal Highness, The Queen of Hearts
Requests Your Presence for Tea
On Saturday, February 14
At 2335 Wellshire Lane
R.S.V.P.

Valentine puzzles, mazes, and love poems make interesting invitations. Include a package of flower seeds: "Love in a Mist" or "Forget-Me-Nots." Valentines or invitations can be sent from Valentine, Nebraska, or Loveland, Colorado, for a special holiday postmark. Send messages at least two weeks before February 14 in a large envelope and ask for the special postmark/logo. Remember to have envelopes addressed and stamped before you send them to Valentine or Loveland.

Chamber of Commerce
Valentine, NE 69201
(ask for postmark)

U.S. Postmaster
Loveland, CO 80537
(ask for logo)

DECORATIONS

- Decorate with **paper** or **balloon hearts.**
- Incorporate lots of **ribbon, lace,** and **flowers** in the decorating scheme.
- Bring out the **silver** and **fine china.** Display it on your finest **lace tablecloths.**
- Light many **candles** and enjoy a candlelight dinner on this romantic day!
- Make a large **banner** of paper or cloth—develop a message from "Sweet Talk" in this chapter.
- Hang **Cupids** carrying hearts with messages.
- Highlight with **heart-shaped garlands.**
- Make sentimental **heartstrings** strung on beautiful ribbon.

- **Tissue hearts** and **tissue balls** are festive.
- On **red tablecloths** add white crepe paper streamers running down the centers.
- Wear **buttons** with valentine captions.
- Design and decorate an **old-fashioned valentine box** (15-inch-square box). Cover in shiny red, white, or pink paper and decorate with cupids, doilies, lace, and hearts. Fill with guest's valentine cards to be exchanged.
- Decorate a **grapevine wreath** with dried flowers, especially dried rosebuds and/or ribbon.

- Put up **love signs**: One Way To Your Heart, Valentine Avenue, Caution—Tender Hearts! Format them inside street signs.

- Create a **heart Maypole.** Place a pole (dowel) in a round piece of Styrofoam. Wrap it with satin ribbon and place a satin heart on top. From the top of the pole drape red ribbons to the base or to each table place setting. Decorate the base with dried flowers or foil paper.
- Remember **Shakespeare**—write out some of his love poems on giant hearts. Generate with computer.
- Create an old **love lantern** out of a gourd or turnip.
- Cut gorgeous **lace doilies** using hearts and diamonds. Fold and cut as a snowflake.
- Display beautiful **love poems** in old assorted frames.
- Roll handwritten **love proverbs** in **little scrolls** and tie them with red ribbons. Line a crystal bowl with a lace doily and fill it with the scrolls. Place it on the tea table for guests to share. Love proverbs can be found in *Apples of Gold* by Jo Petty. Type on a computer.

SWEET TALK

Tender heart	Sweet	Ceremony
Deceit	Lost arrow	Penning (write)
Fantasies	Cupid	Twirling
Heart-to-heart	Cherish	Warm glow
Love nest	Spinster	Candlelight
Aching heart	Jealous	Merrily
Pretty girl	Escort	Bejewel
Sentimental	Bachelor	Aglow
Love ya	Captivating	Elegance
True love	Envy	Lace
Heartthrob	Charming	Romantic
Be mine	Crush	Enchantment
Be true	Romantic	Sugar-coated
Puppy love	Darling	Delicate
Frolic	Heartbeat	Embrace
Love Bug	Kiss me	Bleeding hearts
You belong to me	Contented	Heartfelt
I'm hooked	Sweetheart	Sentiments
Lovingly	Hug	Glitter and glitz
Heartbreak	Knave of Hearts	Whimsical flight
Sugar plum	Guess who?	Frivolous
Kind	Your Casanova	Fanciful
Cool	Queen of Hearts	Fantastic
Health	Hearty	Fascinating

REFRESHMENTS

- Sprinkle red candy hearts on vanilla ice cream.
- Serve heart-shaped sandwiches or cookies.
- Make red punch or pink lemonade.
- Fortune valentines—write special valentine messages on paper hearts (pliable paper). Roll and insert inside Pepperidge Farm Pirouettes.
- Create a heart-shaped cake or ice-cream cake from a square and round cake pan.
- Serve heart-shaped cinnamon toast for breakfast!
- Attach Bit-O-Honey pieces to a heart … "You are my Bit-O-Honey."
- The "Queen of Hearts" and the "Knave of Hearts" may serve refreshments or your candlelight dinner. Create costumes with felt, tights, turtleneck shirts, and white boots.

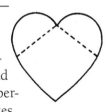

FAVORS

- Valentine button pins
- Stuffed animals
- Decorative soap
- Horoscope
- Chocolates
- Red/pink clothing accessory
- Lace handkerchief
- Flowers

ACTIVITIES/GAMES
Valentine Exchange

Ages: 2–6 years
Time: 10–15 minutes
Materials Needed: Paper punch, yarn, doilies, assorted sequins, glitter, sewing notions, markers/crayons, glue, scissors, construction paper, and foil paper.

Advance Preparation: Create sample valentines. For younger children have valentines cut out.
Activity: Children create a valentine, punch two holes near the top, thread with yarn, exchange, and wear special valentines like pendants.

Autographed Valentines

Ages: 4–adult
Time: 30 minutes
Materials Needed: Doilies, assorted sequins, glitter, foil paper, sewing notions, markers/crayons, yarn, construction paper, wrapping paper, scissors, glue, tag board, wrapping paper, crisp white or red paper for pin-prick valentines, bulletin board tacks, and a paper punch.
Advance Preparation: Have all materials ready and make up some sample valentines.

Activity: Decorate large valentines leaving space for guest signatures. Pass valentines to secure signatures/message from all the guests. Children may want to wear their signed valentines as large pendants. Make pendant out of yarn.
Variation: Adults and older children may want to create a pin-prick or rubber-stamp valentine. Use good quality white paper, prick design with large needle, and glue on dark background paper. Use an assortment of rubber stamps.

Pleated Hearts

Ages: 5–adult
Time: 20–30 minutes
Materials Needed: Assorted paper, markers/crayons, sewing notions, scissors, glue, and lace/doilies.
Advance Preparation: Create samples of pleated valentines and have all materials gathered.

Activity: Accordion-pleat 4-inch strips of paper. One pleat makes one heart—make as many pleats as you want hearts. Draw a half heart on first/top pleat. Cut around heart pattern leaving small area of heart on the fold uncut. Open the pleated hearts and decorate.

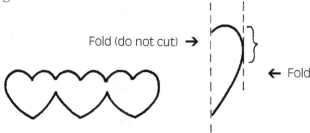

Fold (do not cut) →   ← Fold

Mend a Broken Heart

Ages: 3–adult
Time: 10–20 minutes
Materials Needed: Poster board (red/pink/white), scissors, pencil, and large envelopes.
Advance Preparation: Cut large hearts from tag board. Draw and cut each heart into a giant puzzle. Make puzzle difficulty appropriate to the age of guests. Keep puzzles separated by placing them in large envelopes.

Activity: Give each person/group an envelope of puzzle pieces. See which person/group can put the puzzle together the fastest. You may use the floor for this activity—especially if you are putting together (mending) giant-sized hearts.
Variation: For giant hearts, tape together sheets of newspaper to form a large 5 foot by 6 foot sheet of paper. Draw a giant heart on the sheet of paper and cut into puzzle parts. Transpose puzzle patterns onto red/pink/white poster board.

Heart Tree

Ages: 3–adult
Time: 10 minutes
Materials Needed: A tree branch or decorative silk tree, narrow ribbon, and a paper punch.
Advance Preparation: In the invitation ask each guest to bring a heart/valentine message or poem to be hung on a tree of hearts.

Activity: As guests arrive have them hang their valentines on the tree. Share special messages or poems sometime during the party.
Variation: Hang love verses/poems on the tree and as guests leave they take home a sentimental verse. Dangle ribbon pieces all over the tree.

Post Office Valentine Exchange

Ages: 5–12 years
Time: 15–20 minutes
Materials Needed: Large cardboard box, decorative sacks, red, white, or pink butcher paper/glossy gift wrap, markers, glue, scissors, serrated knife, strapping tape, festive holiday rubber stamp, and a good imagination.
Advance Preparation: With the help of your family, create the post office well in advance of the party. Draw plans and then construct the post office. Cut out the window front and decorate your post office. Place individual post office boxes (decorative sacks) on the floor behind the window—one box for each guest.

Activity: As the guests arrive they should give the postmaster (guest of honor) their valentines for exchange. The postmaster postmarks the valentines with a rubber stamp and places them in the individual boxes (sacks). Toward the end of the party the postmaster passes out the boxes to guests for the valentine exchange.
Variation: Let Mr. Sperry Sparrow, postmaster general, deliver miniature cards for dolls and animal friends.

Clothespin Heart Relay

Ages: 3–9 years
Time: 10–15 minutes
Materials Needed: Scrap fabric pieces (red, white, pink), wood spring clothespins, yarn, scissors, and a small wicker "laundry" basket (one for each team).
Advance Preparation: Out of red felt cut 4-inch hearts. Each guest should have two or more hearts. String yarn to create a clothesline (two adults may hold the line).
Activity: From a basket, children pick up a heart and

clothespin, run to the line, and hang the heart. Then they run back and tag the next team member and repeat. Be very clear when giving relay directions—walk through the relay once. Young children should just hang hearts as an activity. Simply hanging the hearts will be enjoyable for them.
Variation: Instead of hearts, cut long underwear from the red felt.

Animal/Character Valentines

Ages: 3–12 years
Time: 15–20 minutes
Materials Needed: Yarn, construction paper, scissors, glue, markers, and pencils.
Advance Preparation: Cut many assorted hearts—very tiny to 5 inches. Make samples of a few animals.
Activity: Guests create animal or character valentines—snakes, elephants, cats, flowers, etc.

Cupid's Shooting Arcade

Ages: 6–adult
Time: 15–20 minutes
Materials Needed: Poster board, clear plastic yard goods, construction paper, scissors, markers, toy bows and arrows (with suction tips), score pad, and pencils.
Advance Preparation: Create a large dartboard of poster board and vinyl yard goods. Designate target areas with hearts of various degree values—center circle 75 degrees (enamored), middle ring 25 degrees (heartthrob), outer ring 0 degrees (aching heart), and outer edge -25 degrees (deceit). Color code all the arrows in two or three different colors.
Activity: Guests shoot color-coded arrows at the heart target—two or three guests may shoot simultaneously. Guests continue to shoot until all have had a turn. When participants finish shooting, they tally their score and tell the scorekeeper. Highest scores win. Were you stung by cupid's arrow?
Note: Suction arrow tips will stick better if dampened.

Valentine Puzzles

Ages: 6–adult
Time: 10 minutes
Materials Needed: Old valentine cards, envelopes, and scissors.
Advance Preparation: Cut old valentine cards into puzzle pieces and place each puzzle in an envelope.
Activity: Guests each put a valentine puzzle together.

Fortune Telling

Ages: 6–adult
Time: 30–45 minutes
Materials Needed: Gypsy fortune-teller or palmist, fortunes written down for the fortune-teller, a palmistry booth or table, a costume for the fortune-teller (Queen of Hearts), a crystal ball, a scarf, and a palmistry book from the library.
Advance Preparation: Write or type fortunes, create the fortune-teller's costume and booth. Personalize fortunes by seeking out "interesting facts" about each guest before the party.
Activity: Fortune-teller or palmist gives guests some prophecy of what will happen in their futures. "Love life" is fun for many groups but other interest areas can also be fun.

Musical Hearts

Ages: 4–teen
Time: 20 minutes
Materials Needed: Giant hearts made of red poster board, a tape, and tape player.
Advance Preparation: Cut out the giant hearts and lay them on the floor.
Activity: As music is played, guests dance around the hearts. When it stops, all run to stand on a heart. Repeat play removing one heart each time. Play until one heart remains and guests must try to gather on one heart … Heavy Heart!

Arrow Hunt

Ages: 8–adult
Time: 10–15 minutes
Materials Needed: Pink and white construction paper, marking pens, and scissors.
Advance Preparation: Cut many pink and white arrows—same number of each color. On each arrow write one of the following valentine messages: sweet, puppy love, heartthrob, and heartbreak. The arrows must have the same number of phrases in each color. Hide the arrows about the party room.
Activity: Guests are divided into two groups—a pink team and a white team. At a given signal, both teams begin hunting for arrows. The pink team collects only the pink arrows and the white team collects only the white arrows. The hunt is ended after 2 minutes. A leader from each team collects all the team's arrows. Now tell each team that the arrows score as follows: heartthrob—10 points, puppy love—5 points, sweet—2 points, and heartbreak—minus 5 points. The team with the most points wins the hunt.
Variation: For more teams add colors.

Candy Charades

Ages: 8–adult
Time: 30–45 minutes
Materials Needed: Valentine candy with captions.
Advance Preparation: Purchase the valentine candy.
Activity: Guests select a piece of candy and play charades pantomiming the message. The players who guess the correct saying win a point for their team. This is a very funny activity as guests act out "Heartbreak," etc.
Variation: Play charades of famous lovers—Li'l Abner and Daisy Mae, Antony and Cleopatra, Isaac and Rebecca, Dagwood and Blondie, Hamlet and Ophelia, Romeo and Juliet, Popeye and Olive Oyl, Snow White and the Prince, Mickey and Minnie Mouse, Sampson and Delilah, John Smith and Pocahontas, Cinderella and Prince Charming, Dale Evans and Roy Rogers, and others. Put together a costume box from which guests may create a character costume. Remember safety pins.

Broken Hearts

Ages: 7–adult
Time: 10 minutes
Materials Needed: Red, pink, and white construction paper, scissors, heart doilies, lace, and glue.
Advance Preparation: Create one broken heart (half a heart) for each guest. There should be equal numbers of red, pink, and white hearts. Decorate hearts and cut each heart in half with a special puzzle cut. Hide the broken hearts throughout the party area.

Activity: Guests search for one broken heart and then try to find a partner who has the other half of the broken heart. When all the broken hearts are mended (matched), the game is ended. This can also be done at the beginning of the Clothespin Heart Relay. All the red hearts are one team, pink hearts another, and white hearts another relay team.

Alice in Wonderland Croquet

Ages: 7–adult
Time: 20–45 minutes
Materials Needed: Croquet set, poster board, colored markers, wire, and scissors.

Advance Preparation: Create characters from the story of Alice in Wonderland and attach them to the wire wickets. Review the story for ideas.
Activity: Play croquet.

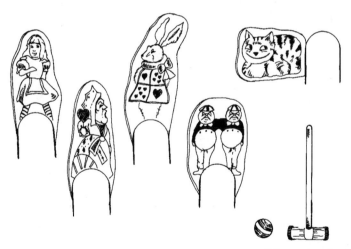

Visit a Nursing Home or Hospital
(Make a Homemade Valentine)

Ages: All
Time: 2 hours
Materials Needed: Glue, paper, doilies, etc. A paper bag for trash.
Advance Preparation: Select ideas for a simple valentine. Collect materials needed and have children make a sample valentine.

Activity: Make a homemade valentine with a senior or hospital patient.

Valentine Treasurers

Ages: 3–adult
Time: Spontaneous
Materials Needed: Red/pink paper, scissors, pen, and special "love" presents.
Advance Preparation: Cut assorted hearts and arrows. Write those special "love" notes to family members and hide them everywhere—in the car, in the refrigerator, in a drawer, etc. Shaving cream makes an excellent medium for a message on a mirror. One note may give clues (directions) in locating that special present!
Activity: Family members discover "love" notes under their pillow, in a shoe, and wherever!

HAVE FUN WITH THESE HEARTY IDEAS!

19: April Fools' Day

April Fools' Day is celebrated on the first day of April. It is a day of harmless jokes and silly antics when the victim is called an "April Fool." The origin of this holiday is not clear but it is thought to have started in France after the implementation of the Gregorian calendar in 1564. Until this time, the New Year was celebrated beginning March 21 (vernal equinox) and ending April 1. It was customary to exchange presents on April 1, but when the date was changed people were disgruntled and began to exchange mock presents on this day. They also showed their unhappiness by inviting people to nonexistent parties. Sometime later, the custom reached England and Scotland. Here one of the pranks was to send someone on a gowk (cuckoo) hunt. "Gowk" is derived from "geck" which means: someone who is easily duped.

All Fools' Day is observed today in English-speaking lands, western Europe, and India. It is loved best by children who adore tripping up a teacher or two.

INVITATION

Place the invitation in envelopes graduated in size from small to large.

ONLY FOR FOOLS IS THIS SPECIAL DAY
FOOLS' FEAST
April 1, 1997
7:00 P.M.
Merry pranks and folly await you at
_____
R.S.V.P.

DECORATIONS

Display posters with **old fools' proverbs:**

"None but a fool is always right"
"Fools rush in where angels fear to tread"
"Fools' names and fools' faces appear in public places"
"By outward show let's not be cheated, a fool should like a fool be treated"
"A fool and his money are soon parted"

Joke and **riddle books** should be easily accessible.

Hang **posters/pictures** of medieval jesters and fools … include Frans Hal's *The Lute Player*.

Make **newspaper comic place mats.**

Decorate with **jester hats** and **bells.**

Arrange a collection of **jesters/fools** as the table centerpiece.

Lay a piece of **fake dog doo-doo** under a dining room chair.

Use a **Thanksgiving** or **Christmas centerpiece** on the table.

- From the chandelier, suspend brightly colored **ribbons** with a bell tied on the end of each ribbon.
- Place **silly signs** about the party room—"No Loafing" on the sofa, "Detour" on the bathroom door, "Keep Off" on the chairs, "Slow" in the hall, "Quick Sale," placed on a moldy loaf of bread, "Beware Dangerous Dog," etc.

FOOLS' TERMS

Ludicrous	Gag	Dupe
Carnival spirit	Loony	Wacky
Prank	Jokers	Utterly foolish
Jolly	Witticism	Absurd
April's Gowk Day	Folly/frolics	Crazy/zany
Gaiety	Fool's paradise	Silly
Merry pranks	Mock	Tomfoolery
Jestering	Daze	Preposterous

FOODS

- Cut up pieces of string and mix into cooked cereal or pancake batter.
- Dip a wad of cotton into melted chocolate for a fools' chocolate truffle.
- Dip a piece of wax/candle into melted chocolate for a simpletons' piece of chocolate-covered caramel.
- Purchase and serve chocolate-covered ants, etc.

FAVORS

- Baby rattles on jester sticks.
- Booby prizes of any kind.
- Foolish or crazy books such as a foolish dictionary.

PREPOSTEROUS PRANKS

- Greet guests or students with an artificial arm or hand borrowed from a store mannikin. Let the arm fall out of the sleeve during the handshake.
- Cautiously affix paper signs on friends' backs bearing assorted inscriptions ... "Please tell me my name," "Kick me," "Pinch me," "Make me giggle," "Kiss me," "For sale," etc.
- Tie a fishing line to a wallet placed alluringly on the sidewalk or front porch. Jerk it away as someone attempts to pick it up.
- Affix a "Wet Paint—use the back door" sign on the front door. On the back door hang another sign that says "You April Fool—use the front door."
- At the office, invent a contest a week before April 1. Announce the rules and the prize—free chicken dinners for the winner's family or friends. On April 1, present the winner with a small sack of cracked oats.
- Place a brick in a hat laying on the ground. As a person gives it a swift kick, he stubs his toe.
- From a novelty store, purchase "dribble" drinking glasses, rubber peanuts or hot dogs, extra-hot red hots, bugs for ice cubes, rubber snakes, onion gum, joy buzzers, whoopee cushions, phony arrows through the head, squirting rings, dog doo-doo, etc.
- Set the dinner table using ridiculous tableware—spatulas, serving pieces, wire whips, platters for plates, bowls for cups, etc.
- Tie all the dining chairs together at the base with strong cord or fishing line.
- Serve breadsticks in a toy log truck.
- From a novelty store, purchase a long rubber tube with a little bulb at each end. Place it under the tablecloth—one bulb under a guest's plate and the other bulb at your place setting. During dinner squeeze the bulb and the bulb under the guest's place will bulge up causing her plate to dance around.
- Glue old silverware together at each place setting.
- With a long basting stitch, sew the dinner napkins together.
- As guests enter and sign the guestbook, they will struggle signing it with a trick pencil.
- Hang a distorting mirror in the bathroom.

Glue a quarter to the floor.

Attach a toy mouse to a curtain or drape.

Send an unsuspecting person on a tomfool errand—pick up a quart of sweet vinegar or buy some rabbit's milk.

Tell a young man that his fly is open.

If you deliver newspapers, deliver old newspapers and place the new paper in a less conspicuous place. Select your clients carefully—those with a sense of humor.

Put today's cover on yesterday's newspaper.

Glue the newspaper pages together.

Fill a candy box with fiberfill.

Give someone a bouquet of fresh green onions.

Glue the secretary's pens and pencils together.

Replace the shaving cream can with a can of whipping cream.

Substitute oil for liquid soap.

Fill pill vial with plastic bugs.

Hide an open carton of Limburger cheese in an unused desk drawer. Substitute another smell if you cannot find the cheese.

Link the secretary's paper clips in a chain.

With soap write "APRIL FOOL" across all the mirrors in the house.

Ask silly questions … "What is that little thing on your face?"

Set alarm clocks to go off at varying times throughout the night.

Create a room of webs. String thread in a friend's office or room.

Short-sheet the beds—fold the top sheet in half and tuck it in.

Wear a dark jacket and place a spool of light thread in the pocket. Run the thread though the back of the jacket and let a little hang out. People will try to remove the conspicuous piece of thread but instead they pull more and more thread.

Tape and play eerie sounds … have them coming from weird places.

Send out three different dinner invitations. One for a tennis theme, one for a hobo theme, and one for a formal sit-down dinner. As guests arrive, they show up in different attire and wonder if they read the invitation correctly.

Send invitations for dinner or dessert. When guests arrive have your children answer the door and very innocently tell the guests that their mom and dad have gone out for the evening. The guests are confused as they also see magazines lying on the floor and things in a bit of disarray. Suddenly as they are about to leave, the host/hostess pop out and yell "April Fools!" After the guests have arrived they must keep out of sight until all the guests have come.

Transmitting sound waves has always been fascinating to children. Have two participants hold the ends of a long string or phone cord. As they visit with one another, ask others if they would like to hear their conversation by putting the line between their teeth. One by one they gather on the line. The conversation continues and the first person asks,

"Where have you been?"
The second person replies, "I have been fishing."
The first one inquisitively asks, "Did you catch any fish?"
The second person responds, "Yes, a whole line of suckers!"

Set up a simpleton obstacle course using buckets, chairs, broom handle, a jump rope, etc. Everyone makes a trial run through the course with eyes open. Now blindfold the first two players who must move through the course without touching any of the obstacles (deduct one point for each touch). As the players are being blindfolded, remove the obstacles!

At dinner guests tell stories about the most foolish thing they ever did.

Have an artist draw caricatures of the guests.

Park your spouse's car sideways in the garage.

Put two chairs together. Instruct guests to "take off your shoes and jump over 'em." This is an easy forfeit for those with their wits about them! Of course it is the shoes that are jumped over!

After everyone has gone to bed, rearrange chairs/furniture!

Proverbs on April Fools' Day

"Laugh and the world laughs with you."
"Hang sorrow! Care will kill a cat. And therefore let's be merry."
"A merry heart doeth good like a medicine."
"A little nonsense now and then is relished by the wisest men."
"I had rather have a fool to make me merry than experience to make me sad."

—*Shakespeare*

"Laugh and be merry, better the world with a song."

"The most exquisite folly is made of wisdom spun too fine."

—*Benjamin Franklin*

"Nay, I shall ne'er beware of mine own wit till I break my shins against it."

—*Shakespeare*

"Seest thou a wise man in his own conceit? There is more hope for a fool than of him."

"If any one among you thinks that he is wise in his age, let him become a fool, that he may be wise." —*I Corinthians 3:18*

"Foolery, sir, does walk about the orb like the sun; it shines everywhere."

"Jesters do oft prove prophets." —*Shakespeare*

"The secret source of humor is not joy but sorrow; there is no humor in heaven."

—*Mark Twain*

"Hence it appears that among mortals they who are zealous for wisdom are farthest from happiness, being by the same token fools twice over."

—*Desiderius Erasmus*

"When a thing is funny search it for a hidden truth."

—*George Bernard Shaw*

"The more one suffers, the more, I believe, one has a sense for the Comic. It is only by the deepest suffering that one acquires the authority in the art of the Comic; an authority which by one word transforms as by magic the resounding creature one calls man into a caricature."

—*Soren Kierkegaard*

"By their merry talk they cause sufferers to forget grief." —*The Talmud*

April Fools' Day
1 April

The first of April, some do say
Is set apart for All Fools' Day
But why the people call it so
Nor I nor they themselves do know
—"Poor Robin's Almanack," 1760

BE A LITTLE FOOLISH!

20: Easter

The Easter season, in addition to its religious significance, is the spring festival for Christians. It begins with Shrove Tuesday and culminates on Easter which celebrates the Resurrection of Jesus Christ. Easter is on the Sunday following the first full moon after the vernal equinox, between March 22 and April 25. Some of its symbols and traditions originate in pre-Christian spring festivals that celebrated the return of the sun and its warmth. Its name may have come from Eostre, a Teutonic goddess of spring or a spring festival called Eostur. Sunrise church services may relate to ancient hilltop spring fires welcoming the sun god.

The egg was symbolic in many pre-Christian cultures. Some believed that the universe descended from an enormous egg. It was a symbol of rebirth and regeneration, thus fitting to the celebration of the Resurrection. The custom of dying eggs probably arrived in Europe after the Crusades—an ancient tradition brought back from the Egyptians, Persians, and Greeks. Even today, Chinese parents announce the arrival of a newborn with a red egg.

Wearing "Easter outfits" may date back to the custom of bathing and putting on clean clothes after shedding winter clothes worn for several months. In fact, Maundy Thursday is also called Pure or Clean Thursday; it was on this day that people bathed their whole bodies in preparation for Easter.

The Mardi Gras or Carnival may have derived many of its customs from the Roman Saturnalia feast when social roles were reversed. Mardi Gras means "fat Tuesday" in French—it was the day when all the forbidden Lenten foods were eaten. Carnival is Latin meaning "farewell to meat." Hot cross buns, associated with Good Friday, are from pre-Christian times. Cross-marked cakes were used by the ancient Greeks in celebration of Artemis, the goddess of the hunt. Similar cakes were used by the Egyptians in the worship of Isis, the mother goddess. These cakes symbolized to early Christians the unleavened bread of the Last Supper—the Eucharist. The symbol of the lamb comes from the Jewish Pesah (Passover) holiday when the Jews sacrificed a Paschal lamb during their traditional ceremony in the Temple in Jerusalem. The Paschal lamb was later interpreted by Christians as a forecast of Christ's sacrifice on the cross.

More Easter customs evolved during and after the Middle Ages as the numbers of Christians grew. One such custom was that of taking an "Easter Walk" after the Easter church service. A procession of people would walk through the town, into the fields and forests with a leader carrying a lighted candle. The group would stop to pray and sing hymns at designated spots. Young German and Austrian farmers decked their horses with flowers and ribbons and became part of the procession. Easter is a festival of hope and renewal—a time for joy.

INVITATION

Write invitation on colored stationery, roll or fold, and insert into a plastic or sugar egg. Hand deliver invitations.

SOME BUNNY WANTS YOU
Come to an Easter Party

Date _____

Time _____

Place _____

_____

Bring a basket to fill with "egg-stra" special surprises.

DECORATIONS

- Adorn your home with beautiful **spring flowers** at Easter—include white Easter Lilies, tulips, daffodils, narcissus, pussy willow, hyacinths, and blossoming branches.
- Decorate a large **grapevine wreath** with dried or silk flowers and miniature stuffed bunnies.
- Fill **baskets** with **Easter paraphernalia** and place them about the house.
- For a festive touch, hang **Easter posters** or **cutouts.**
- Hang a **wide-brimmed straw bonnet** on the front door with a garland of dried flowers glued to the band. Add trailing ribbon streamers for an old-fashioned look.
- Nestle **stuffed bunnies** about the house.
- Fluttering **butterflies** are beautiful at Easter.

- Dangle **hand-painted eggs** (wooden or hollowed shells) on a silk tree, painted branch, or from tree limbs outside.
- For an impressive centerpiece, arrange a **gigantic Easter basket** filled with many eggs—as many as 200.
- A **large Paschal candle** takes the place of Easter fires of early times.
- Nestle a large fabric **hen** or **duck** with **babies** or **eggs** in a large basket.
- Display your **Beatrix Potter figurines** in pink Easter grass.

EASTER TERMS

Eastertide (Easter time)
Easter bells
Eastre/Easter/East (sun rises)
Frills
Easter Eve (Night of Illumination)
Alleluia
Egg (symbol of rebirth and regeneration)
Peace
Chicken (symbol of new life)

Love
Rabbit (symbol of new life)
Joy
Lamb (symbol of Jesus)
Sunrise
Cross (Christ's crucifixion/resurrection)
Messiah
Lighted candles (love/service/holy things)

Hope
Paschal/Easter Candle (large—30" tall)
Dawn/sunrise
"Eggs-travaganza"
"Eggs-citing"
"Eggs-ceptional"
"Eggs-pecially"
"Eggs-traordinary"
"Eggs-cellent"
"Eggs-tra-terrific"
"Eggs-ercise"

COLORS

- White—light, purity, and joy
- Yellow—sunlight and radiance
- Purple—royal/religious mourning
- Green—maturity and hope of eternal life

FOODS

- Easter breads
- Fruits
- Lamb
- Eggs
- Ham
- Soft Pretzels

Hot cross buns are baked each Friday during the 40 days of Lent in The British Isles and many other countries. Each bun is iced with a cross on it. In ancient times they had magical powers.

Hot cross buns, hot cross buns,
One a penny, two a penny,
Hot cross buns;
Smoking hot, piping hot,
Just come out of the baker's shop;
One a penny poke, two a penny tongs,
Three a penny fire-shovel, hot cross buns!

FAVORS

- Easter baskets
- Plastic wheelbarrow
- Canvas tote
- Flowers
- Plastic watering can
- Beach pail
- Recordings
- Beatrix Potter books, etc.

ACTIVITIES/GAMES
Shrove Tuesday Pancake Supper

Ages: All ages
Time: 1 hour
Materials Needed: Ingredients for pancakes/crepes.
Advance Preparation: Prepare for a pancake supper.
Activity: There is an old ritual of using all the fats, eggs, and butter before the Lenten fast (Mardi Gras).

Guests enjoy a feast of pancakes. For a more formal dinner, serve crepes.
Variation: Try pancake races—contestants must run and flip the pancake three times! This is an old English custom.

Pretzels

Ages: 7–adult

Time: 1 ½ hours

Materials Needed: Ingredients for bread and coarse salt.

Advance Preparation: Make yeast dough ahead of the party.

Activity: Make pretzels by forming dough-ropes into the familiar shape of a pretzel.

Note: The pretzel dates back about 1,500 years in southern Europe. The shape of the pretzel is said to have reminded someone of a child's arms folded in prayer. The Christians first used the pretzel as Lenten bread in the fifth century. They used pretzels because they contain no milk or eggs, which were forbidden during Lent.

Dissolve 1 package of dry yeast in 1 ½ cups lukewarm water. Add and knead 4 cups flour. Form into a large roll and cut into 18 pieces. Roll into ropes and twist into the shape of pretzels. Place on lightly greased cookie sheets and brush pretzels with a beaten egg. Sprinkle with coarse salt and bake 15 minutes at 400 degrees.

Mr. McGregor's Vegetable Patch

Ages: 4–10 years

Time: 20 minutes

Materials Needed: Vegetables (carrots with greens, zucchini, radishes, etc.), a low garden fence or low boxes with a corrugated paper fence border, baskets, a recording of the song "Here Comes Peter Cotton Tail," a tape player, a bandanna, and an old straw hat for Mr. McGregor.

Advance Preparation: Create two or three small garden patches filled with vegetables. Mark places encircling the vegetable patches with baskets .

Activity: Guests/rabbits form a large circle and stand by their baskets. They sneak up to Mr. McGregor's garden patches when the song "Here Comes Peter Cotton Tail" begins to play. Mr. McGregor is standing watch and rabbits must try to fetch a vegetable and return to their baskets without being caught by Mr. McGregor. If a rabbit is caught, it must freeze and return the vegetable to the patch. Guests/rabbits return to their baskets and repeat play when the music begins to play. Continue until all vegetables have disappeared from Mr. McGregor's garden.

The rabbit with the most vegetables wins. Choose a new Mr. McGregor and play again.

Easter Egg Hunt

Ages: 3–adult

Time: 20 minutes

Materials Needed: Colored boiled eggs or plastic eggs filled with pennies, raisins, nuts, gum balls, candy, or prize-winning coupons.

Advance Preparation: Color/fill eggs and hide them in the leaves, shrubbery, in nests/baskets, and in the garden.

Activity: Guests hunt eggs and place them in baskets. Give prizes for the most eggs gathered and prize coupons.

Variation: Hide "fortune eggs." Coordinate fortunes to the egg color. This is a good adult hunt.

Egg Rolling

Ages: 4–12 years

Time: 20 minutes

Materials Needed: A grassy slope and hard-boiled eggs.

Advance Preparation: Hard boil and color the eggs.

Activity: Guests roll hard-boiled eggs down a slope.

The winner is the one with an unbroken egg reaching the bottom of the hill first.

Variation: Guests roll eggs with spoons across the lawn. The first person to reach the finish line is the winner.

Hole in One

Ages: 4–12 years
Time: 15 minutes
Materials Needed: A large circle (40-foot diameter) with a hole in the center, colored hard-boiled eggs, and spoons.

Advance Preparation: Carefully dig a small hole (3-inch diameter) in the center of a large circle.
Activity: Guests roll/putt eggs toward the hole. The guest with the fewest putts wins.

A Big Yoke

Ages: 9–adult
Time: 20 minutes
Materials Needed: An obstacle course of wire croquet hoops (coat hangers), boxes, etc.
Advance Preparation: Set up obstacle courses, one for every five guests.

Activity: Contestants must roll a hard-boiled egg through an obstacle course with their noses. For added laughter, decorate a few raw eggs. It will be a "big yoke" when the egg breaks. Be ready to replace broken eggs with hard-boiled eggs so it doesn't interfere too much with the relay.

Quest for the Golden Egg

Ages: 9–adult
Time: 20 minutes
Materials Needed: Colored hard-boiled eggs and metallic gold foil.
Advance Preparation: Color eggs and cover one egg with gold metallic foil. Hide eggs in shrubs, garden, behind trees, and crevices.
Activity: Guests hunt for the eggs. When all eggs are

found, tell them that the eggs have different values by their color. Have points written on a poster board to display right after the hunt. The highest score wins.
Purple egg = 50 points
Blue egg = 25 points
Red egg = 10 points
Green egg = 5 points
Golden egg = Minus 25 points

Bunny Tracks

Ages: 3–6 years
Time: 10 minutes
Materials Needed: Cornstarch, flour sifter, and a cardboard stencil of a rabbit's footprint or use a fork to create it.
Advance Preparation: Make bunny tracks throughout the house, even up and down the staircases.

Activity: Children will be enchanted by the bunny tracks as they hunt for their baskets Easter morning.

Bunny Trail

Ages: 3–8 years
Time: 15 minutes
Materials Needed: Colored/plastic Easter eggs.
Advance Preparation: Hide eggs along the bunny's trail in backyard or woods.

Activity: Children hop down the bunny's trail and gather eggs. The person gathering the most eggs is the winner.
Optional: Make bunny tracks along the trail.

Hunt for Flopsie's Tail

Ages: 4–8 years
Time: 20 minutes
Materials Needed: Fuzzy tail, rabbit ears, and the musical recording of the story "Peter Rabbit and the Hunt for Flopsie's Tail."
Advance Preparation: Hide Flopsie's tail.

Activity: Children listen to the music and story about Peter Rabbit and the hunt for Flopsie's tail. The hunt begins and all search for the tail. The child finding the tail becomes Peter Rabbit and may wear rabbit ears.
Variation: Hide tails enough for each guest or play "Catch a Monkey's Tail" in the Safari Party chapter.

Easter Eve Dinner

Ages: All ages
Time: 1 hour
Materials Needed: One large Paschal candle and votive candles for each guest.
Advance Preparation: Make preparation for an Easter Eve dinner and purchase candles.

Activity: Guests light a votive candle from the Paschal candle and place it in front of their place settings. Read a scripture or story about the Paschal candle.
Note: The Easter candle represents early Easter fires. The lighting of the Paschal candle on Easter Eve is a ceremony called "striking the new fire."

Easter Eve Dance

Ages: Teen–adult
Time: 2–3 hours
Materials Needed: Recordings for dancing and a blazing bonfire (fireplace). Rent a portable dance floor or use the patio.
Advance Preparation: Make preparations for a dance.

Activity: Guests dance on Easter Eve. This is an old German custom—they danced around a blazing bonfire. Remember to do "The Bunny Hop."
Variation: You may wish to add an old Dutch custom of people parading with candles/lanterns lit from the Easter fires.

An Easter Parade

Ages: 3–10 years
Time: 20 minutes
Materials Needed: Irving Berlin's recording of "Easter Parade" and a Polaroid camera.
Advance Preparation: Indicate in the invitation that guests are to dress for an Easter Parade. Set up a "runway" through the backyard flower garden.

Activity: Guests model their Easter frocks in the garden terraces, etc. Take Polaroid pictures as they walk through the gardens. Accompany with the song "Easter Parade."
Variation: Have an afternoon tea.

An Easter Riddle

Oh, what am I, whom children hide,
Round, hard and smooth, yet soft inside?
Who's born all white, yet, strange to say,
Turns red and blue on Easter day?
Who has a yolk, but not a shirt,
Whose head when cracked does not feel hurt?
Who's boiled alive, unless too bad,
Whose dyeing makes the children glad?
Now, what am I? Pray guess, I beg.
Of course I am an _____!
—The Delineator, 1923

A German Folktale

It is said in a German folk tale that a poor lady dyed eggs for her children and hid them in a basket. When the children found the eggs, a little bunny hopped out of the basket. This folk tale has prevailed and today's Easter Bunny excites children all over the world.

MAY YOUR
EASTER BE
EGGSTRA-
SPECIAL!!

21: May Day

May Day is a festival observing the coming of spring—the revival of life. Some people believe May Day celebrations began with the tree worshipping of the Druids in ancient England. Their spring festival honored the sun with fires on hilltops. Origins can also be found in both the Norse legends and the ancient Romans'. The Norsemen celebrated yearly festivals. In Sweden, a grand procession (May Ride) featured a flower-decked May King (Odin) who was pelted with blossoms. The Romans honored the goddess of flowers, Flora, in their spring festival. They featured blossoms in parades and dances. Later, when the Romans occupied the British Isles, the celebration customs merged and the Maypole dance was added. The Maypole soon became the center of all festivities. It was beautifully decorated with May flowers (hawthorn blossoms) and made ready for dancing.

Young and old danced around the gaily decorated Maypoles. Little girls, each hoping to be selected Queen of the May, wore their prettiest dresses. The legend of Robin Hood was an important part of the May Day festivities. Plays, games, and jousts represented Robin Hood and his Merry Band. English fervor for May Day kept this holiday very much alive. May Day never became significant in the United States as it was in Great Britain because early Puritan settlers frowned on frivolous dancing around the Maypole. Later, however, the custom of filling May baskets with flowers and distributing them to friends sprang up in many parts of the country.

INVITATION

Roll up the invitation and place it in a basket of flowers.

You're Invited to a May Day Breakfast
Come After Eight and Celebrate!

DECORATIONS

* **Streamers** and **ribbons** are beautiful hanging from trees.
* Display **flowers** and **garlands** of flowers.
* Hang **flags** (national or ornamental).
* Make **wreaths** much like Christmas evergreen boughs.
* Scatter **gold foil chocolate pieces** (Robin Hood).
* Make a **miniature Maypole** with little storybook dolls.
* Decorate small, colorful **Hula Hoops** with ribbons and dried or fresh flowers. Suspend with ribbon from an arbor or arches.

For each of the Maypole dancers create **flower headpieces.** Use floral wire, ribbons, baby's breath and daisies (use assorted dried 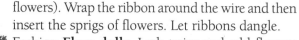 flowers). Wrap the ribbon around the wire and then insert the sprigs of flowers. Let ribbons dangle.

Fashion **Flora dolls.** Lash twigs and add flowers for the head, hands, and skirt. Tulips make great skirts and the twigs support the stems!

TERMS

May baskets	Streamers	Parades
Hawthorn (May) blossoms	Lord of the May	Robin Hood and Sherwood Forest
Secret	May magic	Merriest day
Adorn	Coming of spring	Merrymaking
Maypole	Garlands of flowers	Maytime or
Gilded crowns	Dancing	Maytide
Queen of the May	Flora, the goddess of flowers	May wine

FAVORS

- May baskets
- Hula Hoops
- Flowers
- Robin Hood story

ACTIVITIES/GAMES

May Day Breakfast

Ages: 8–adult
Time: 2 hours
Materials Needed: May Day baskets filled with flowers and an invitation to breakfast tucked inside.
Advance Preparation: Make the baskets and deliver early in the morning on May Day.
Activity: Guests will enjoy a spontaneous breakfast to celebrate May Day. This works best if May Day falls on a weekend but it can be celebrated on a day near May Day also.
Variation: An old tradition of the Hobby Horse rollicking into every house and cottage, bringing summer and May, can be a fun way to deliver the early morning invitations.

May Baskets

Ages: 3–adult
Time: Not applicable
Materials Needed: Doilies, wrapping paper, lightweight construction paper, glue, scissors, and assorted ribbons. Candy, popcorn, or flowers may be used to fill the baskets.
Advance Preparation: Make and fill baskets with treats or flowers.
Activity: Warm the hearts of special friends. Secretly deliver baskets filled with flowers/candy/popcorn to friends and relatives. Hang the basket on the doorknob, ring the doorbell, and run.

Cut two hearts. Fold and staple forming cone. Use wrapping paper, etc.

Decorate a paper cup with ribbon, etc.

Cone-shaped baskets can be formed from doilies.

Purchase decorative gift boxes or baskets. Fill with flowers, popcorn, nuts, or candy.

Paper plates and doilies make pretty flower baskets.

Floral Crowns

Ages: 3–adult
Time: 30 minutes
Materials Needed: Daisies, dandelions, ivy, tulips, buttercups, floral wire/tape, dark green paper plates.

Advance Preparation: Gather materials and make a sample crown.
Activity: Fashion floral crowns with wire or paper plates. Intertwine flowers and ivy around the circular piece of wire or slash slits in the outer rim of green paper plates (remove centers) and insert flowers.

Legend of Robin Hood

The Legend of Robin Hood was very important in Medieval England May Day festivities.
Ages: 7–adult
Time: 20 minutes
Materials Needed: Puppets, story of Robin Hood, and a puppet stage.
Advance Preparation: Make puppets and set up the puppet stage.

Activity: Read or tell the story of Robin Hood and let the children work the puppets to the story.
Variation: Adults may wear the costumes of the Robin Hood characters. Children may dress as the Robin Hood legend characters and walk in a short May Day parade. Remember Robin Hood is Lord of the May and his faithful Maid Marian is Queen of the May. Their attendants are such characters as John, Friar Tuck, and a jolly band of yeomen.

Friar Tuck

Robin Hood

Maid Marian

Maypole Dance

Ages: 5–10 years

Time: 15–20 minutes

Materials Needed: A 7-foot pole/tree, tuft or wreath of flowers for pole top, green crepe paper, and an even number of ribbons tacked at the top of the pole. Use a volleyball or tetherball standard. Also bells, ribbons, hats, streamers, bell bracelets, disc/tape player, and dance music. Resource: "All Time Favorite Dances," KIM 196 Kimbo Educational, 800-631-2187.

Advance Preparation: Children gather a few flowers to adorn the Maypole. Decorate a beautiful flower-wreathed pole.

Activity: Dancers (6 to 12), wearing bells around their ankles and streamers from their hats, each hold a ribbon and face alternately left and right. The dancers facing right pass under the dancers facing left. Dance continues by alternately passing over and under the ribbons. Re-enact the Morris (peasant) dancers—tap sticks, wave handkerchiefs, jingle bells, and dance with high leaps and jumps.

Note: Other dances that can be used around the Maypole include: "Seven Steps," "Patty-Cake Waltz," "La Raspa," any stately minuet, and the traditional "Maypole Dance" to the Elizabethan tune of "Bluff King Hal."

One of the earliest circle dances is the "Sellinger Round," an English dance in which couples skip in and out of a circle around the Maypole. Check your library for music.

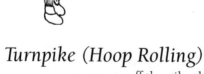

Turnpike (Hoop Rolling)

Ages: 4–teen

Time: 15 minutes

Materials Needed: Hula Hoops, green ribbons, little bells, 18-inch-long dowels, and large stones/bricks.

Advance Preparation: On the inside of the Hula Hoops, glue or tie little bells with green ribbons. Build a turnpike in a circle or along a path placing pairs of stones about 6 inches apart at regular intervals. Each pair of stones is guarded by one of the participants.

Activity: Children roll the hoops with sticks, steering carefully through the turnpike. If they miss a gate and go off the pike they become a guard and give the guard the hoop at that point. If the child steers well without a miss, she may go through the course again.

Variation: Create the turnpike by mowing grass paths very short!

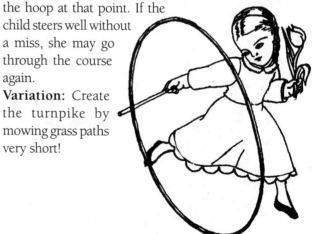

May Day Procession

Ages: 3–adult
Time: 15 minutes
Materials Needed: Assorted costumes, flowers, and a small wagon decorated with flowers.
Advance Preparation: Organize the procession and gather May Day paraphernalia.

Activity: Children carry bouquets of spring flowers as they escort a May Queen through the village streets. Shepherds, shepherdesses, dancers, chimney sweeps, jesters, tumblers, the other characters—such as Robin Hood—join the procession.

Robin Hood Roving Tourney

Schools in England celebrated the first of May with field days or other sporting events. Medieval England enjoyed the Robin Hood Roving Tourney re-enacting the games of Robin Hood and his band of Merry Men deep in Sherwood Forest. Contestants race through Sherwood, seize gold coins in Nottingham, and escape to Robin Hood's hideout. They rove from one event to another with a scorecard in hand (points for events vary). Station a scorekeeper at each event.

EVENT I: Hoop Jousting
Need: Five hoops and five batons for driving the hoops.
Preparation: Mark 5 lanes about 4 feet wide with goal lines at both ends.
Activity: Contestants drive the hoop down and back passing over the goal lines and giving the hoop and baton to the next player. They must stay within the lane, the hoop cannot fall over, and the hoop may be lifted around the turn.
Score: Hoop falling over -5 points, successful drive 10 points, and first-place team 20 points.

Variation: Contestants roll the hoop using their hands.

EVENT II: Tug O' War
Need: Sturdy rope and a colorful piece of cloth.
Preparation: Tie the cloth in the center of the rope and mark lines which must be crossed to win the tug.
Activity: Each team attempts to pull the other side over the line.

EVENT III: Casting Stones
Need: Aluminum pie pans (stone disk), large nails/washers, and plenty of stones.
Preparation: Arrange pie pans three distances from a toe line. Stabilize the pans by pounding large nails and washers through the pan and into the ground.
Activity: Contestants tell the scorekeeper which disk they're trying to hit. If they successfully cast the stone in the disk, they get another turn and continue until they miss.
Score: Nearest disk 5 points, middle disk 10 points, and the farthest disk 15 points.

EVENT IV: Casting a Lance

Need: Wooden poles about 5 feet long or a toy spear.
Preparation: Mark various distances from the toe line (determine the distance by the age of the contestant).
Activity: Cast the lance for distance. Rock it back and forth several times before throwing with a good thrust. The contestant must reach the required distance at least once in three throws to score.
Score: 5 points for each successful cast.

EVENT V: Shooting Darts

Need: Rubber-tipped darts/real darts (if the activity is well supervised by adults) and a dartboard. A toy safety crossbow would work well for this activity.
Preparation: Purchase or make a dartboard with at least three concentric circles. Hang or display on a tripod.
Activity: Contestants have five tries to shoot the board.
Score: Bull's eye 20 points, next circle 10 points, next circle 5 points, and the outside circle 2 points.

EVENT VI: Archery Target Shooting

Need: Arrow-filled quivers, bows, and targets (straw bales).
Preparation: Set up targets and mark toe lines for varying distances.
Activity: Archers shoot three arrows from two or three distances. Record the total points earned.
Note: Roving was popular during the Middle Ages. Archers from the city and townsmen roved the suburbs and countryside shooting at targets. Sometimes prizes were awarded.
Safety: It is imperative that this activity be well supervised by adults. All archers must put down their bows and retrieve their arrows at the same time. The targets should be set up in a place where people are not wandering about. It is best to have an experienced archer coordinate the archery shooting contest or use toy safety arrows.

EVENT VII: Puff-the-Arrow Target Shooting

Need: Dried peas and peashooters or hairpins and tufts of yarn. You will also need cardboard and colored paper for the target.
Preparation: Cut a large target (36 inches in diameter) and cover it with green paper. Cut eight small circles from yellow paper and glue them on the large target with no particular pattern. Give them a value of 5 or 10. If using hairpins for the feather-weight arrow, tie the yarn tuft to the ends of the pins.
Activity: Contestants blow peas or feather-weight arrows through a paper tube or pea shooters. The toe line should be about 3 feet from the target. The object is to hit as many circles as possible in five attempts.
Note: In Medieval Europe, a needle with a tuft of wool was used to create a feather-weight arrow.

EVENT VIII: Carousel

Need: 20+ small Nerf balls or tissue balls.
Preparation: Purchase or make balls.
Activity: When eight contestants have gathered, the scorekeeper gives half the players (four) the Nerf/tissue balls. He instructs the eight players to stand back to back. At the signal to start, the players take six steps away from one another, turn and face one another. Quickly the players, with the balls, begin pelting the other players (half) with the balls. Allow 1 minute for throwing the balls. Now the other players have the missiles and play is repeated. All contestants must keep a set stance. Score 1 point per hit.
Note: The original version of this game came from the French. The cavaliers riding horseback pelted one another with balls until one or the other was driven from the field. Many of the Medieval European games were rough and crude, and have tempered as the world has become more civilized.

EVENT IX: Kayles

Need: A skittles game which can be purchased at some sporting goods stores and game stores. Skittles is a game in which spinning tops knock down pins of varying values.
Preparation: Purchase a skittles game.
Activity: In France, kayles was played much like skittles we play today. Contestants play a game or two of skittles and record their scores.

EVENT X: Dice

Need: Several pairs of dice.
Preparation: Choose a favorite dice game—craps, etc. or make one up using several pairs of dice.
Activity: Play your favorite dice game.

EVENT XI: Pillow Joust

Need: Two soft pillows and a log (18-inch diameter and 5-feet-long).

Preparation: Select pillows filled with foam or feathers. Pile lots of leaves or straw on either side of the log.

Activity: Combatants stand balanced on the log and swing pillows (joust) at one another attempting to throw the other off balance. Hits should be below the head. The contestant falling off the log first is the loser.

Variation: Play without a log. Players may run and hide among the trees of "Sherwood" to avoid being jousted with a pillow.

EVENT XII: Stilt Race

Need: Stilts and various obstacles.

Preparation: Lay out an obstacle course (see Backyard Sports Fest chapter).

Activity: Play follow-the-leader or compete in races through obstacle courses.

Variation: Hang cakes or candies from cords strung from tree to tree. Participants on stilts must keep their balance while biting off a morsel (without using their hands, of course!).

EVENT XIII: Jackstones (Jacks)

Need: Jacks and ball.

Preparation: Purchase sets of jacks.

Activity: Play one or more games of jacks ... downs and ups, eggs in the basket, scatters, or pigs in the blanket.

Note: In ancient times children played without a ball. They used pebbles instead of metal jacks.

EVENT XIV: Skipping Stones

Need: Carpet squares and poles to be used for vaulting.

Preparation: Lay carpet pieces to resemble stepping stones across a stream. Secure with large nails.

Activity: Contestants skip with both feet from one stone to another. The number of stones skipped successfully without missing (both feet on the carpet) constitutes your score.

Variation: For older contestants, make the skipping more difficult and vault from stone to stone.

EVENT XV: English Hopscotch

Need: Snail-shaped hopscotch court on dirt/concrete and pucks.

Preparation: Mark the court and gather stones for pucks.

Activity: Players jump on both legs holding the puck between their feet. Instead of a rectangular court a snail-configured court is used.

Note: You may use regular hopscotch rules—directions are in the Water/Beach chapter.

EVENT XVI: Besiege the Castle Grounds

Need: Wooded backyard/park (Sherwood Forest) and old socks filled with 1 or 2 cups of flour.

Preparation: Mark two plots of land like a volleyball court. Create more plots to accommodate larger numbers of players. It is important to keep the size of the armies down so the players are not eliminated for a long time.

Activity: Divide participants into two armies (three to five on a team). Using trees as castle battlements, besiegers attack the enemy by hitting them with a sock filled with flour (a flour mark designates a hit). Hits must fall below the waist. Players who have been hit with a sock must drop out of the game. The first army to hit all the enemy besieges the other army's plot of land. Repeat several times.

EVENT XVII: Royalty Tennis

Need: Playground balls and chalk.

Preparation: Mark a court 5 feet by 10 feet (two 5-foot squares).

Activity: Two players re-enact a game of early tennis played like handball. Play as modern-day "four square" using two squares and two players. Serve the ball with a bounce.

GO A-MAYING IN THE WOODS!

GATHER WILDFLOWERS FOR MAY BASKETS!

22: Halloween

Goblins, ghosts, trick-or-treaters, haunted houses, costumes, and fortune-telling are all a part of a most magical and fun-filled holiday called Halloween. It's a time when reality and illusion mix … when anyone can assume any identity or accomplish any mystical feat. Most of the Halloween superstitions and symbols date back to festivals celebrated thousands of years ago by the ancient Romans and Greeks. However, the Druid religion practiced by the Celtic people in Northern France and the British Isles had the most impact on modern Halloween customs.

The Celtic people celebrated the New Year on November 1 and their "New Year's Eve" was marked by the autumn festival call Samhain, after the Lord of Death. The Celts believed that Samhain caused souls of the wicked to be reincarnated as animals—especially black cats. They believed that the spirits of those who died during the preceding year returned to earth for a few hours to mingle with the living and warm themselves by a fire. The mystical Druids believed that elves, fairies, ghosts, spirits, and witches would come out on this night to haunt the people. It was a common belief that these malevolent spirits feared fire, so, on the eve of this feast, priests commanded the people to burn huge bonfires on which animals were sacrificed to appease the dreaded Samhain. Some people would dress in costume and tell fortunes.

From A.D. 600 to 1100, Christianity spread throughout Europe and eventually reached the Celts. Missionaries were appalled at the pagan practices, especially Samhain. Realizing that the Celts would not give up these customs altogether, they decided to turn Samhain into a Christian holiday. Church leaders proclaimed November 1 as All Hallows' Day, a day to honor all the saints who did not already have a feast day of their own. The night before then became All Hallows' Evening—later shortened to Halloween. During the Middle Ages most people spent Halloween around home fires in prayer for protection against the devil.

Different countries held different Halloween superstitions and customs. In England, leaves, pumpkins, and cornstalks were used as decorations for the feasting at summer's end. People would also sit around the fire and tell spooky stories while eating apples and nuts. In Ireland, Scotland, and Wales, costumed children marched in parades and begged for food while masked villagers representing the souls of the dead paraded to the outskirts of the town, frightening away witches and other mischievous spirits. The Irish passed along an old tale about the jack-o'-lantern: There once was a man named Stingy Jack who was not able to enter heaven because he was a miser. He could not enter hell because he played practical jokes on the devil. So Jack had to wander in darkness as a lost soul carrying his lantern until Judgment Day.

Around 1800, immigrants from the British Isles brought these ancient customs with them and marked the beginning of Halloween in the United States. Over time, people's perceptions have changed. Today most people no longer believe in these superstitions. The focus of Halloween is on the festivity, mystery, fun-filled spirits, and goblins.

INVITATION

A ghost, skeleton, pumpkin, tombstone, or a black cat may be used to create a "haunting" invitation.

WHOOOOOO'S INVITED
TO A
HALLOWEEN PARTY?

YOOOOOOO
ARE!

JOIN THE SPOOKS
At Jay's "Haunted
House"
155 Western Drive
Friday, October 31
6:00-10:00 P.M.
Admission: One Hallow-
een treat, costume, and
a strong heart!

DECORATIONS

- Place stuffed costumed "**scarecrows**" around the yard or party area. For example: a farmer, hobo, etc.
- Create **ghosts.** Stuff the center of a large sheet with newspaper and tie it at the neck for the head; stuff handkerchiefs with a small Styrofoam ball and tie at the neck for the head. Cut ghosts of assorted sizes from tag board or heavy paper—punch holes to hang.
- Rig a **ghost** on a pulley. Tie a wire from a tree to the house and hang a large ghost on the pulley. Inexpensive pulleys, cable, or cord can be purchased at a hardware store. Use a ball for the ghost's head.
- **Jack-o'-lanterns** and **pumpkins** come in many mediums. Select from plastic, ceramic, etc.
- Drape **gauze** (dyed black) over chairs, pictures, etc.
- Light lots of **candles** and **lanterns** to create flickering shadows in the enchanted night.
- Line a wall or ledge with **votive candles** and **moss.**
- Stage the party in an **old haunted building/historical home.** Before you sign a contract, read it thoroughly.
- Tie a bundle of cornstalks together to make a **corn shock.** Surround it with pumpkins, squash, and gourds.
- Rent several **straw** or **hay bales** and use them for seating and decorating.

- Cut and hang assorted **bats** and **skeletons.**
- Paint **spooky Halloween posters/murals** with luminous paints. Illuminate with black-light bulbs.
- For a **cemetery scene,** create tombstones from boxes, tag board, or Styrofoam with funny captions such as "Here lies_____ She is at rest now and so am I."

- Illuminate **farolitos** (little lamps) decorated as **ghosts** or **tombstones.** Fill white paper bags with 2 inches of sand. Place old candles in the sand and light for luminous effect. A lighted graveyard is fantastic. **Note:** Place bags in an area of the yard where children are not apt to come into contact with the farolitos.
- Create a **secret trap door.** Use a real door or make-believe door and write the word "Beware" on it.
- Place a lamp and strange figures behind a hanging sheet to create **spooky shadows.** Black or orange light bulbs will cast a spooky glow.
- Weave string, thread, or yarn to create **webs** in windows, ceiling corners, doorways, etc. You can also purchase webbing for this purpose. Remember to

add spiders. For more permanent webs, pull pieces of string through white household glue, weave and place on waxed paper to dry for 1 hour. Add interest by painting webs with glow-in-the-dark spray paint.

Hang or use as table runners **pleated skeletons** and **skulls.** Pleat long strips of paper (each pleat is 8 inches x 4 inches). Draw skeletons and skulls. Cut out the shaded area carefully with sharp scissors.

  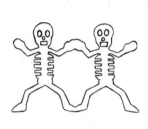

Hang **jointed skeletons.** Cut out skeleton parts, punch holes, and hold the joints together with brass tacks. Draw skeleton parts on tag board or fluorescent paper. You may also use glow-in-the-dark paints.

Hang **masks** around the party room and on a hall tree.

Create a **witch** using a plastic garbage bag, a broom, hat, and mask. Stuff with newspapers.

Fabricate a **coffin.** Paint two large boxes tied together.

For **special effects** display old bottles, flasks, poison jugs, and crossbones. Orange Christmas lights placed around the front door can also add a special touch to your Halloween setting.

Drown a **gremlin** in your bathtub. Stuff clothes to resemble a gremlin or character of your choice. Add a rubber mask filled with towels. Place in a water-filled bathtub. Place a flashlight on the side of the tub near a soap dish and shine the light onto the face. Pull the shower curtain shut. When guests use the bathroom, they will investigate the light source from behind the curtain. Listen for the shrieks!

Note: When using **candles** for your Halloween decorations, use extreme care and thought. In some situations, it may be preferable to use electrical bulbs, especially if small children are present in the party area.

SPOOKY TERMS

Dracula	Goblin	Beware
Cemetery	Mummy	Bewitched
Cat eyes	Bones	Haunt
Dark	Outrageous	Witch's brew
Ghoulish	Miser	Clank
Graveyard	Mummies	Shrieks
Fangs	Brains	Jug
Terrified	Spooky	Blood
Frankenstein	Ghost	Rigor mortis
Coffin	Thriller	Gremlins
Hovel	Sorcerer	Terrible
Shaky	Shiver	Magic
Trap door	Fierce	Eerie
Corpses	Black of night	Monstrous
Skeleton	Raging	Tombstone
Moaning	Moon	Spine
Headless	Secret	Stiff
Bat	Transylvania	Vicious
Chilling	Werewolf	Witching hour
Groaning	Howl	Gruesome
Scary	Gargoyle	Cast a spell

Roar	Creepy	Fright night
Chant	Hoot	Doom
Rattle	Creaking	Screaming
Screech	Numskull	Skulls
Lurk	Phantom	Frivolity
Scream	Owl	Enchantment
Haunted	R.I.P.	Spirits
Whooo	Lurk	Beckon
Horror		

REFRESHMENTS

- Create jack-o'-lantern centerpieces. Tie favors on yarn pieces coming out of the jack-o'-lantern and stretch to each place setting. Serve refreshments from a "closed coffin."
- Ladle magic potion (beverages) from a bowl placed inside a large jack-o'-lantern (add rubber worms, etc. to the brew).
- Swizzle black licorice sticks in orange fruit punch.
- Your menu may include "blood berry" punch, "cool brew," popcorn, caramel corn, popcorn balls, donuts, apples, jelly beans, corn candy, peanuts, marshmallow ghosts, decorated cookies or cupcakes. Pumpkin seeds can be dried in the oven and used for snacks when guests finish carving pumpkins.
- Add 6 black pipe cleaners (legs and 2 pinnacles) to chocolate-iced doughnuts to create fabulous spiders.

FAVORS

- Goblins or jack-o'-lanterns filled with goodies: Create them by inserting the bottom of a 3-inch milk carton into the center of a double piece of tissue paper (white or orange). Pull tissue paper up and around the milk carton base. Gather paper at the top, tie with a bright Halloween ribbon, and finish by decorating the goblins and jack-o'-lanterns with black cut-out facial features.
- Lollipop ghosts can be created by covering a round Tootsie Roll lollipop with white tissue paper tied with an orange ribbon. Make eyes with a fine-point marker. You may use gum balls instead of lollipops.

ACTIVITIES/GAMES
Haunted Spook House/Horror Chamber
(Convert a Cellar Into a Cavern)

Eerie Sounds: Make or buy a tape of eerie sounds—screams, moans, rattles, wind, train whistle, horse clopping, hysterical laughs, rhythmical rubbing of sandpaper, a toilet flushing, heavy breathing, blow into a mike for an explosion sound, electronic synthesizer, crashes, creaking boards, and instruments. Play at the entrance of the haunted house. Use a continuous-play cassette.

Tunnel: Use a child's play tunnel, two card tables with sheets, or large boxes tied together. Hang ropes, cords, and furry critters in the tunnel and tunnel entrance.

Enter the Morgue: Create a dead body with a sheet leaving only feet (rubber feet) sticking out. Identify the body with a large name tag attached to a toe. Fill buckets or plastic tubs with body parts. "Brains" (spaghetti), "spiders" soaking in formaldehyde (rubber spiders in water), "werewolf's blood" (water with lots of red coloring), "vampire's teeth" (golf tees), "Dracula's eyes" (green olives, boiled eggs, or grapes), "skeleton bones" (dowels or sticks), "witch's hair" (old wig), "hand" (wet rubber glove filled with cooked rice), "ears" (dried apricots), "heart" (peeled plum), "liver" (soggy sponge), and "coffin nails" (large nails). Guests feel all the body parts as someone narrates frightful stories about the morgue and its corpses.

Spider's Escape: Attach a piece of wood or cardboard from the top of an entry. Dangle hundreds of black threads. Create large webs throughout the area by criss-crossing strings. Place spiders strategically in the webs and spot a dim light on the spider maze. You may wish to incorporate fish nets.

Bat's Cavern: Hang many paper or rubber bats all over the cavern. Light with a very dim light.

Boneyard: Decorate with graves and tombstones. Add paper-mache skulls, severed heads, and other missing body parts lying about the graveyard. Fake blood dripping from a head is scary. Create a skeleton out of iridescent paper or paint with fluorescent paint. Tie strings on the hands and feet of the skeleton. When guests come through the boneyard, have someone jerk the skeleton and rattle a bag of bones (place wooden dowels, sticks, and spoons in a large bag or pillowcase). **Variation:** Add strobe lights to create a surreal and disorienting effect!

Spooky Characters: Spooky characters (pirate with rubber knife, ghosts, eerie person dressed in black) jump out, scaring guests as they come through the spook house.

Dragon's Den: Create the stomach of a dragon by using an air- or water-filled mattress (guests must remove shoes before crawling across the dragon's stomach). Make gurgling noises by filling a large pan with water and blowing air into the water with straws. Crawl quiety across the dragon's stomach—don't wake the dragon!! Create the dragon's mouth with a rubber door mat.

Moon Room: Cover walls with black material/paper. Randomly insert white Christmas lights creating a star field. Using glow-in-the-dark paint, spray a large moon and planets. Toss mini glow-in-the-dark flying saucers. Add spaceships and space sound effects.

Fairy-Tale Village: Create castles, gingerbread houses—something out of the ordinary. Doors fly open and characters pass out treats to young children!

Count Dracula's Chateau: Create a shadow by hanging a sheet and placing a lamp or flashlight behind it. Place a person or object behind the sheet to make the desired shadow. A hanging ghost on a pulley is fun in Dracula's chateau. Someone should operate the pulley as guests arrive. Dracula's coffin can add the finishing touch to the chateau. Make a coffin from a large refrigerator box or two smaller boxes tied together. Cut the lid so it folds outward and paint the coffin. You may line the coffin with dark red or black cloth. When guests arrive, Count Dracula suddenly sits up in the coffin to scare the spooks.

Black Cat Alley: Cut from black tag board assorted cat eyes about 4 inches high. Create eyes out of reflective or florescent tape and stick them on both sides of the eyes. Punch holes in the top and hang the pairs of cat eyes throughout the alley.

Lion's Den: Purchase a large piece of long fake fur and

attach it to a dowel. When guests arrive in the den touch an arm or leg with the fake fur. If you do not want to use a stick, a person can hide and jump out touching the guests with the fake fur. For added effect in the den, add a few small eyes and a tape of lions' roars.

Junkyard: Arrange tin cans in a little yard through which guests must travel. As guests walk and kick the cans, they will cause rattling and clinking sounds.

Walk the Plank: With a brick, raise one end of a plank which guest must walk and step off at the end. This is scary done in the dark—assist young children.

Chain Gang: Suspend assorted chains through which guests must walk. The clanging sounds are eerie in the dark.

General Instructions for Your Spook House: To create walls in your spook house, use old sheets, blankets, or painters' dropcloths. They can be stapled up or hung on rope or wire strung across the garage or basement. For varied lighting effects, use old lamps, flashlights, trouble lights, and black lightbulbs. Fog can be created with dry ice in water. Remember luminous paint for masks, posters, etc. Some children are easily frightened—use discretion.

Hayride (Trick or Treat)

Ages: All ages
Time: Varies
Materials Needed: Flatbed or wagon, straw bales, horse, tractor, or vehicle, tape of Halloween music/sounds, tape player, and a flashlight.

Advance Preparation: Locate and find materials needed. If you are using a flatbed, you will have to line the edges with bales leaving the back end open for access.
Activity: A ride through the open countryside is great

fun at any age. A nice variation to trick-or-treating is taking the children around in a hay wagon to friends' houses. This solves many trick-or-treat problems and the children have a great time. Be sure to set some firm ground rules concerning safety. Determine signaling procedures between the driver and the adults on the wagon.

Witch's Hovel

Ages: All ages
Time: Throughout the evening
Materials Needed: Black cloth (dye an old sheet), witch's costume, broom, cauldron, treats, chair, dry ice, water, and a little old table for cauldron.
Advance Preparation: Drape and stretch black cloth over a simple frame to create the witch's hovel. Just before little spooks come to trick-or-treat, prepare the cauldron for the bowl of treats by placing dry ice in the cauldron and adding water. Do not add all the dry ice at once—keep adding it throughout the evening.
Activity: The witch sits inside her hovel and visits with the trick-or-treaters as they arrive. Play Halloween music/sounds in the background. The witch is surrounded by her friends hanging down from the ceiling. She introduces the little bats, spiders, etc. to the trick-or-treaters. Giving the creatures names adds more fun … Myrtle, Hilda, Gertie, Lena, Mag, etc.

Peanut Search

Ages: 4–10 years
Time: 15 minutes
Materials Needed: Wading pool or large sandbox, straw/leaves, and peanuts in the shell.
Advance Preparation: Fill pool or tub with straw/leaves and peanuts.
Activity: Children search for peanuts and put them in their goodie bags.

Bone Hunt

Ages: All ages
Time: 20 minutes
Materials Needed: Wrapped candy that resembles bones and goodie bags.
Advance Preparation: Hide bones throughout the graveyard.
Activity: Guests search for bones in the well-defined graveyard.

Poison Broom

Ages: 6–adult
Time: 20 minutes
Materials Needed: Four or five toy brooms, Halloween music, disc/tape player.
Advance Preparation: Gather all materials.
Activity: Children form a large circle. Place five brooms with children throughout the circle. Play Halloween music while the guests pass the brooms around the circle. Each time the music stops, those holding the brooms are poisoned and must leave the game. Play until there are four or five players left in the game—they are the winners. Keep the game moving quickly so you can play several times. Poisoned goblins should come back into a new game as quickly as possible. Very young children stay in the circle and continue play.

Ghosts in the Haunted House

Ages: 3–young teen
Time: 20 minutes
Materials Needed: Large box, tempera paints, markers, old sheet, beans, rubber bands, construction paper, and scissors.
Advance Preparation: Decorate the box like a haunted house with large windows and an open roof for younger children. Make bean bag ghosts from small squares of white fabric, filling the center with beans. Wrap the fabric around the beans and tie with a rubber band. Use a marker to draw ghost eyes.
Activity: Throw bean bag ghosts through the windows and roof. Play as a relay for older children. Younger children toss ghosts into the haunted house through the roof.

Witches' Brew

Ages: 4–10 years
Time: 10 minutes
Materials Needed: Cauldron, wrapped candy or pennies.
Advance Preparation: Set up cauldron and mark toe-lines from which guests must throw pennies into the cauldron. Test distances for varied ages.
Activity: Throw candy or pennies into the witches' cauldron. Give each guest three throws. Guests then go to the end of the line before having a second turn.

What's Your Fortune

Ages: 7–adult
Time: Spontaneous
Materials Needed: Large box about 26 inches high, black crepe paper, aluminum and gold foil paper, paper plate markers, thin bolt, nut and washer, tongue depressor, glue, tape, and large nail to punch hole in depressor for bolt.
Advance Preparation: Decorate the fortune box with black crepe paper and foil stars/moons. On top of the box make a wheel of fortune with a paper plate and tongue depressor. Divide it into 8 segments and number each. Fortunes correspond with the numbers on each segment and the spin determines which fortune you receive.
Activity: Guests spin a number on the fortune wheel. The witch or fortune-teller gives the guest a fortune that corresponds to that number.
Optional: Use a fortune-teller (Madame Sasha) seated at a table with her crystal ball (brandy bottle), pen light, and scarves. Under the scarves, place little cards that tell something about guests and then their fortunes. The guests will be amazed at the fortune-teller's ability!

Unwind the Web

Ages: 4–adult
Time: 20 minutes
Materials Needed: Varying colors of yarn or string and a prize for each guest.
Advance Preparation: Intertwine 60-foot yarn pieces (one color for each guest) about the party room. Tie a prize at the end of the web. Each web should be the same general length with shorter lengths for smaller children.
Activity: The guests simultaneously unwind their webs until they reach the end of the string where there is a special prize for each.
Note: Play first so the web can disappear and not interrupt other activities.

Eerie Sounds

Ages: 5–teen
Time: 30 minutes
Materials Needed: Tape recorder, tape, and assorted sound effects—creaky doors, siren, screams, groaning, banging pots, scary laughter, shower running, assorted household items, etc.
Advance Preparation: Check all equipment and supplies. Make a list of some eerie sounds to get the activity rolling.
Activity: Guests produce an eerie sound tape contributing as many sounds as they can. Add spooky music.

Costume Parade

Ages: All ages
Time: 20 minutes
Materials Needed: Ribbons with captions enough for each guest. Polaroid camera and film.
Advance Preparation: Make up ribbons with caption stapled to top. Captions may read "sweetest," "ugliest," "most awesome," "funniest," "scariest," "craziest," "most creative," "cutest," "most horrible," etc.
Activity: Costumed merrymakers proceed around the block or backyard. Select a winner for each category. Take pictures of each guest.

Mummy Wrap

Ages: 6–adult
Time: 20 minutes
Materials Needed: Two rolls of toilet tissue for each group of three people.
Advance Preparation: Purchase tissue paper.
Activity: Two people from each group wrap the third person with the tissue paper. Wrap as quickly as possible. Cover the person from head to toe except for eyes, nose, and mouth. The first group to wrap the mummy, have it checked for completeness, and then unwrap the mummy is the winner.

Skeletons in the Trunk

Ages: 6–teen
Time: 20 minutes
Materials Needed: Old trunk, body parts (see "Enter the Morgue" in the Haunted House section of this chapter) dry ice, stick, container for dry ice, and water.
Advance Preparation: Gather and prepare body parts and put them in an old trunk. Purchase dry ice. Just before you play the game, place dry ice in a bowl of water inside the trunk.
Activity: Guests sit on the floor in a circle. The room should be dimly lit. Pass the body parts stored in the trunk. To make the game move quickly, pass the same parts in two directions. Tell ghostly stories as the parts are passed. Stir the brew occasionally.

Moon Volley

Ages: 8–adult
Time: 30 minutes
Materials Needed: Glow-in-the-dark paint, white sheet, and two beach balls (expose one ball to light while playing with the other).
Advance Preparation: Paint the beach balls with glow-in-the-dark paint and put up the volleyball net.
Activity: Play moon ball (volleyball) in the dark.

Pumpkin Patch

Ages: 3–10 years
Time: 20 minutes
Materials Needed: Mini pumpkins (gourds).
Advance Preparation: Hide mini pumpkins throughout the yard.
Activity: Children hunt for pumpkins in the "pumpkin patch."

Pillow Fight

Ages: 7–adult
Time: Spontaneous
Materials Needed: Two soft pillows, a large log about 6 feet long, and lots of leaves.
Advance Preparation: Gather equipment and bunch the leaves around the log.
Activity: Guests have pillow fights two at a time while balancing on the log. The object is to knock one another off the log.

Ghastly, Ghostly, Ghoulish Walk

Ages: 7–12 years
Time: 20 minutes
Materials Needed: A scary story, good storyteller, and props.
Advance Preparation: In the woods or neighborhood set up haunted house scenes that pop out as goblins walk by. Neighbors can each set up one part of the walk.
Activity: Tell a scary story as goblins walk through the woods or neighborhood and encounter spooky scenes like witches, skeletons, pirates, ghosts, etc.
Optional: Mark direction arrows with glow-in-the-dark chalk.

Safety Tips

- Hold a block party or a private party in the neighborhood. Throw a haunted house party or rent a video movie.
- Children should trick-or-treat at familiar houses in your neighborhood. An adult or responsible teen should accompany children. Travel in groups of four or five.
- Children should carry flashlights and use reflective tape on their costumes.
- Masks should have large eye openings.
- Keep costumes simple and easy to wear.
- Stay on sidewalks and be cautious.

CHILLS AND THRILLS ON HALLOWEEN NIGHT!

23: Thanksgiving/ Native American Indian

Ever since crops have been cultivated, people have held harvest festivals after they are gathered. These celebrations are referred to in the Old Testament, ancient Chinese history, Greek mythologies, Native American folklore, etc. From Edward Winslow's writings we catch a glimpse of our nation's first Thanksgiving in 1621:

> Our harvest being gotten in, our governor sent four men on fowling, that we might after a special manner rejoice together after we had gathered the fruit of our labors. The four in one day killed as much fowl as, with a little help beside, served the company almost a week. At which time, amongst other recreations, we exercised our arms, many of the Indians coming amongst us, and among the rest their greatest king Massasoit, with some ninety men, whom for three days we entertained and feasted, and they went out and killed five deer, which they brought to the plantation and bestowed on our governor, and upon the captain and others.

The first American Thanksgiving was probably an agricultural holiday patterned after the English harvest-home celebrations. After the last of the year's harvest had been reaped, the English people celebrated with dancing, feasting, and games. Exactly what the Pilgrims ate and did, historians are not sure. The first feasting foods were undoubtedly simple, lacking wheat/rye flour and sugar. It was a few years after the first Thanksgiving that Pilgrims gave the day a religious slant with prayer and thanksgiving for a bountiful harvest. It became a primary holiday reflecting their Puritan beliefs.

In 1863, President Lincoln made Thanksgiving Day a national holiday after Mrs. Sarah Hale, the editor of Godey's Lady's Book, worked 30 years promoting the idea. However, the concept is not unique to the United States. The Native American has left a rich heritage in the United States, much of which is just being tapped. Some lived very simply while others developed advanced civilizations. One of the important gifts of the Native Americans was food, especially corn and sweet potatoes. They taught early immigrants how to grow avocados, beans, peppers, squash, tomatoes, and peanuts. Maple sugar was also introduced to the early settlers by the Native Americans. Our language also reflects the Native American culture—succotash and chipmunk are examples of words incorporated into English. More than half of our states have "Indian" names, along with hundreds of cities, towns, mountains, and rivers.

Games of chance and dexterity were very important in the daily lives of the Native American. Many were played only by adults. Women played games of chance resembling dominoes and betting was popular among both men and women. Games were very much a part of the ceremonies and celebrations, such as the hoop and pole games. The hoop sometimes symbolized the sun but also represented the globe with different colors to represent the four quarters of the earth. Today we can find North American Indians assimilated into the modern world though some, especially in the Southwest, are still living much as their ancestors did. In honor of these Native Americans, the fourth Friday in September has been designated American Indian Day.

INVITATION

Use a scroll for a Thanksgiving decree. Invite guests to wear Native American Indian and Pilgrim costumes.

*CELEBRATE Thanksgiving Dinner With Us
2:00 P.M. November 23, 1997
21 Bird Lane
Come as Pilgrims or
Native American Indians*

*A POWWOW!
Come Celebrate
Chief Matthew's
Birthday
2:00 P.M.
June 20, 1997
at the Wigwam
3200 Apache Drive*

DECORATIONS

⚪ Nestle a **life-size tepee** among the trees.

> One heavy cotton dropcloth approximately 12 feet x 17 feet.
> Five bamboo poles 1 foot taller than the sides of the tepee.
> Cotton ribbon pieces for ties.
> Stitch and decorate with Indian symbols.

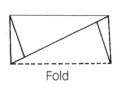

Ties

Fold

⚪ Create an **Indian village** with miniature tepees.

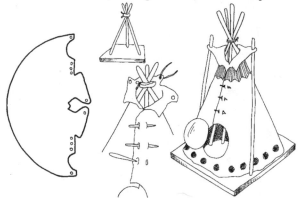

⚪ Use a **travois** as a table centerpiece. Create with a toy dog, sticks, leather shoelaces, twigs, and hide/fabric. Fill with Indian mementos.

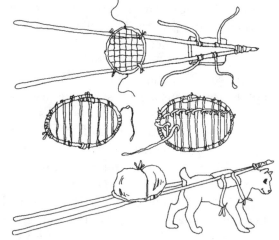

⚪ Display **prayer feathers** and other **Indian paraphernalia.**

⚪ **Cornhusk dolls** will adorn any party room.

⚪ A **bearskin rug** (fake furs) will add a finishing touch to tepees.

⚪ Fill **canoes** with Indian foods.

⚪ **Apples/turnips/gourds** may be used as candle holders.

- Fill **baskets** with gourds or Indian corn.
- Hang **Indian corn wreaths** or **Indian corn** with husks braided.
- Fill **cornucopias** with miniature pumpkins, gourds, and miniature Indian corn for a Thanksgiving centerpiece.
- Adorn the party tables with **drums, tom-toms,** and **Indian rattles** made of gourds.
- Place **paper arrows** up the walkway.
- Stick **large arrows** in the front yard (use long sticks and poster board).

- Create **totem poles** with poster board, markers, and construction paper. Juice cans work well for smaller totem poles.

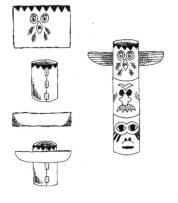

TERMS

Tepee/wigwam	Bow and arrow	Kiva
Totem pole	Pottery	Powwow
Hunt	Baskets	War paint
Peace pipe	Wampum	Braves/maidens
Medicine man	Tomahawk	Smoke signal
Canoe	Toboggan	Warpath
Moccasin	Buffalo	Princess
Ceremony	Travois	Warrior
Trading post	Snowshoes	Paleface
Chief	Ceremonial dancing	Circle
Weaving	Hogan	Sacred hoop
Arrowhead		

FAMOUS NORTH AMERICAN INDIANS

Black Hawk	Sacagawea	Red Cloud
Pontiac	Squanto	Lone Wolf
Jim Thorpe	Crazy Horse	Wild Horse
Hiawatha	Powhatan	Maman-ti
Pocahontas	Sitting Bull	Iron Shirt
Geronimo	Cochise	Satank (Sitting Bear)

INDIAN NAMES

Lost Feather	Running Bear	Gray Wolf
Lone Eagle	Crow	Big Tree
Red Fox	Morning Dove	Kicking Bird
Lone Elk	Blue Fox	Stumbling Bear
Morning Star	Silver Moon	Blue Bird
Swift Water	White Dove	Good Moon
Red Star	Running Water	American Eagle
Left Hand	Happy Bear	White Buffalo
Sleeping Wolf	White Cloud	Grey Wolf
Morning Mountain	Sunrise	Sunflower

TRIBES

Abenaki	Iroquois	Seminole
Apache	Menominee	Seneca
Arapaho	Natchez	Shasta
Blackfoot	Navajo	Shawnee
Cherokee	Nez Perce	Shoshoni
Cheyenne	Ojibway	Sioux
Chickasaw	Omaha	Tlingit
Chippewa	Osage	Tuscarora
Comanche	Penobscot	Twana
Crow	Pima	Umatilla
Delaware	Pomo	Wampanoag
Hopi	Ponca	Wasco
Illinois	Powatan	Winnebago
Inuit	Pueblo	Zuni

INDIAN SYMBOLS AND THEIR MEANINGS

 Thunderbird— Happiness

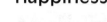 **Arrow—**Protection

Four ages—Infancy, youth, middle, and old age

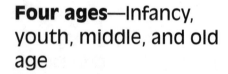 **Arrowhead—**Alertness

Bird—Carefree

Horse—Journey

Man—Human life

 **Snake—**Wisdom

Hogan—Permanent home

Tepee—Temporary home

 Sun rays—Constancy

Deer track—Plentiful game

 Eagle feather—Chief

 Lightning—Swiftness

Bear track—Good omen

 Butterfly—Everlasting life

 Headdress— Ceremonial dance

Sun symbols— Happiness

 **Rain cloud—**Good prospects

 Day and night—Time

 Crossed arrows— Friendship

 Mountain—Abundance

 Medicine man's eye— Wise, watchful

 Rain—Plentiful crops

 Peace

 Water

FOODS

- Peppers
- Wild berries/juice
- Wild rice
- Squash
- Nuts/seeds/raisins
- Chili
- Avocados
- Maize (popcorn)
- Venison
- Beans
- Leaves/cabbage
- Coconut
- Succotash
- Grits, hominy
- Maple sugar candy
- Pumpkins/seeds
- Corncakes
- Corn chips
- Tomatoes
- Wild turkey
- Rabbit
- Wild fruit

- Buffalo/jerky
- Fish
- Tea and cranberry drinks are nice for Thanksgiving because they represent treasured foods of the early immigrants.
- Serve refreshments in baskets or Indian pottery.
- Serve soup in a large pumpkin.
- Corn bread with maple syrup was an Indian favorite.
- Thanksgiving turkey made with cookies and candy.

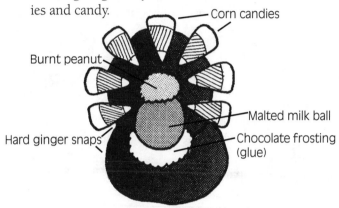

Corn candies
Burnt peanut
Malted milk ball
Hard ginger snaps
Chocolate frosting (glue)

FAVORS

- Feathered headband from the game "Feather Hunt"
- Amigo bands (knot-tying friendship band)

- Indian humming toy (loop a 48-inch string through a large button)

INDIAN COSTUMES

Large paper bags/burlap bags/tan fabric.
Use a pajama top for a pattern.
Fold.
Decorate with felt, yarn, and markers.
Cut top (allow for seams) and stitch. Fringe sleeves and bottom.
As braves and maidens arrive, help them decorate their faces with "peace" paint. Caran D'ache works well.

ACTIVITIES/GAMES
Indian Dances/Folklore

Ages: 8–12 years
Time: 30–40 minutes
Materials Needed: Indian recordings and instruments. Resource: Authentic Indian Dances and Folklore, 9070C Kimbo Educational, 800-631-2187.

Advance Preparation: Purchase recordings or check them out at your library. Practice the dance or activity.
Activity: Guests enjoy Indian music or dancing.

Rabbit Dance

Ages: 5–9 years
Time: 15 minutes
Materials Needed: Indian rattles and tom-toms.
Advance Preparation: Purchase or make the rattles and drums.
Activity: Children hop like rabbits/bunnies using two feet in the hop. They may incorporate an Indian dance step of hopping from one foot to another. As the young rabbits hop, they put their hands (thumbs inward) to their heads forming ears. Some may even flap their ears to the tempo of the dance. This was a Plains Indian dance.

Ring Pitching

Ages: 7–adult
Time: 20 minutes
Materials Needed: Tree saplings and two limbs for stakes.
Advance Preparation: Stick two stakes into the ground far enough apart that contestants can pitch the ring. Make rings 4 ½ inches in diameter with the tree saplings. Wrap with yucca leaves or masking tape. Paint half of the ring white and leave the other half green.
Activity: The object of the game is to toss the ring over the peg for 5 points. If the green side of the ring touches the peg, score 3 points, and if the white side touches the ring, score 1 point. Accumulating 15 points wins the game.

Place Snatching

Ages: 7–adult
Time: 20 minutes
Materials Needed: Fabric pieces/bandanna handkerchiefs—one for each participant.
Advance Preparation: Place pieces of fabric about 2 inches apart in a large circle.

Activity: Each player stands on a "blanket" (fabric piece). One player stands in the center without a blanket. As the players constantly change places with one another, the center player attempts to step into a place left vacant momentarily. If he is successful, the player displaced must go to the center and seek a vacant spot.

Indian Jacks

Ages: 8–13 years
Time: 20 minutes
Materials Needed: Large pile of smooth rocks (2-inch diameter).
Advance Preparation: Children gather rocks plus a special rock for tossing into the air.
Activity: Two to four players sit around the rock pile, each taking a turn to toss the "special rock" into the air and pick up a rock from the pile while it is still suspended in the air. The player continues to toss and reach for a rock from the pile until he misses. The game ends when all the rocks from the pile are gone. The player with the most rocks is the winner.

Create Indian Jewelry

Ages: All ages
Time: 30–50 minutes
Materials Needed: For younger children use simpler materials such as shoelaces, beads, macaroni, shells, etc. Older guests may string more authentic materials such as shells, corn kernels, acorns, pumpkin seeds, bones, nuts, and gems/rocks. Check your nearest craft store for stringing materials.
Advance Preparation: Gather all materials needed and create sample necklaces.
Activity: Make Indian jewelry.

Mill a Meal

Ages: 5–adult
Time: 10–20 minutes
Materials Needed: Shelled corn, large flat rocks, and smaller round rocks.

Advance Preparation: Gather all materials needed. Make a sample of the cornmeal.
Activity: Guests try their hand at grinding corn between the rocks and making cornmeal.

Indian Story Time

Ages: 3–7 years
Time: 10–20 minutes
Materials Needed: Large tepee and an Indian story.
Advance Preparation: Make a tepee (see "Decora-

tions"). Select an Indian story. Read it and practice telling the story.
Activity: Sit inside the tepee and tell the Indian story.

Wild Turkey Hunt

Ages: 3–9 years
Time: 10 minutes
Materials Needed: Decorated turkey-shaped sugar cookies (in a sandwich bag) and a turkey caller from a sporting goods store. You may also use tag board or colored paper to make turkeys.
Advance Preparation: Hide turkey cookies through-

out the party area. Purchase a turkey caller. This game is best played outside.
Activity: While guests hunt for turkeys, someone blows the turkey caller.
Variation: Hide geese and use a goose caller. On each goose, write out a special poem, prize, or number.

Wild Turkey Shoot

Ages: 7–adult
Time: 20 minutes
Materials Needed: Large decorative turkey covered with glass or clear adhesive vinyl and a toy bow and arrow set (suction-type arrow). One target and arrow set for every five guests.
Advance Preparation: Put up target and purchase arrow set.

Activity: Guests shoot at a turkey. The team making the most hits wins. Each guest may have 3 to 5 attempts at the target. Younger children just shoot at the target. They do not keep score.
Variation: Make and throw whirlibobs or use a toy crossbow.

Stone Toss

Ages: 16–adult
Time: 15 minutes
Materials Needed: Seven flat rocks 5 inches in diameter, fourteen small rocks 1 inch in diameter. Prizes are optional.
Advance Preparation: Locate rocks and arrange the seven large rocks about 1 foot apart in a straight line. Scratch a throwing line 12 feet away from the line of rocks. Place a small rock on each of the flat rocks.

Activity: Each guest receives five rocks. The object of the game is to knock the small rock off the flat rock. Indians take turns standing behind the throwing line (12 feet away) and tossing their rocks. Score 1 point for each successful toss. Younger children should play this as an activity without keeping score. The distance may also be less.

Graffiti at Thanksgiving

Ages: 4–adult
Time: Spontaneous
Materials Needed: Butcher paper, markers, rubber stamps, and tape.

Advance Preparation: Attach paper to a wall which is easy to view and access. Gather all materials needed.
Activity: Write/draw/stamp your expressions of Thanksgiving.

Stick Ball

Ages: 8–adult
Time: 15–45 minutes
Materials Needed: One 12-inch broomstick, one 24-inch broomstick, and four bases.
Advance Preparation: Set up bases like a baseball diamond. Select two teams as in softball. Mark 10-foot distances for each base progression: 10 feet to 1st base, 20 feet to 2nd, 30 feet to 3rd, 40 feet to home. Test the distances for varied ages. Shorten the distances for younger children.
Activity: Player goes to home base and sets up for the kick: player lays a short stick on the ground and places the tip of the longer stick under the short stick. Player kicks the longer stick (at lower end) sending the shorter stick flying through the air. The distance kicked determines the base earned. 10 feet=1st base, 20 feet=2nd base, etc. Like baseball, the second kicker moves the first kicker on to the next bases. No steals. Score like baseball. An inning is completed when each player has a turn. Play three or more innings.

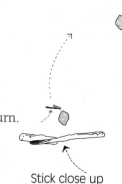

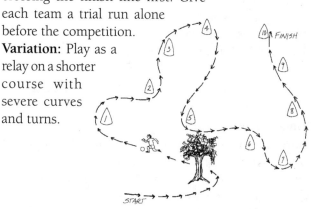

Stick close up

Indian Kickball

Ages: 8–adult
Time: 30–40 minutes
Materials Needed: Two soccer balls (each a different color), 8 to 10 cone markers, and a large playing field/park.
Advance Preparation: Lay out a large winding trail for two teams to follow. Create curves and turns with the markers or sticks. Make the trail as long as possible (100 to 300 yards).
Activity: Each team receives a ball. The players of each team work the ball through the course as quickly as possible. Team members dribble and pass (as in soccer) to the finish line. The winning team is the one crossing the finish line first. Give each team a trial run alone before the competition.
Variation: Play as a relay on a shorter course with severe curves and turns.

Cob Dart Throw

Ages: 6–adult
Time: 20 minutes
Materials Needed: Safety darts and rope or long vine.
Advance Preparation: Cut corn cobs into 4- to 5-inch lengths. Insert three feathers in one end of cob and a screw into the opposite end of cob for weight. Make a 1-inch diameter circle of vine/rope for the target.
Activity: Place the target on the ground. Mark a toe line from which players must toss three darts. There should be a target for every three or four guests. The winner is the one who places the most darts in the ring. This activity must be played with adult supervision if using a sharp point.
Note: The corn dart game was originally played with a point on the end of the dart. The Hopi Indians used a ring made of corn husks, dropped it on the ground, and then threw cob darts at it.

Indian Corn Toss

Ages: 6–adult
Time: 15 minutes
Materials Needed: Twenty-four-inch-square heavy vinyl cloth/paper, permanent marker, and Indian corn kernels.
Advance Preparation: Draw a target consisting of four concentric circles. Give each circle a different value.
Activity: Guests toss five kernels onto the circles. Tabulate scores earned by each player. The player with the highest score wins. For younger children, play as an activity and do not keep score.

Sticks and Stones

Ages: 6–adult
Time: 15 minutes
Materials Needed: Large can, paper/contact paper, markers, five small stones (1 ½ inches), many little twigs/toothpicks.
Advance Preparation: Mark stones with numbers 1 through 5. Decorate can with paper and Indian symbols.

Activity: Players stand several feet away from the can and toss five stones into the can. Total the number of stones landing in the can. The highest score wins. Use one target for each three to four guests. Keep track of wins with twigs/toothpicks. Repeat play.

Spear a Hoop

Ages: 8–adult
Time: 15 minutes
Materials Needed: Hula Hoop and safety spears. Original hoops were 18 inches in diameter and made from tree saplings fastened together with sinew or buckskin.
Advance Preparation: Lace a Hula Hoop with cord/twine. Weight the leading end of a dowel or purchase spears.
Activity: Contestants throw spears through a netted

wheel attempting to send it though the center or bull's eye. Be safety conscious. Guests should all remain behind the throw line and all throw in the same direction toward the target. This is only one of many variations of hoop and pole games.
Note: The Hula Hoop may be left open rather than laced, especially for younger children.

Indian Pottery

Ages: 5–9 years
Time: 10–15 minutes
Materials Needed: Molding clay.
Advance Preparation: Create a sample clay pot (olla).
Activity: Guests roll clay into a long fat snake and then

form a pot by coiling it around and around. Keep enlarging and heightening the coil to build sides. Older guests may smooth the coils forming a more perfected pot.

Indian Nation Shields

Ages: 6–10 years
Time: 15 minutes
Materials Needed: Flat paper plates, markers, feathers (from a hobby store), construction paper, scissors, glue, yarn, and masking tape.

Advance Preparation: Make a sample shield and illustrate some simple Indian designs.
Activity: Each guest creates a shield representing an Indian nation. Hang as party decorations.

Pass a Moccasin

Ages: 7–teen
Time: 15 minutes
Materials Needed: Box of toothpicks/small sticks and a pebble for each clan of Indians.
Advance Preparation: Count out a dozen toothpicks/small sticks for each guest. Find pebbles.
Activity: Each clan of eight Indians gathers in a circle, sits Indian style, and each person takes off one shoe. Designate one player as "It." Indians pass their shoes around in the circle and at the same time sing an Indian chant. The shoes (moccasins) are passed in rhythm

(Hi ya ye hi ye ye, etc.). "It" hides a pebble in one shoe/moccasin. Pass the shoes/moccasins around the circle a couple of times before stopping the chant. Now, the Indians each guess which moccasin holds the pebble. A wrong guess means giving up one stick (counter) to "It." A correct guess wins six sticks (counters) from "It." At the end of each round, the pebble is revealed. Rotate "It" each round and play until each Indian has had a turn at being "It." You may wish to add another pebble (have two "Its").

Feather Hunt

Ages: 4–10 years
Time: 10–15 minutes
Materials Needed: Assorted large feathers, ribbons enough for guests to tie around their heads, and a hot glue gun or masking tape.
Advance Preparation: Hide the feathers about the party area or yard. One feather is marked as a prize feather and the finder of that feather is designated the Indian Chief.

Activity: Guests hunt for the feathers and then make headbands with the feathers they have discovered. An adult should glue the feathers on the ribbon/felt for each guest. Braves and maidens may wear the headbands during the party.

Take Your Troubles Away

Ages: 4–10 years
Time: 10–15 minutes
Materials Needed: Sticks/dowels 1 ½ inches in length, twine, black felt-tipped pen, and round fabric pieces (6-inch diameter).
Advance Preparation: Cut sticks/dowels into 1 ½-inch pieces enough for each guest to have six dolls. Make a sample doll by creating a simple face on the little stick. Decorate the stick with a fabric pieces. Ancient dolls were very simple. The round fabric piece creates the bag for the dolls. Trouble Dolls can be purchased.

Activity: Guests create faces on each of their six dolls. Tell the story and custom of the Guatemalan Indian girls. There it is taught that when you have troubles, you share them with your dolls. Take one doll from the bag for each trouble. Share the trouble with your doll. As you sleep the little dolls will attempt to solve your worries. There are only six dolls—six troubles.

Which Hand?

Ages: 4–12 years
Time: 10–15 minutes
Materials Needed: Pebbles and Indian music (chanting).
Advance Preparation: Gather a few pebbles.
Activity: Guests form two lines facing one another. Each guest in one line is given a pebble. The players with the pebbles are "It." The "Its" pass the pebble from one hand to another in the rhythm of an Indian chant. The opponent (person directly opposite) guesses which hand holds the pebble. If the guess is right, the opponent gets the pebble in the next chant. If the guess is wrong, the same person repeats the game. Use sticks as counters. You may choose not to keep track of the wins and losses. Do not keep score with children under 7 years.

Kick the Stick

Ages: 7–adult
Time: 10 minutes
Materials Needed: Eight-inch sticks enough for each guest.
Advance Preparation: Gather sticks for each guest. Mark a start and finish line 125 feet apart. Allow plenty of space between each player.

Activity: Players stand behind a starting line with a stick in front of them. On the signal "Go," guests kick their sticks toward the goal line. The first guest to reach the finish line with her stick is the winner.

Kachina Doll Ornament

Ages: 7–12 years
Time: 20 minutes
Materials Needed: Balsa wood pieces, acrylic paints (red and white), black markers.
Advance Preparation: Cut wood into simple doll-shaped pieces—one for each guest. Purchase paints and black markers.

Activity: Guests decorate a Kachina Doll ornament. This style was the first Kachina doll a baby girl would receive.

Exploring

Ages: 3–9 years
Time: 15–20 minutes
Materials Needed: Story about Indian children in the woods, by the sea, or by a river.
Advance Preparation: Learn the story well enough to tell the children as you take them to explore. This will give you ideas as you explore special treasures in nature.
Activity: Guests/Indians explore by a creek, in the woods, or by the sea.

Weaving

Ages: 3–adult
Time: 15–60 minutes
Materials Needed: Basket/cloth weaving materials and a specialist who can demonstrate or teach weaving. Check hobby stores and community class schedules.
Advance Preparation: Make arrangements to have someone demonstrate or teach simple weaving techniques.
Activity: Guests enjoy learning about basket/cloth weaving.

Top Spinning

Ages: 7–teen
Time: 15 minutes
Materials Needed: One top for each guest.
Advance Preparation: Purchase tops.
Activity: This is an Eskimo game in which players attempt to run around the house while their tops are spinning.

Note: Indian boys made tops from wood or bone which were often spun with a string. Younger children twirled tops (a seed or berry with a stick through its center) with their fingers.

Indian Clues

Ages: 7–teen
Time: 35 minutes
Materials Needed: Pencil and paper.
Advance Preparation: None.
Activity: Play begins with two teams of Indians. One team hides, sends its leader back to the other team.

The leader draws a map on the ground revealing where his team is hidden. The searching team now attempts to discover the hidden Indians from the map clues. When the team is discovered, both teams race back to the tepee (starting point). The team whose members arrive first is the winner. Repeat play reversing roles.

Flip a Pit

Ages: 7–adult
Time: 20 minutes
Materials Needed: Wood bowls/small baskets, many peach/plum pits, and a black permanent marker.
Advance Preparation: Mark a black band across one side of each pit. You will need 5 or 6 pits for each group. Find lots of little twigs to be used for keeping score. Put 5 or 6 pits in each bowl—one bowl for every group.

Activity: Groups of six people sit in a circle. Guests take turns holding the bowl in one hand and giving it a slight toss flipping the pits into the air. They catch the pits in the bowl and count the pits that land with the banded side up. Each pit with the exposed band counts 1 point. Keep score with twigs. Game ends after each guest has 10 tosses. Tally final scores and the team with the largest score wins.

Skipping

Ages: 8–adult
Time: 20 minutes
Materials Needed: Rope 16 feet to 18 feet long, a large piece of fake fur (originally, caribou skin was used), and polyfill.
Advance Preparation: Sew fur piece to resemble small sleeping bag and stuff with polyfill. Wrap around the center of the rope two or more times and sew together.
Activity: Indians jump the obstacle as two people turn the rope. They must jump higher and sometimes duck to miss the caribou skin. The Inuit Indians varied the twirling of the rope. They sometimes changed direction or swung it like a pendulum.

Ball Juggling

Ages: 8–adult
Time: 15 minutes
Materials Needed: Juggling balls (tennis balls).
Advance Preparation: Purchase the balls.
Activity: Determine a goal: a tree, a post, etc. Contestants juggle their balls as they walk toward the goal. The first juggler to reach the designated goal without breaking the rhythm of the juggle is the winner.

Note: Two or three balls may be used. The Indians used water-worn stones about 2 inches in diameter.
Note: Running, rope skipping, hide-and-seek, hunting, tag, high jumping, long jumping, and cat's cradle are a few examples of Native American play. Stilts and shuttlecock games were also played among the Native Americans.

Indian Proverbs

"May the warm winds of heaven
Blow softly on this house
May the Great Spirit
Bless all who enter here."

"May your moccasins make
Happy tracks in many snows
And the rainbow always
touch your shoulder."

"Oh Great Spirit
Grant that I may never
find fault with my neighbor
Until I have walked three moons
In his moccasins."

Indian Resources

- Indian Museums can be found thoughout the United States, including:
  Heye Foundation (Museum of the American Indian), New York City
  American Museum of Natural History also in New York City
  The Peabody Museum at Harvard University
  The Field Museum in Chicago, Illinois
  The Denver Art Museum in Denver, Colorado
  Indian City, U.S.A. in Anadarko, Oklahoma
  Mesa Verde National Park near Durango, Colorado
  Indian Museum in Flagstaff, Arizona
- Local historical societies may publish periodicals that contain excellent information about Indians.
- Arts and crafts shops on Indian reservations throughout the United States.
- Local libraries have books on Indian crafts, costumes, lore, and Indian music recordings. *Brother Eagle Sister Sky* by Susan Jeffers.

HAVE A POWWOW!

24: Christmas/Hanukkah/ Epiphany/Winter Solstice

The winter solstice, which marks the transition from darkness to light and cold to warmth, has long been a time for merrymaking. Early celebrations focused on bonfires to drive out evil spirits and hasten the sun's return ending the long, dark days of winter in Northern Europe. The Norse mythology tells us of one such winter solstice celebration involving the yule log. One early form of this was a straw-wrapped wheel set ablaze and rolled down the hillside into a stream. The wheel symbolized the sun and the warm growing season to come. Later, a large yule log was decorated and brought into the home to burn. It originally was used to worship the sun as the light of the world. The church changed the ceremony so that the blazing fire represented the new Light of the World, Christ. The festival of Santa Lucia (Festival of Lights), originated in Italy, is another winter solstice/Christian celebration. The Swedish custom of Santa Lucia is the most charming. Santa Lucia (oldest daughter wearing a crown of lighted candles and a white gown) awakens her family members and regales them with song, coffee, and saffron buns on the morning of December 13.

Christianity and the observance of Christmas spread throughout Europe from A.D. 600 to 1100. Pagan tribes were willing to give up their pagan gods but they were not willing to give up their important folk customs and merry festivals. Religious missionaries, recognizing this, allowed the people to continue their festivals and gradually these customs became part of Christmas. During the Middle Ages, Christmas time became the merriest of seasons. Grand feasts held in castles and great houses of kings and nobleman featured poets and traveling singers. Christmas was the only celebration in which the peasants were included. During the twelve days between December 25 and January 6 leading up to Epiphany, everyone could celebrate and forget the struggles of daily living. A magnificent finale, the Twelfth Night, marked the end of the Christmas season. It was the most elaborate of the Christmas festivities and included processions, wassailing, banners, costumes, traditional music, juggling, magic, dance, food, and drink. A Twelfth Night King and Queen of Bean were ceremoniously crowned and reigned throughout the evening. Christmas greens were burned and a blessing of life and health for the coming year was bestowed upon the guests. Rekindle a celebration of the past with family and friends. Blend a little of the old with the new. Celebrate, in fellowship and song, the simple message of Christmas—loving and giving. Cherish family traditions and exchange gifts of laughter and happiness.

INVITATION

Holiday note cards make great, quick, and easy invitations. Old Christmas cards can be used for invitations. Write the message on the back and cut into puzzle parts.

DECORATIONS

🎅 **Poinsettia plants** and the **English Christmas rose** always add a festive touch at Christmas.

🎅 **Snowflakes** create a feeling of wintry merriment. Use **doilies** as a variation.

🎅 **Gingerbread-man garlands** can be hung across a wall or fireplace mantle. (Spray gingerbread men with a lacquer and glue to a festive ribbon).

🎅 A **toy train** chugging around the Christmas tree is a fun decorating touch!

❄ Display a **bell collection.** By the Middle Ages, bells had become a very important part of the Christmas celebrations.

❄ Unveil an **antique Santa/Father Christmas** collection.

❄ Arrange **antique toys** on the fireplace mantel.

❄ Snuggle **teddy bears** around the house at a child's table, in a child's rocker, or in an antique sleigh.

❄ Fasten **sheaves of grain** in a tree or atop poles stuck in the ground. This is an old Norwegian tradition—placing bundles of grain above every gateway, gable, and barn door to feed the birds at Christmas.

❄ Display a **gingerbread house** at Christmas.

❄ For a bit of nostalgia, hang your children's **baby booties** on the Christmas tree. Embroider names and birth dates.

❄ Adorn the holiday table with **pleated paper angels** decorated with white glitter or hang the angels as a garland.

❄ String **lights** on trees and roof lines. Try battery-operated **twinkle lights** in your decorating scheme inside or outside.

❄ **Advent calendars** are enjoyed by children and may be used as part of the holiday decorations. Save and display as a collage on a large wall.

❄ **Aromas** are a must for the festive holiday celebrations. Scents of potpourri, evergreen, cloved fruit, rosemary, thyme, sage, scented candles, peppermint sticks, and all the wonderful scents of the kitchen will delight the senses. Also simmer cinnamon sticks/cloves in water or drip cinnamon oil on a hearth broom.

❄ Fill **mini baskets** with potpourri; first line the baskets with lace doilies. Fill a basket with cloved fruit.

❄ **Candles, candles, candles**—place vanilla-scented tapers in assorted candleholders. Add ribbon for accent.

❄ **Oil lamps/lanterns** create a wonderful warmth at Christmas.

❄ **Torches** and **bonfires** were used in winter solstice rites centuries before Christ's birth and during medieval times.

❄ **Christmas wreaths** are beautiful holiday decorations. The Romans exchanged holly wreaths as tokens of friendship.

❄ Deck your home with natural **greenery.** Greens have always been symbolic of life's continuity. A variety of greens may be used—laurel, rosemary, ivy, mistletoe, holly, and garlands of evergreen.

❄ **Sprigs of mistletoe** are symbolic of love and friendship. Hang mistletoe for a special touch of fun and celebration. A kiss under the mistletoe is a token of love.

❄ Lay a simple **dried rose** with stem across a Bible open to the Christmas story.

❄ **Yule logs** are inexpensive and great for large gatherings that need many centerpieces. Decorate with greens and holly. Snuggle a few **nuts** among the greens.

❄ **Farolitos** (little lamps) can be made by filling a large lunch bag with 2 inches of sand and placing an old candle or votive candle in the sand. Line your walkway with the little lamps. Light the lamps for a beautiful luminous effect.

❄ **Tablecloths** of **Mylar** or **plaid taffeta** are especially nice with crystal candlesticks and red candles.

❄ **Ice candles** are delicately radiant as they are snuggled in the snow along the front walkway or front porch. Ice candles are made by filling large plastic 5-quart buckets with water to about $^{3}/_{4}$-inch from the top. Place the buckets outside to freeze—about 5 hours in near zero temperatures. Take the ice candles out of the buckets before they freeze completely. When you place the ice candle in the snow upside down, you will notice a small well in which to place a votive candle.

❄ Nestle a **doll collection** on window ledges, in a child's rocker, or around a play table creating a whimsical tea party setting. Small dolls may be anchored on the branches of a Christmas tree with pipe cleaner. Doll collections will bring back heartwarming memories at Christmas.

❄ Place **old lanterns** along the walkway or on an outdoor porch.

❄ For a simple centerpiece, surround a **candlestick** with **greens** and **nuts.**

❄ Roast **chestnuts** on an open fire. Boil nuts briefly. This makes roasting easier.

Note: Celebrate and decorate creatively and personally rather than compulsively. Enjoy your preparations. If time is limited, make a list and prioritize. Be realistic!

WINTER HOLIDAY TERMS

Revelers
Snowball
Holly
Aroma
Garlands
Reindeer
Savories
Noel
Yule log
Gingerbread men
Joy
Jingle bells
Elves
Peace
Silver bells
Gnomes
Dazzle
Christmas tree
Yuletide
Tinsel
Angels
Round the hearth

Radiant
Sentimental
Candlelight/flickering
Father Christmas
Wassail
Stars/twinkle
Santa
Twelfth Night
Festival
St. Nicholas
Hanukkah/Chanukah
Kindness
Gleeful
Menorah
Sleigh
Love/love feasts
Shamash (servant candle)
Bustling
Sharing

Wintry
Hope
Festival of lights
Cheer
Merriment
Glow
Ho-ho-ho
Feasting
Star of David
Olde Tyme Christmas
Dazzle
Bountiful
Kindliness
Glitter
Brilliance
Snow/silent/deep
Advent
Mummers (short wordless plays)
Jingle Bell Junction
Ringing

FOODS

☃ Cocoa/cider/cranberry juice
☃ Holiday breads
☃ Ethnic specialties
☃ Christmas cookies and candy

Santa Lucia Buns

5 cups flour
½ cup sugar
1 tsp. salt
2 pkg. yeast
¾ cup lukewarm milk
½ cup water

½ cup margarine
3 eggs (room temp.)
½ tsp. ground cardamom
½ tsp. powdered saffron
½ cup raisins

Dissolve yeast in warm water. Stir in milk, sugar, margarine, eggs, cardamom, saffron, salt, and 3 cups flour. Mix until smooth. Add remaining flour and knead on a lightly floured surface. Let rise until double in size. Punch down the dough and divide into 24 parts. Shape each into a **S**-shaped rope and add a raisin inside each coil. Let rise on a greased cookie sheet until doubled. Brush lightly with 1 egg and 1 T. water mixture. Sprinkle with sugar and bake at 350 degrees for 15 minutes.

Note: Substitute "ready to bake" breadsticks from the grocery store.

CHRISTMAS ACTIVITIES/GAMES
Gingerbread Men

Ages: 3–10 years
Time: 45 minutes
Materials Needed: Gingerbread dough packaged individually for each guest, raisins, and nuts. Purchase little rolling pins from a variety store—one for each guest. Buy gingerbread men and women cookie cutters of varying sizes. Have plenty of soap and water for cleanup!
Advance Preparation: Find a favorite gingerbread recipe and make a trial batch of cookies. Mix the gingerbread dough and package it for each guest. Refrigerate if necessary.
Activity: Children wash hands. Each guest is given a package of dough to roll and cut gingerbread men and women. Decorate with raisins, nuts, etc. Bake. When the cookies are cooled, place them on a paper plate in a plastic bag. Send cookies home with the guests as they leave.

Chimney Bound

Ages: 3–6 years
Time: 10 minutes
Materials Needed: Red fabric, beans, narrow ribbon, a tall box, and brick-design paper.
Advance Preparation: Make Santa's "bean bags" by cutting circles of fabric, filling with beans, and tying with ribbon. With brick paper, decorate a tall box as a chimney.
Activity: Guests toss Santa bean bags in the chimney. The older guests may play this game as a relay.

Piñata

Ages: 4–adult
Time: 15–30 minutes
Materials Needed: Purchase or make a piñata. You will also need a heavy cord, pulley, broom, and blindfolds.
Advance Preparation: Fill piñatas with novelty items, candy, and nuts. Hang the piñata from a hook in the ceiling, or over a basketball hoop or a tree limb. A pulley system may also be used.
Activity: Blindfolded guests take turns whacking the piñata with a broom, trying to break it open. Each turn consists of three whacks. When the piñata breaks, all guests dive for the treats.
Variation: Hang ribbons (one for each guest) from the piñata. One is attached to an object which will break open the piñata. When the "hot" ribbon is pulled, the piñata will break open, spilling the treats. For a little added excitement, fill a few walnut shells with $2 bills. Glue nuts back together with a hot glue gun.

Family Surprise

Ages: All ages
Time: 1 hour
Materials Needed: Baked goods, novelty items, Christmas recordings, basket, etc. From your church or community outreach programs, learn of a family in need.
Advance Preparation: Family members prepare a special basket or giant stocking filled with surprises.
Activity: On the Sunday before Christmas or on Christmas Eve, deliver all the goodies to the family in need. Quietly pile all the offerings on the porch and ring a loud bell. Hide until the presents are discovered. You may remain anonymous or you may reveal yourselves by caroling for the special family.

Wandering Minstrels

Ages: 6–adult
Time: 1–2 hours
Materials Needed: Flashlights/lanterns, song booklets, pitch pipe, children dressed as jesters or elves. Children also enjoy percussion instruments such as bells, triangles, chimes, wood blocks (trotting horses), and tambourines.
Advance Preparation: Develop the list of people you wish to carol. Select jesters who may juggle, dance around, or do a bit of tumbling during a lively carol.
Activity: The minstrels stroll the neighborhood and sing carols. Elves may ring the doorbells!
Variation: Sing a few ethnic carols in a foreign language. Accompany your singing with a small portable stereo.

Carolers

Ages: Teen–adult
Time: At the beginning of the celebration (open house, etc.) and spontaneously throughout the party
Materials Needed: None.
Advance Preparation: Contact a high school or college music department. Ask if they have a small group of carolers in costume who could be hired to sing. Schedule and make arrangements with the group.
Activity: As guests arrive, carolers greet them with songs. Later in the evening, carolers stroll around singing for the guests.

Parade of Lights

Ages: 6–12 years
Time: 30–45 minutes (less hectic after December 25)
Materials Needed: Lanterns (make or purchase) or penlights/battery-operated electric candles, and Christmas costumes such as elves, snowmen, Dickens' characters, jesters, shepherds, kings, angels, etc.
Advance Preparation: Make or purchase lanterns/penlights. Send invitations indicating costumes needed.
Activity: Children stroll down the street or sidewalk, ringing bells, singing revels, and carrying lights aglow. Little elves run ahead and ring doorbells heralding Christmas greetings and inviting the neighborhood to view and listen to the parade of children. Children gather for snacks and cocoa after the parade.

Carol Sing-a-long

Ages: All ages
Time: 30–45 minutes
Materials Needed: Piano/violin, songbooks, and cheerful voices. May also use flutes or guitars.
Advance Preparation: Arrange for someone to play the piano or violin. Purchase song sheets.
Activity: Sing Christmas carols around the fireplace/piano.
Variation: Children enjoy percussion instruments such as bells, triangles, wood blocks (trotting horses), and tambourines.

Elves/Gnomes

Ages: 8–adult
Time: During an open house or business party
Materials Needed: Felt, large and small bells, tights, and turtleneck shirts.
Advance Preparation: Create costumes for elves. A basic tunic pattern can assist you in making a costume.
Activity: Elves/gnomes greet guests, help serve the dinner, replenish the serving table of an open house, or pass out presents at a business party.

Cookie Exchange

Ages: Adult
Time: 2 hours
Materials Needed: Invitations with cookie exchange information. Indicate quantities.
Advance Preparation: Send invitation.
Activity: Guests exchange Christmas cookies and recipes. Cookies are sampled by the guests.

Sleigh Ride

Ages: All ages
Time: 30–50 minutes
Materials Needed: In the invitation, remind guests to wear warm clothing and bring blankets.
Advance Preparation: Arrange for the sleigh ride. Check the Yellow Pages and winter sport's resorts for possible rental. Check city ordinances for regulations concerning horses.

Activity: Slide though the streets or meadows to a favorite place—a small restaurant, a cabin, or a campsite where you can build a bonfire.
Variation: Ride a carriage driven by horses. Check the Yellow Pages.

English Tea

Ages: 3–adult
Time: 2 hours
Materials Needed: Play tables and chairs for children, child's tea service, fine china, lace, flowers, silver tea service, and everything nice! Etiquette book for reference and someone to play the harp or piano during the tea.

Advance Preparation: Set a beautiful tea table—one for children also if they are invited.
Activity: Bring the generations together for an English tea party. Enchant your guests with a beautiful table, delicious food, and music.

Taffy Pull

Ages: 8–adult
Time: 2 hours
Materials Needed: Ingredients for taffy, a metal hook (purchase from a hardware store), and a plastic dropcloth.
Advance Preparation: Put up one or more taffy hooks

in an area where cornstarch can fall on the floor. A basement or heated garage are good places to pull taffy. The floor can be covered with a dropcloth.
Activity: Cook taffy, pull, and cut into pieces. Store in airtight containers.

Favorite Taffy

3 cups granulated sugar
1 ½ cups white corn syrup
¾ cup water

Boil these ingredients to 264 degrees. Pour taffy onto a buttered marble slab or buttered pan to cool. When the taffy is cool enough to work, pick it up and begin pulling it on the taffy hook. Use cornstarch on your hands to prevent sticking. Pull taffy as lightly as possible, allowing lots of air in the candy. Add an oil flavoring and coloring when pulling the taffy. When using cocoa, pour on hot taffy so it melts a little. When the taffy becomes hard, cut into pieces. The taffy will be hard but chewy when eaten.

Candy Cane Search

Ages: 5–12 years
Time: 15 minutes
Materials Needed: Candy canes.
Advance Preparation: Hide candy canes throughout the room.

Activity: Search for candy canes.
Variation: Combine with the "Trim a Tree" activity.

Trim a Tree

Ages: All ages
Time: 2–3 hours
Materials Needed: Cranberries, popcorn, doilies, raffia, cinnamon sticks, ribbon, buttonhole thread, and large needles.
Advance Preparation: Collect materials needed. Pop

the corn and string lights on the tree. Day-old popcorn strings best.
Activity: Guests string popcorn/cranberries, make cornucopias with paper doilies or wrapping paper, tie bundles of cinnamon sticks together with ribbons, and trim the tree with all the handmade ornaments.

Christmas Eve Candlelight Celebration

Ages: 3–10 years
Time: 20 minutes
Materials Needed: Candles with holders, penlights for very young children, a large nativity scene, and a vigil light near the infant Jesus. Recordings of "Away in the Manager" and "Joy to the World."
Advance Preparation: Gather materials needed.
Activity: Children gather around the creche and, one by one, light their candles from the vigil light. When all the candles are lighted, the children sing "Away in the Manger" and "Joy to the World." After singing, children carry the candles to their bedrooms and are tucked into bed.

Trim a Travel Tree

Ages: All ages
Time: Vacations
Materials Needed: Travel mementos that can be used as Christmas tree ornaments.
Advance Preparation: When vacationing, purchase an ornament reminding you of the vacation spot.
Activity: Trim your Christmas tree with travel memento ornaments. As you trim your tree, you will be reminded of the special memories and stories of your travels.
Variation: Purchase an ornament each year that commemorates a very special event of that year.

International Feast

Ages: Teen–adult
Time: 1 ½ hours
Materials Needed: Invitations.
Advance Preparation: Send invitations asking guests to bring their favorite ethnic dishes and come in ethnic clothes.
Activity: Guests enjoy an international dinner.
Variation: Feature one particular ethnic culture. Greet Christmas guests in traditional costumes, tell stories, dance, and sing folk songs.

Secret Santa

Ages: 9–adult
Time: 1 week
Materials Needed: Names to be drawn among the participants.
Advance Preparation: Everyone draws a name and is Secret Santa to the person drawn.
Activity: Each day Secret Santa writes a poem, clue, etc. and has it delivered or mailed anonymously to the recipient. On the last day, the Secret Santas give a small present and reveal themselves.

Children's Tree

Ages: 4–12 years
Time: Not applicable
Materials Needed: Miniature cars, trucks, dolls, paper dolls, stuffed animals, or choose ornaments depicting a theme (origami, a legend, a hobby/collection, paper cut-work [snowflakes], space paraphernalia, etc.)
Advance Preparation: Select tree and ornaments chosen by the child.
Activity: Children enjoy decorating a small tree of their own. Snuggle stuffed animals around the base of the tree.
Variation: If your child celebrates a birthday around Christmas, transform the small tree into a birthday tree. Add party blowers, whistles, serpentine streamers, and a "HAPPY BIRTHDAY" banner. Top the tree with numbers showing the age of the birthday child.

Holiday Wishes

Ages: 6–adult
Time: 20 minutes
Materials Needed: Decorated box/can and note cards.
Advance Preparation: Family members prepare one or two wishes on a note card. These wishes should be expressions of love or service. Family members place their wishes in the decorated container.
Activity: On New Year's Day share the family wishes during a holiday meal.

Gingerbread Houses

Ages: 6–adult

Time: 1 to several hours

Materials Needed: Milk cartons and graham crackers, small red cinnamon candies, miniature candy pieces, nuts, powdered sugar, frosting ingredients, and cake-decorating tubes/plastic mustard dispensers. To glue these houses together use decorators' frosting recipe—many magazines feature gingerbread house recipes at Christmas.

Advance Preparation: With frosting, attach crackers to the sides of the milk cartons. Then put on the roof using frosting as the glue.

Activity: Guests decorate the gingerbread houses with frosting and candy. Adults may create gingerbread houses from gingerbread cookie dough and decorate with fancy cake-decorating tubes. This can be a simple or more elaborate activity. Keep it appropriate to the ages creating the houses. Younger children have an attention span of about 30 minutes to an hour.

Holiday Searchers

Ages: 6–14 years

Time: 10 minutes

Materials Needed: Hiding places!

Advance Preparation: Hide one of each child's presents in a cupboard, cubby hole, etc.

Activity: Children look for a present which has been hidden.

Santa Lucia

Ages: 8–young adult (girls)

Time: 15 minutes

Materials Needed: Saffron buns/small coffee cakes, a basket lined with a festive cloth, white loose-fitting robe/gown with a crimson sash, lingonberry or leaf crown with white candles (may be wax or battery operated).

Advance Preparation: Prepare buns/small coffee cakes, decorate basket/tray, and purchase crown and robe/gown.

Activity: Santa Lucia awakens family members and regales them with song, coffee, and saffron buns on December 13. When all the family members are dressed for the day, they gather for breakfast in the dining room, which has been lighted with lots of candles.

Variation: Santa Lucia and her band sing Yuletide songs as they visit homes in the neighborhood or serve cakes

among the guests celebrating an open house, etc. The band may include all the children in the family. The daughters don white gowns, wear silver tinsel in their hair, and carry candles. The sons (called "star boys") don white robes and high pointed caps with silver stars. The star boys may hold illuminated star lanterns.

Saint Nicholas

Ages: 3–7 years

Time: 45 minutes

Materials Needed: Costumes for Saint Nicholas and Black Peter (Saint Nicholas' assistant). Black face paint for Black Peter, coal, a bag of presents, and note cards.

Advance Preparation: Make or rent Saint Nicholas and Black Peter costumes. On note cards, gather information about each guest (something nice and something not so nice) for Saint Nicholas and Black Peter.

Activity: Saint Nicholas and Black Peter come to visit on the eve of December 6. St. Nicholas talks with each of the guests questioning them about their behavior

(use the information cards). If guests have had a good year, they receive a present from St. Nicholas. A lump of coal is given to the person who hasn't had such a good year (best to select a good-natured adult for the lump of coal). On St. Nicholas' Eve, children put out their wooden shoes filled with carrots for Sleipner, St. Nicholas' horse. Black Peter replaces the carrots with candy and treats for the children.

Note: The tradition of St. Nicholas comes to us from the Netherlands.

Whose Is It?

Ages: All ages
Time: 15–20 minutes
Materials Needed: Packages wrapped in many layers with each layer revealing a different name.
Advance Preparation: Wrap packages enough for each guest. Place names and trinkets such as balloons between each layer.
Activity: Unwrap presents. Each present goes through many hands before finding its owner. This is an old Dutch custom. Guests or family members love the excitement of this tradition.
Variation: Wrap presents and put "obviously wrong" names on the packages—a baby rattle for an 11-year-old boy, a pipe for an 8-year-old girl, a basketball for a newborn baby, etc. After the gifts have been opened and many puzzled looks are exchanged, family members will catch on to the trickery and pass presents to the right people.

Treasure Maps

Ages: 7–adult
Time: 20 minutes
Materials Needed: Festive recipe cards or paper.
Advance Preparation: Create maps or clues which will lead to a special present!
Activity: Each guest/family member receives a map or clue which will lead to a present. They read the clues and search for the present. This can be an exciting way to find a large gift that will not fit under the tree or in the house.

Yule Feast
(Yule Log)

Ages: All ages
Time: 2 hours
Materials Needed: Large Yule log.
Advance Preparation: Prepare a feast featuring pork, symbolic of the boar's head important to Norse Yule ritual.
Activity: Re-enact a Norse Yule feast. The Norse celebrated the return of the sun with a Yule Feast which began on the longest night of the year (called "Mother Night"). The Yule, meaning "wheel," symbolized the sun which was thought to resemble a fast-moving wheel as it moved across the sky. In England and Germany celebrants gathered on a mountain, set fire to a large wooden wheel entwined with straw, and sent it down the mountain-side. The wheel ended its journey when it plunged into a stream or lake at the foot of the hill. Later, burning a large Yule log replaced the wheel.

Holiday Collage

Ages: Adult
Time: 30 minutes
Materials Needed: Picture frame with glass and a glue stick.
Advance Preparation: Gather Christmas pictures of friends and family from holiday greeting cards and letters.
Activity: Create a collage of photos and indicate the year of the collage.

Surprise Ball/Package

Ages: 5–14 years
Time: 30 minutes
Materials Needed: Surprise balls/packages, rolls of crepe paper streamers, holiday recording, disc/tape player.
Advance Preparation: Purchase surprise balls or make surprise packages by wrapping a package with many layers of crepe paper. Between each layer of paper, tuck a balloon, a piece of gum, a riddle/joke, a coin, dice, trinkets, etc.
Activity: Guests gather in a circle with a surprise ball/package given to every fourth or fifth person. Guests pass the balls as the music plays. When the music stops, guests holding the balls/packages begin to unwrap them. They

continue to unwrap until the music plays again. The balls/ packages are then passed until the music stops. Play continues until all the balls/packages are unwrapped. Guests may keep the surprises that are revealed as they unwrap the various layers of paper and ribbon. The winners share the surprises with those who have not received a surprise. **Note:** This is a exciting way to wrap children's presents they exchange with friends. Create a giant ball!

"Come Seven"

Ages: 8–adult
Time: 30 minutes
Materials Needed: A present wrapped in many layers of paper boxes and cord, several pairs of dice, several pairs of Christmas mittens, table knives and forks. Be sure to use string or cord between layers—otherwise the package is opened too easily.
Advance Preparation: Wrap the presents (one for each table) and gather all materials needed. Decorate mitts with old family buttons, lace, etc.

Activity: Each table of guests begins throwing the dice until someone throws a seven. That lucky guest puts on a pair of mittens, picks up the knife and fork, and begins to open the package with the utensils, continuing to unwrap until another person throws a seven. That person is then given the mittens, knife, fork, and the present, and continues to unwrap the package. Play goes on until the gifts are unwrapped. This is a great activity. Guests enjoy its fast-moving and funny qualities!

Package Exchange

Ages: 8–adult
Time: 20–30 minutes
Materials Needed: A present for each guest and a basket filled with their names (give guests a funny name along with real name). Gifts may be white elephants, gag gifts, or tree ornaments.
Advance Preparation: Purchase and wrap an assortment of gifts—one for each guest. You may have everyone bring a white elephant, etc. Indicate this on the invitation.
Activity: The activity begins by drawing the first name from the Christmas basket. The guest whose name is drawn receives a package and opens it. A second name is drawn, and that guest may choose the package that was opened by the first person or may choose one from the pile. If the second player chooses the opened present, the first player must select another gift from the pile and open it. Play continues with names drawn from the basket one at a time; the guest may choose an opened present or a wrapped bundle from the pile. Everyone has a great time with this activity. Your gift is never safely yours until the end of play!

Variation: Guests each receive a Christmas package. They do not unwrap them but trade wrapped presents. One or two of the presents may be "hot" with five dollar bills hidden inside. The object of the trading is to end up with the presents containing the five dollar bills. The other presents should also have fun items inside but are not worth five dollars.

A Tree for the Young at Heart

Ages: Adult
Time: 2–3 hours
Materials Needed: Red satin Christmas ball ornaments, a gold metallic pen, and a small pine tree (real or artificial).
Advance Preparation: Write in gold script all the names of the children, grandchildren, and great-grandchildren on the satin balls. Hang the ball on the small tree.
Activity: Often older people do not want to fuss with a Christmas tree even though they would enjoy one. The gift of a decorated family tree delivered to a grandparent, aunt, or uncle is a very thoughtful gesture.
Variation: Decorate and use small photos as ornaments.

Living Holiday Present

Ages: Adult
Time: 1–3 hours
Materials Needed: Video camera or tape recorder. Rentals available.
Advance Preparation: Make a list of interesting topics and interview grandparents. Tape the live interview and duplicate it for relatives.
Activity: Send videotapes to family members.
Variation: You may wish to exchange a videotape at Christmas with a distant member of your clan.

How Many?

Ages: 5–adult
Time: 5 minutes
Materials Needed: Note pad and pencils.
Advance Preparation: Gather pad and pencils; be sure you count the ornaments while hanging them on your tree.
Activity: Participants guess the number of ornaments on the Christmas tree. They write the number on a piece of paper. Remember to put names on the paper. The winner is the person guessing the right number of ornaments.

Gift of Time

Ages: 8–adult
Time: 10 hours
Materials Needed: Blank coupons created on your computer or with colorful markers.
Advance Preparation: Make up several redeemable coupons with tasks or time.
Activity: This is a nice present for the elderly or for people who are handicapped. Coupons can be a thoughtful gift for children to give within the neighborhood—no transportation needed.

HANUKKAH ACTIVITIES/GAMES

Hanukkah (Festival of Lights) celebrates the Jewish victory over persecution in Jerusalem 21 centuries ago. Eight candles symbolize the eight days during which a one-day oil supply kept the Eternal Light burning after that victory.

Hanukkah Gelt

Ages: 7–adult
Time: 10–15 minutes
Materials Needed: Large bowl/basket filled with new pennies, chocolate coins, and nuts.

Advance Preparation: Fill the bowl or basket with the pennies and treats.
Activity: Each child takes one "hand dip" into the bowl/basket collecting as many pennies and treats as possible.

The Horah

Ages: 7–adult
Time: 30–40 minutes
Materials Needed: Music and directions for "The Horah" dance. Resource: All-Time Favorite Dances, KIM 9126C Kimbo Educational, 800-631-2187.

Advance Preparation: Practice the dance.
Activity: Dance the "The Horah"!

Dreidel

Ages: 5–12 years
Time: 20–40 minutes
Materials Needed: Dreidels—one for each group of four children—and prizes of nuts, raisins, pennies, or candy.
Advance Preparation: Gather materials needed.
Activity: Children take turns spinning the dreidel.

Nun means player takes nothing (nisht).
Gimel means player takes all the kitty (ganz).
Hay means player takes half of the kitty.
Shin means player puts a penny/treat into the kitty.

When the dreidel stops spinning, a Hebrew letter appears and tells the player what to do. Play continues until one player has all the pennies/treats. This has been a Jewish family favorite since medieval times.
Note: There is the "Dreidel" song which can be found at most music stores.

Dreidel Surprise Box

Ages: 5–12 years
Time: 15–20 minutes
Materials Needed: Large cardboard box, holiday wrapping paper, several pieces of ribbon, and a surprise for each child.
Advance Preparation: Decorate a large box, wrap presents, and attach each gift to a ribbon. Place presents in the box and drape ribbons from each side of the box (equal numbers on each side).

Activity: Children spin the dreidel and when the top stops, it will reveal a Hebrew letter that corresponds to one side of the box. When the child pulls a ribbon from that side of the box, it will reveal a surprise!

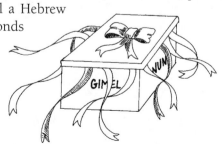

EPIPHANY CELEBRATIONS
English Dinner

Ages: All ages

Time: 1 hour

Materials Needed: English Christmas crackers, recipes for a traditional English dinner, and recording of "The Twelve Days of Christmas." Frankincense and myrrh are optional.

Advance Preparation: Prepare Beef Wellington, Yorkshire pudding, plum pudding, etc. for the dinner. Purchase or make Christmas crackers. Decorate tissue or paper towel tubes with crepe paper, foil paper, doilies, stickers, ribbons, etc. Fill Christmas crackers with sweet love mottos, sugared almonds, whistles, balloons, trinkets, etc.

Activity: On January 12, many Christians celebrated the coming of the Magi to Bethlehem. This is a nice time to celebrate with a festive dinner and burn frankincense and myrrh. Delight guests with Christmas crackers. These decorative touches at each place setting are broken open after the dinner. To break the crackers, guests form a circle grasping the Christmas crackers between them. Trinkets/novelty items are suddenly released from the crackers as everyone pulls simultaneously.

Variation: Experience a Dickens Dinner with everyone coming in costume.

Twelfth Night

The most magnificent of all the medieval celebrations was the Twelfth Day (Twelfth Night, January 6). Medieval Christmas was a twelve-day festival with the Christmas finale on the Twelfth Night. It was a festival of many performers—a chief cook, wine tester, pages, musicians, mimes, jugglers, magicians, minstrels, and more. The director of all the festival ceremonies was called the Surveyor (head actor and master of ceremonies). All the guests came in medieval finery and were masked. The performers were in costume and also masked. The Surveyor was the only performer not masked.

Invite your guests to a feast with entertainment, dance, and games as in the medieval Twelfth Night. Guests may also be invited to come costumed and masked. Check your local library for costume ideas or a nearby college drama department for costumes. The decorations may include large banners hanging from long brass horns/dowels and twelve candles divided

and placed in the four corners of the banquet room. One large candle or candelabra is placed in the center of the room or on the high table. In medieval times, the meal was served on trenchers (bread platters). A few knives were sometimes used at the head table but forks and spoons did not exist. Ale was served from large festive bowls and guests drank from tankards. Adapt these customs to your feast.

The pages introduce the guests (as they are costumed): Lord, Lady, Count, Duke, Knight, Squire, Bishop, Peasant, and Serf from the kingdom of _____ (town where they reside). Guests also participate in the hand-washing ritual.

Baron
A knight and nobleman whose job it was to protect the land he owned, keep order and peace. Many knights are under his leadership.

Noble-woman
A woman of noble birth who helped teach young girls who served her in the castle.

Knight
A knight is a fighting man. He is raised to an honorable military rank and pledged to do good deeds.

Troubadour
Knightly poet and musician.

Squire
A young man of noble birth. He attends a knight until he becomes one.

Page
A young man training to be knight. At 7 he joins the household of his father's lord or some great noble, bishop, or king.

Minstrel
A singer or musician in the house of a lord. Wandering minstrels went about to sing and recite poems.

Jester (Court Fool)
Often wearing caps and bells, jesters amused the family of a king or nobleman. They were clever and sometimes gave advice to their king.

Bishop
The bishop has charge of many parishes and a cathedral (great church). The priest is the religious leader of a parish.

Friar
A friar is a priest but does not have a parish—he travels about.

Monk
Monks and nuns are religious people who serve God by prayer, work, teaching, and helping people.

Man-at-Arms
A heavily armed soldier on horseback but does not have the title of a knight.

Foot Soldier
A foot soldier is a fighting man but is not of noble birth.

Steward
A steward is the head servant.

Servants
Servants live in the castles devoting service to their masters whom they must obey.

Peasants
A farmer who belongs to the land owned by a lord. They sometimes farmed some land for themselves.

Serfs
Often children, captured in wars and sold to the wealthy. A slave who could not be sold off the land, but passed from one owner to another with the land.

Banners and Invitation

Hang banners from all the kingdoms about the great hall. Use brightly colored butcher paper or felt.

Key

	Yellow
	Green
	Red
	Blue

Twelfth Night

Supper and Revelry

Saturday,
January 4, 1997
6:00 P.M.
GREAT HALL
3820 Mountain Drive
In the Land of Evergreen, CO
Wear your medieval finery.
R.S.V.P. 555-3555

Twelfth Night Program

Hand Washing (Aquamanile)
Pages at the entry

Welcome Wassail
Surveyor

Grand Procession and Singing
Revelers stand and sing the Wassail Song

Crowning the King and Queen of Bean
Royal procession

Cutting the Upper Crust
Pantler

Presentation of First Remove (Apples and figs)
Hand bells

Presentation of Second Remove (Pâté and little breads)
Jugglers

Presentation of Third Remove (Fresh vegetables)
Minstrel singers

Presentation of Fourth Remove (Salmon in onion and wine sauce)
Mummers

Presentation of Fifth Remove (Barley fruit soup)
Procession outdoors for wassailing

Presentation of Sixth Remove (Cheese)
Dancers

Presentation of Seventh Remove (Chicken or pheasant wings)
Reading of poetry or Shakespeare's Twelfth Night *(Abridged edition)*

Presentation of Eighth Remove (Cakes with honey and spice)
Instrumental music (four temperaments—sanguine, phlegmatic, choleric, melancholic)

Presentation of Ninth Remove (Sliced turkey)
Tumblers and jesters

Presentation of Tenth Remove (Artichoke hearts)
Song fest

Presentation of Eleventh Remove (Small crullers in imaginative shapes—doughnuts)
Magician

Presentation of Twelfth Remove (Parade of Subtleties like marzipan, etc.)
Coming of the Magi *playlet. Burning and blessing of the greens.*

Aquamanile Ritual

Before each meal a ritual of hand washing is practiced. Pages bring a basin and pitcher to the high table. Other guests wash in basins near the door. As guest enter the hall, pages/laverers help guests wash their hands with spiced and herbed warm water. Water is poured from a pitcher (aquamanile) into a bowl. As each feaster eats with fingers, the ritual continues into the meal as pages carry a towel and bowl to the guests for hand washing. **Note:** Use an antique washstand with pitcher and bowl for the hand washing at the hall entry.

Cutting the Upper Crust

The surveyor summons the pantler (servant in charge of bread) who ceremonially carries a round loaf of bread and special knife to the head table. With much fanfare, he cuts the top of bread horizontally and presents it to the most honored guest. This demonstrates that he or she is the "upper crust."

The Guise Procession

Surveyor signals musicians for the guise procession fanfare (led by the surveyor, everyone displays their clever masks and guises by walking in rhythm about the great hall).

Twelfth Night Fires

Before Christianity, fires signified hope for a bountiful crop and drove away evil spirits. Historically the Twelfth Night Fire was a central place for drink and song. Later, in the transition from paganism to Christianity, the Twelfth Night fires (light) came to signify Christ. Some think of the twelve fires as representing the twelve Apostles and one large candle/fire dedicated to Christ himself. For your Twelfth Night fire, use twelve candles (three in each corner of the room) and a candelabra on the head table. A glowing fire in the fireplace can also symbolize the Twelfth Night Fire. The burning of the greens comes from a very old tradition. It was unlucky to have old, dry greens in the home. To prevent bad luck, the tradition of burning greens evolved. People threw their greens on the fire and made a wish. Today people throw a sprig from their Christmas tree onto the fire and make a wish or blessing.

Twelfth Night King and Queen of the Bean

Only on the Twelfth Night is the high table empty for a while. The places of honor are not taken by the noblest or richest but by the most honored revelers, the King and Queen of the Bean, who are revealed with the help of the Twelfth Night Cakes. In one cake, a gold/jeweled bean is hidden and, in the other, a small jewel the size of a pea has been placed. A real bean and pea may be used and hidden in the frosting decoration rather than the cake. All the guests are served a piece of cake. The men are served from the cake containing the bean and the ladies are served from the cake containing the pea. The King and Queen are revealed as the cake is eaten when the bean and pea are discovered. With a majestic fanfare, the King and Queen are escorted by the surveyor to the high table, crowned, introduced, and seated. A lively march is played during the escort. The Surveyor shouts "Wassail!" The King and Queen are the most honored revelers of the evening.

Note: On top of the Twelfth Night Cakes are decorations of stars, crowns, flowers, dragons, and little kings.

Twelfth Night Performers

During the feast, revelers are treated to a variety of entertainment acts. With each remove (course) comes a new performer. Plays, sonnets, poems, music of all kinds, and magic are an important part of the celebration. Performers move about the banquet room entertaining the King and Queen and the Twelfth Night Revelers.

Twelfth Night Wassailing

Throughout the evening, revelers celebrate with wassailing. Wassailing is a very important ritual of dance and singing around fruit trees for a bountiful harvest. "Wassail" comes from the old Gaelic words "was hael," which means "good health." It also signifies special food and drink with which we wish each other well. After the first few courses of food have been served, the revelers bundle up and head for the orchard. They walk rhythmically around a fruit tree chanting this old rhyme or other wassailing songs.

Hail to thee, old apple tree!
From every bough
Give us apples enow;
Hatsful, capsful,
Bushel, bushel, sacksful,
And our arms full, too!

Wassailers march a second time repeating the rhyme. After the third procession, end with shouts of "hurrah," stamping, noise making, and emptying cider on the tree.

Variation: Wassail around an indoor tree or around the banquet tables. English farmers wassailed their animals, bee hives, etc.

Mulled Apple Cider

3 quarts apple cider
1/4 teaspoon nutmeg
1/8 teaspoon thyme

1/2 teaspoon ginger
7 sticks of cinnamon
1 tablespoon sweet basil

Simmer juice, nutmeg, thyme, ginger, and cinnamon sticks. Remove the cinnamon sticks and serve in a tankard/glass. Sprinkle sweet basil on each portion.

Note: Check your library for *Medieval Holidays and Festivals* by Madeleine Pelner Cosman, published by Charles Scribner's Sons, New York. It is an excellent book for additional information on the Twelfth Night Celebration.

CELEBRATE A MEDIEVAL TWELFTH NIGHT

Favorite Holiday Stories

Follow the Star by Mala Powers
Dawne-Leigh Publications

A Child's Christmas in Wales by Dylan Thomas
Holiday House Publisher

The Best Christmas Pageant Ever by Barbara Robinson
Tyndale House Publishers, Inc.

The Polar Express by Chris Van Allsburg
Houghton Mifflin Co.

"The Miraculous Staircase" by Arthur Gordon
Woman's Day, December 14, 1982

Miracle in the Wilderness by Paul Gallico
Delacorte Press

"The Nut Cracker" by T. E. A. Hoffman

"The Gift of the Magi" by O. Henry
Ladies Home Journal, December 1985

The Story of Holly & Ivy by Rumer Godden
The Viking Kestrel

The Littlest Angel by Charles Tazewell
Ideals Publishing

Madeline's Christmas by Ludwig Bemelmans
The Viking Kestrel

How the Grinch Stole Christmas by Dr. Seuss
Random House

The Twenty-Four Days Before Christmas by Madeline L'Engle
Harold Shaw Publishers

"Christmas in Lake Wobegon" by Garrison Keillor
Saturday Evening Post, December 1987

Hans Brinker, or the Silver Skates by Mary Mapes Dodge
Del Publishing

Favorite Christmas Songbooks

Carols for Christmas. Edited by Sir David Willcocks. H. Holt & Co., 1983.

Christmas Revels Songbook. Compiled by John Langstaff & Nancy Langstaff. David R. Godine, Publisher, Inc., 1985.

Wee Sing for Christmas. Pam Beall & Susan Nipp. (Children's cassette and songbook). Price Stern, 1984.

Tomie dePaola's Book of Christmas Carols. Tomie dePaola. Putnam Publishing Group, 1987.

Merry Christmas Songbook. Readers Digest Assoc., Inc.

Holiday Song and Rhythms. Hap Palmer Ed. Activities, Box 392, Freeport, N.Y.

CELEBRATE YOUR FAMILY HERITAGE AND PASS A SCEPTER TO THE YOUNGER GENERATION!

Happy Holidays!

Section Three
SPECIAL OCCASIONS

25: Anniversaries/Reunions

A wedding is one of society's oldest and most important celebrations. It is the beginning of a new family unit, a rite of passage to adulthood, a religious sacrament, a legal contract, and a time of romance and joy. Even for children, dreaming of a wedding is very magical and fanciful. It is appropriate to commemorate annually an event of such societal and personal importance. Special anniversaries may also prompt family reunions. These occasions nurture family bonds as well as give families a time to experience the simple pleasures of anticipation and celebration. What would our life be without family holidays to enrich us?

Family reunions are regaining popularity and people are connecting with their ancestors and relatives. Reunions celebrate each family's special heritage and provide a time for relatives to renew old ties and meet new clan members. Family trees, genealogies, heirlooms, photographs, and ancestral stories passed on from generation to generation are precious and can become an important part of the reunion connections. These stories and old records enrich people's lives in very special ways. They reveal family values and define family interest areas such as politics, business, education, acting, music, etc. Family rituals and traditions, no matter how simple, give drama to living and confirm the importance of each family member as well as providing an important link between the past and present. Cherish this family lore and heritage.

INVITATION

- Write a poem about the couple incorporating their wedding picture. Photocopy the marriage certificate on parchment paper and use as the cover for the invitation.
- If your family has a family crest or a sign/symbol, use it in the invitation.
- Photocopy baby pictures of some older guests/relatives with the caption "Guess Who?" Make known their identities at the celebration.

DECORATIONS

Anniversary

- Create an **indoor garden setting** with rented flowers and greens from a florist.
- A **dove tree** is beautifully symbolic of the celebrated couple. (Hang as ornaments paper dove cutouts or doves from a florist/craft store.)
- Enhance the celebration with a **family time line** of pictures highlighted with romantic or funny captions.
- Decorate using the **traditional anniversary themes.** Cover the table with confetti for the first anniversary, use aluminum foil for table covering and gift wraps on the tenth anniversary and serve dinner in aluminum pie tins; and go Oriental for the twentieth "China" theme.
- For less formal settings use **balloons** in basket bouquets.
- Display **photograph collections/collages** around the party room with descriptions of memories. Remember the wedding album.
- Serve foods, flowers, candy, etc. in silver, etc. given as wedding presents.
- In calligraphy, write on parchment paper some **great proverbs** from *Apples of Gold* published by The C.R. Gibson Company. Display on the walls, in picture frames, etc.
- Remember a **guest book.**
- People enjoy seeing your **wedding dress, bridesmaid dress, groom's tie,** and other **wedding paraphernalia** displayed.
- Play some of the **songs** from your wedding ceremony.

Reunions

- Remember a **guest book**.
- Use **name tags** for large reunions. Sometimes it is helpful to designate relationships to family patriarchs and matriarchs—Mary and Fred Smith's son-in-law.
- Welcome guests by tying large **yellow ribbons** on trees and posts. Purchase **Americana print table-cloths** (blue or red and white checked) which can be used year after year.
- Have each family bring a **bunch of flowers** from their flower garden. Provide containers or have family members arrange in family heirloom vases.
- Have each guest bring a small **flag** from the countries of their heritage. Display in baskets with florist's clay.
- Display **family pictures** on a large piece of Styrofoam insulation or on a large wall. You may also include pictures of historic homes/schools/old landmarks.
- A **sharing center** with family albums, stories, and heirlooms is a wonderful way for connecting people. Remember clothing, even some made of old feed-sack fabric. Dolls and old toys are also wonderful remembrances. Identify their original owners.
- Play **musical recordings** of a theme, era, or heritage.

ANNIVERSARY/REUNION TERMS

Love	Romance	Hearts
Family tree	Memory	Ancestors
Stories	Traditions	Clan
Share	Doves	Heritage
Trivia	Mementos	Cherish
Heirlooms	Reminiscent	Family holiday

YEARLY ANNIVERSARY THEMES

First Year—Paper	**Fourteenth**—Ivory
Second—Cotton	**Fifteenth**—Crystal
Third—Leather	**Twentieth**—China
Fourth—Books/Fruits & Flowers	**Twenty-fifth**—Silver
Fifth Year—Wood	**Thirtieth**—Pearl
Sixth—Iron	**Thirty-fifth**—Coral/Jade
Seventh—Wool/Copper	**Fortieth**—Ruby
Eighth—Bronze	**Forty-fifth**—Sapphire
Ninth—Pottery	**Fiftieth**—Gold
Tenth Year—Tin/Aluminum	**Fifty-fifth**—Emerald
Eleventh—Steel	**Sixtieth**—Diamond
Twelfth—Linen/Silk	**Seventy-fifth**—Diamond Jubilee
Thirteenth—Lace	

REFRESHMENTS

- Most reunions are held in a large hall or outdoors. Welcome families as they bring favorite ethnic food dishes. The hosting family may provide the drinks and paper goods.
- For a more formal anniversary celebration, re-create the original wedding cake (check your wedding album for pictures). Include your wedding cake ornament.

FAVORS

An anniversary poem may be written by the honored couple thanking the guests for coming. Roll the poems into scrolls, tie with ribbons, and place in baskets. Grandchildren will enjoy passing the little scrolls out as guests leave.

A story could be told by one or more of the elder family members at the reunion. A copy of the story for each guest is a wonderful remembrance and the beginning of a family story collection.

ACTIVITIES/GAMES

Book of Memories

Ages: Teen–adult
Time: Several weeks before the event
Materials Needed: A letter with the invitation explaining the "memoirs" needed for the book and a large photo album.

Advance Preparation: Put collected memoirs into a memory book.
Activity: Present the honored couple with a book of memories.

April 1997

Dear Family and Friends,

As a special surprise for our parents' 50th Wedding Anniversary, we request your help in compiling a "Book of Memories" from their first 50 years of marriage.

Write a letter or note (long or short) in which you recall a special memory or experience shared with Mom and Dad. For example, you might recall a funny story, special visit, a trip, or perhaps enjoying some of mother's "famous" food—anything you would like to share. Include, if possible, a photo. It might be current or an old snapshot or perhaps even one including Mom and Dad. On the back of the photo, identify subjects and indicate date and location.

Please write your note or letter in black ink on one side only so it can be placed in the scrapbook, and send to:

> Allen Smith
> 3100 South Vrain
> Urbana, Illinois

Also, please send no later than April 26, 1997, so that the book can be assembled. Remember, this project is a surprise for Mom and Dad. Please do not send letters and photos to them.

Respectfully requested,

Doris, Walt, Jan, and their families

Dancing

Ages: 3–adult
Time: 2–3 hours
Materials Needed: Large hall/rented dance floor and a live band or recordings.
Advance Preparation: Make arrangements for a band or collect music recordings for dancing. Remember era and ethnic dances.
Activity: Guests dance during the gala event.
Variation: Have dance contests. Award silly ribbons with computer-generated captions attached.

Reminiscing With Video

Ages: 5–adult
Time: Throughout the celebration
Materials Needed: Old movies and videos, television, tape recorder, and patience.
Advance Preparation: Select assorted stories from old movies and videos. Have them copied/recorded at a professional recording service.
Activity: Play recorded video continuously at the celebration for guests to view at their leisure.

Family Stories

Ages: Teen–adult
Time: Allow several months
Materials Needed: Family stories and a computer.
Advance Preparation: Research and collect family stories. Read *Black Sheep and Kissing Cousins: How Our Family Stories Shape Us* by Time Books. Type and print family stories in a booklet.
Activity: At a reunion give guests a copy of the family stories. Stories are wonderful and have a way of explaining even abstract concepts such as racial discrimination. A good example is the story of Helen Forten, a black teacher during the Civil War. Every family has its characters and stories. How interesting it is to learn about these people through stories.

Story Time

Ages: 3–adult
Time: 20–30 minutes
Materials Needed: One of the oldest relatives to tell his/her story. Use a dome tent or improvise a tent with a large blanket for the storytelling area.
Advance Preparation: Ask an older relative to be prepared to tell some stories about his or her life. It is especially nice if they will put them in writing or on video or tape so guests may have a copy to take home as a party favor.
Activity: Guests snuggle on a blanket inside the tent with the storyteller and share family stories.
Note: Remember tales of the more illustrious ancestors and funny anecdotes.

Publish a Family Cookbook

Ages: Adult
Time: Several months
Materials Needed: Family recipes, anecdotes, and pictures.
Advance Preparation: Gather family recipes, organize, and type. Have an artist sketch the family home for the cover.
Activity: Preserve your family's treasured recipes and heritage. Precious memories can be awakened through recipes and cherished photos. Have wonderful family recipe cookbooks ready for the next reunion.

For a free information packet on family cookbooks write:

Cookbooks by Morris Press
P.O. Box 1681
Kearney, Nebraska 68848
800-445-6621
800-652-9314 (in Nebraska)

Song Fest Around a Campfire

Ages: 3–adult
Time: 40 minutes
Materials Needed: Guitarist, song sheets with camp songs, ethnic songs, and a few songs for the children. Wood for the campfire, planks and short logs for benches.
Advance Preparation: Build a fire pit and benches. Make all musical arrangements and photocopy song sheets.

Activity: Sing around a campfire or fireplace.
Variation: If you need assistance in providing musical leadership, use campfire song recordings as your support. This may also be a time to feature special talents among family members—musical, tumbling, jestering, juggling, etc.

Publish Family Highlights

Ages: Teen–adult
Time: 3 months before the reunion
Materials Needed: Brief news story and picture from each family.
Advance Preparation: Ask all families to send a news

story highlighting new family members (marriage or birth), special accomplishments, etc. They should also include a picture. Put together a reunion newspaper.
Activity: Guests enjoy the family highlights of relatives they do not see very often.

Art Festival

Ages: 4–adult
Time: Spontaneous
Materials Needed: Pieces of art, needlework, etc. displayed on large Styrofoam pieces of building insulation and tables.

Advance Preparation: Invite relatives to bring a special piece of art to be displayed at the reunion. Many quiet talents become recognized. It is a delightful way to reminisce.
Variation: Display hobbies.

Family Fashion Show

Ages: 4–adult
Time: 30 minutes
Materials Needed: Clothes, especially hats, from ancestors. Remember accessory items such as shoes, ties, hats, etc. Music to accompany the fashion show.

Advance Preparation: Prepare a script for the fashion show including a bit of history about the person and the garment.
Activity: Relatives enjoy a bit of nostalgia through a family fashion show.

Games

Ages: All ages
Time: Various times throughout the event
Materials Needed: A plan for games to be played and the equipment needed for each game. See other chapters in this book for a variety of ideas. Remember cards, bocce ball, and croquet for the adults.

Advance Preparation: Set up nets for volleyball and other activities. Gather all equipment, prizes, etc.
Activity: Play board games and recreational games. Remember, very young children enjoy nonstructured activity such as a swimming pool, sandbox, boxes, tunnels, and simple play items.

Planning a Reunion

- Update list of relatives and addresses.
- Choose date suitable to most relatives.
- Choose location.
- Work out lodging accommodations.
- Delegate responsibilities—involve as many people as possible.
- Send invitations about six months in advance.
- Allow plenty of time for visiting.
- Escape to a park, large backyard, campground, resort, farm, hall, country club, or restaurant for a wonderful time of reminiscing and catching up.

MAKE YOUR NEXT ANNIVERSARY/REUNION A SPECIAL CELEBRATION!

Happy Remembrances!

26: Special Birthdays

FIRST	❦	SIXTEENTH	❦	TWENTY-FIRST
FORTIETH		FIFTIETH		EIGHTIETH

Golden birthday is that birthday which is the same as your birth date—17th birthday on June 17.

Throughout most of history, birthdays were celebrated only by kings. In earliest times, people did not even know their birth dates. The first calendar was developed by Egyptian astronomers around 4000 B.C. and, because early astronomers were connected to the royal court, birthday celebrations were reserved for kings only. After the fall of the Roman Empire in A.D. 395, birthdays lost importance as personal celebrations. Only in the twelfth century were birthdays again recognized as significant occasions.

The first birthday parties began because it was believed that harmful spirits converged around a birthday celebrant. Friends and relatives gathered, bringing their good wishes to keep evil spirits at bay. Presents brought even more protection. Many ancient people believed that wearing a birthstone brought good luck and strengthened personality traits such as courage, love, and loyalty. Birthday candles seem to have their origins with the Greeks and Romans. They believed flames had mystical powers—a magical ability to convey messages to the gods. The Germans adopted this ancient respect for flame in their use of birthday candles. German birthday pastries were adorned with a large candle (lebenslicht) surrounded by many small candles. Only the birthday child could blow out the candles and his wish would come true in the same number of months as it took puffs to blow out the candles.

The tradition of the birthday cake and candles spread to England and was especially popular with Queen Victoria. In the mid-1800s, postage stamps and the introduction of the first birthday card made the exchanging of birthday greetings very popular and started a whole new era for birthday celebrations. From this time forward, birthdays were celebrated by everyone. From England, birthday traditions made their way to America and other parts of the world.

Birthday customs vary around the world. In China older persons rather than children are held in high esteem and honored on their birthdays. A Brazilian girl's fifteenth birthday is most important—the celebration is much like the coming-out parties in America. Children from the Philippines observe birthday celebrations every seven years—significant years in development are the 1st, 7th, 14th, and 21st. In America, children's parties are very important and adults often celebrate milestone birthdays like the 21st, 30th, 40th, 50th and 80th. Birthdays are important personal celebrations as expressed in excerpts from an editorial in the *Godey's Lady's Book,* 1856:

> What untold delights would be lost to the juvenile world if the celebration of Christmas, New Year's Day, and the Fourth of July was henceforth and forever annihilated! And what minor pleasure and joyful anticipations would fade in dim distance were the family holidays or birthday and wedding-day to be forgotten.
>
> Perhaps the milestones will come too quickly hereafter. If we wreathe them now with garlands, we may then be thankful to sit awhile beside them in the shade, for shadows lengthen as the eventide creeps on the number with thankful recollection, the blessings of the way. A happy childhood carries its own brightness to another generation, springing up with the same glad anticipations and birthdays are among its brightest recollections.

A birthday celebration is one of the most cherished gifts that parents can give their children. Toys are temporary ... memories are forever.

INVITATION

- Insert an invitation into a balloon.
- Blow up and write an invitation message with a permanent marker on a balloon. Deflate and mail.
- Type the invitation message on a narrow strip of paper, roll tightly, and insert into size 000 drug capsules obtained from your local pharmacy.

DECORATIONS

- Fly a **birthday flag.** Create it with colorful fabrics.
- Incorporate **toy cars** in 16th birthday decorations!
- Hang and display **worn-out shoes!** Use wheels instead on your 16th birthday.
- Arrange a **collage of pictures** from birth to 16 years. Incorporate **keys, wheels,** and **driver's license** for the 16th birthday.
- Display **large yard signs** made with poster board and paint sticks.
- Hang a **gigantic birthday banner** made with a large roll of colored butcher paper or wrapping paper. Grandchildren will especially enjoy creating this banner for grandparents. Fill each bubble letter with something different—smile faces, 55th, "love you," "you're great," designs, or whatever fits.

- If using a Gypsy theme, place **gold-covered chocolate coins** and **old jewelry** about the serving table.
- Have a few coins falling out of little pouches.
- Fill a **giant balloon** with helium and tie to the mailbox.
- Make a **giant birthday cake** using a card table. Cover it with an old sheet. Spray-paint "Oh Sheet" on the front and place 40 large candles on the table. This is a magnificent surprise entry.
- Decorate with **black balloons, streamers, pinwheels,** and **serpentine.**
- Spray **old plastic flowers** black.
- Wrap presents with large, **black lacy ribbon.**
- Sprinkle **confetti** on the party table, especially gold and silver metallic.
- Enlarge **baby pictures** into **posters.** Funny poses are best.
- Display **picture albums** and **baby books.**
- Purchase **Happy Birthday banners.**
- Use monthly **birthstones** and **flowers** to decorate tables.

BIRTHSTONES AND FLOWERS

January—Garnet (constancy)—Carnation/Snowdrop

February—Amethyst (sincerity)—Violet/Primrose

March—Aquamarine or bloodstone (courage)—Jonquil/Violet

April—Diamond (innocence)—Sweet pea/Daisy

May—Emerald (love, success)—Lily of the valley /Hawthorne

June—Pearl or alexandrite (health)—Rose/Honeysuckle

July—Ruby (contentment)—Delphinium/Larkspur

August—Peridot or sardonyzx (married/happiness)—Gladioli/Waterlily

September—Sapphire (clear thinking)—Aster/Poppy

October—Opal or tourmaline (hope)—Marigold/Calendula

November—Topaz (fidelity)—Chrysanthemum/Hop blooms

December—Turquoise or zircon (prosperity)—Daffodil/Holly/Narcissus

OLD BIRTHDAY PROPHECIES

Monday's child is fair of face
Tuesday's child is full of grace
Wednesday's child is full of woe
Thursday's child has far to go
Friday's child is loving and giving
Saturday's child works hard for a living
But the child that's born on the Sabbath day
Is bonny and blithe and good and gay.

A dimple on the cheek
Leaves a fortune to seek.

The most talented and luckiest of all children, however, are seventh children of seven children.

TERMS

Life begins at ...
It's all relative
Over the hill
Doing it in style
Ready to roll
The hottest number in town
No one is getting any younger
You are feistier than ever
You now deserve a rest
Character is built by experience; you have had lots of experience
You may never be a grown-up
You have not aged a bit
The best is yet to come
Blast into the past
Soon you will be a classic
Outstanding
Like expensive wine, age brings out the finest

A kid at heart
Awesome
Fire in your eyes
Wrinkles, droop
Like antiques, age adds value
Aged to perfection
Polished and priceless
Mellow
Jolly
Marvelous
Wonderful
Ultra
Terrific
Significant
Witty
Outstanding
Bizarre
Nifty, nifty, Don is fifty

BIRTHDAYS IN OTHER LANGUAGES

Happy Birthday—English
Til Lykke—Danish
Hartelijk Gefeliciteerd—Dutch
Glucklichen Geburtstag—German
Joyeauax Anniversaire—French

Yom Moledet Somayach—Hebrew
Gratulerer Med Dagen—Norwegian
Wesolych Urodzien—Polish
Feliz Cumpleaños—Spanish
Statsny Narozeni—Czech

REFRESHMENTS

- Use trick candles that relight and cannot be blown out.
- Cover a photo of the guest of honor with clear cellophane and place it in the center of the birthday cake.
- Hide fortune charms in the birthday cake/frosting—ring (marriage), button (poor), coin (wealth), and a thimble (old maid or bachelor), etc.
- Check a cake decorating/party store for a variety of fun cake decorations. Use bandages, dentures, etc.
- Serve refreshments in unusual containers—something that may relate to hobbies, etc.
- Serve birthday fortune cookies (sometimes found in specialty stores).

GAG PRESENTS

Wig
Denture cup
Cane/walking stick (add rhinestones)
Full mask
DI-GEL
Adult push toy
Sulfur 8
40 "carrot" necklace
Heet
Sport crying towel
Forties survival kit
Glasses
Adult diapers
Hair dye
Gigantic 16th driver's license
Books for the age

T-shirts
Live animals (use discretion)
Geritol
Magnifying glass
Granny shoes
Coins with birth date
Baby food
Old bifocals
Jelly beans (pills)
Grecian Formula
Hot tub toy
Toothless comb
Giant pins
50 lottery tickets, etc.
Fan (hot flashes)
Gourmet foods

Forties or Fifties Survival Kit for the 90s

In a large tin box, layer each item with tissue paper. Write poems for each item on large plain address labels and stick labels on.

Nasal spray—How's your nose? Can you still smell a rose?

Bottle of Vitamin E—Vitamin E, follow me. We'll climb a tree if you can see!

Avon Facial Mask—Use a facial mask if you must bask in the sun to have fun.

Corn pads—I've never thought you corny! In fact you can't be beat. So take these pads and stick them where else but on your feet?

Chin strap (may use ordinary headband)—Put it on tight all thru the night, for you'll never be a winner sporting a double chinner!

Bathtub appliqués—Who wants to slip and break a hip? Better to sprain—no need to explain!

Dental adhesive powder (KLUTCH)—What more can I say?

Mouthwash—If you can catch your breath use this!

Epsom Salts—For an olde salt!

FAVORS

❦ Mini computer-generated newspapers dedicated to the guest of honor.

EXTRA EXTRA

Special Edition   *November 15, 1997*   *Denver, Colorado*

EVENT: Describe the celebration details

STORIES: Have friends and family write short stories or anecdotes about the guest of honor.

HOROSCOPE/FORECASTS

COMICS

SOCIETY PAGE

WRITINGS BY GUEST OF HONOR

Select a favorite poem or story written by the guest of honor. Check childhood papers and pictures.

THROUGH THE YEARS
Picture on page 2

ACTIVITIES/GAMES
Birthday Flag

Ages: 1–100 years
Time: All day on the birthday
Materials Needed: Waterproof fabric, sewing machine, pattern/design, and a dowel.

Advance Preparation: Design and make a birthday flag. Personalize it for the guest of honor.
Activity: Fly on every birthday.

Time Capsule

Ages: At birth, 1 year, 10 years, 21 years, etc.
Time: 10–15 minutes
Materials Needed: Large decorated can, lock of hair, clothes item, birthday cards, newspaper, magazine, popular toy, calendar from baby's first year, athletic event ticket, *TV Guide,* photographs, special letters, mementos, baptismal candle, stickers, stamps, popular tapes or video movies, list of slang expressions of the day (with definitions).
Advance Preparation: Purchase a large 5-gallon popcorn can and gather paraphernalia for the time capsule.
Activity: Present the time capsule to the birthday child. Let guests see what will be in the time capsule. Store (bury) in a closet, etc.

Note: Type information on a small gift card and glue it on top of the capsule lid.

TIME CAPSULE
Buried by
Mary Elizabeth
January 14, 1996
Do not disturb or open until January 14, 2006

Variation: Gather vintage paraphernalia from the year of the celebrant's birth. Put it in a time capsule that can be opened immediately.

How Tall

Ages: Begin the first year
Time: 5 minutes
Materials Needed: A door or vertical banner 7 feet in height, a tape measure, and a pencil.
Advance Preparation: Select a door to record the height of your child on every birthday. If you are using a banner or stick, purchase appropriate materials.
Activity: Record your child's height on a door jamb or banner each year on his/her birthday.

Sixteenth Special

Ages: All ages, especially 16
Time: Eve of the 16th birthday
Materials Needed: Streamers, serpentine, balloons, and birthday presents.
Advance Preparation: Gather materials and have them ready for decorating. Plan the breakfast menu.
Activity: When the teenager is asleep on her birthday eve, quietly decorate her bedroom and pile gifts at the foot of the bed. Have a special breakfast for the family the morning of the honored guest's birthday.

Keys to the Family Car

Ages: 16 years
Time: Varies
Materials Needed: An additional set of keys to the family car and a scroll with family driving policies.
Advance Preparation: Develop driving policies and write them with a computer on a long scroll. Roll and tie with a ribbon.
Activity: Present the new driver with a set of car keys and the family driving policies.

A Big Haul

Ages: 16 (young men)
Time: 20 minutes
Materials Needed: Plastic toy wagon, assorted plastic guns including suction dart guns, colored paper bags.
Advance Preparation: Put toy guns in the paper bags and fill the plastic wagon with the bags. This may be used as a centerpiece.
Activity: Guests each grab a bag and play with the plastic guns. Set up targets around the party area.
Note: Young men still will be boys and enjoy plastic guns, etc.

"Mille Bornes"

Ages: 16–adult
Time: 45–60 minutes
Materials Needed: "Mille Bornes," a French card game.
Advance Preparation: Read and understand the game.
Activity: Play a card game that takes you across the European countryside. The cards dealt and drawn are miles, obstacles, hazards, remedies, safety, and distances. Rules of the road include light, speed limits, flat tires, out-of-gas, and accidents. The first team to accumulate 5,000 points in several hands wins.

Are We at the Right Place?

Ages: 16–adult
Time: 45 minutes
Materials Needed: Three different sets of party invitations—one formal, one hobo, and one sport. Three table settings—one formal with candlelight, one casual with a sport motif, and one hobo where guests are served on the floor from the bag on the bindle stick.
Advance Preparation: Send guests the invitations—$^1/_3$ receiving formal invitations, $^1/_3$ receiving hobo, and $^1/_3$ receiving a sport invitation. Prepare the three table settings and food appropriate for each.
Activity: Guests arrive confused as they see others coming in different attire. After all have arrived, they are seated at the appropriate table setting. This is a great way to begin a party.

Gypsy Booth

Ages: 16–adult
Time: 30–40 minutes
Materials Needed: Fortunes, Gypsy booth, "Madame Sasha," crystal ball, scarf, and a basket.
Advance Preparation: Make up fortunes and find someone to be Madame Sasha (dramatic and vibrant). Put together a crystal ball in the basket along with scarf and fortunes.
Activity: Madame Sasha tells guests their fortunes. If you have time, gather funny unknown facts about each guest and before the party give these facts to Madame Sasha on a card.
Variation: Invite guests to come as Gypsies. Play ethnic songs such as "Rakoczi March," Liszt's *Hungarian Rhapsody No. VIII, The Fort,* and *The Fortune-Teller* by Victor Herbert. Have someone costumed as a dancing bear re-enacting late medieval Gypsy entertainment.

Gypsy Caravan

Ages: Adult
Time: 30–55 minutes
Materials Needed: A Gypsy wagon (limousine, van, or motor home), two dramatic ladies, the guest of honor's favorite drink, and large signs that say "GYPSY WAGON."
Advance Preparation: Make arrangements for the wagon and find two dramatic women to play the role of Gypsies. Decorate the wagon with flowers and signs. Tell the plan to others at work so they are not alarmed.
Activity: Kidnap the guest of honor as he leaves work and escort to the "Gypsy wagon." Take the guest on a ride about town and serve his favorite drink. In the meantime, the Gypsy ladies, highly animated and energetic, entertain the guest of honor. After a fun-filled tour about town, take the guest of honor to his surprise party.
Note: It is important that the Gypsies say things immediately so the guest of honor will know the "kidnapping" is a gag. For example, they may do a little Gypsy dance as they approach the honored guest and then say, "We are here to find a treasure that has been buried for 40 years." Gypsies should know other tidbits about the guest!
Optional: Invite all guests to come dressed as Gypsies.

Remember??

Ages: "Milestone" birthdays
Time: 30–40 minutes
Materials Needed: Tape recorder, scripts from each grandchild, and a loudspeaker system.
Advance Preparation: A month before the celebration, ask grandchildren to prepare remarks about something interesting or special in their relationship with the guest of honor. Have each grandchild write the remarks on a sheet of paper to be put in the memory book.
Activity: Grandchildren stand and tell their special stories.

A Special Walk

Ages: All ages
Time: 30–55 minutes
Materials Needed: Map.
Advance Preparation: Plot places of important events in the life of the honored guest. Gather stories, etc. about these special places and events.
Activity: Walk, if possible, to all the places where special activities took place. Tell about each event—engagement, wedding, farm, place of work, school, etc. You may have to drive and walk.
Variation: If places are in different communities and states, create this same walk on video with a narrator.

Newspaper Advertisement

Ages: 50th birthday and older
Time: A week before the birthday
Materials Needed: Money to place a full-page ad in the local newspaper.
Advance Preparation: A week before the big cerebration, arrange for a full-page advertisement to be placed in the edition closest to the celebration date. Do not tell the guests/relatives about your advertisement. Make it a surprise to all. Many may see it when the paper is delivered to their motel rooms if they are from out of town.

> To: Mintie Paulson
> Rigis Retirement Center
> Happy 100th Birthday
> Grandma Paulson
> From your favorite Grandson!

Note: Signing your name and closing in a clever way will cause a great deal of excitement for all guests gathered for the special occasion. "From your favorite grandson" could be from the one who was always mischievous!

Trivia

Ages: 6–adult
Time: 30–45 minutes
Materials Needed: Family/relatives each bring several trivia cards about their family, pets, special holidays, gatherings, trips, accomplishments, favorite colors, talents, etc. Remember to write the question on one side and the answer on the back side. Recipe cards and a file box.

Advance Preparation: Remind families to bring the trivia cards to the celebration.
Activity: Many wonderful moments are remembered as guests play "Family Trivia."
Note: This can be done every year and the trivia game will become a family history.

Singing Telegram

Ages: 16–100 years
Time: 20 minutes
Materials Needed: None.
Advance Preparation: Locate a company that sends singing telegrams. Arrange for them to come to the celebration.
Activity: Singing telegram people arrive. They present balloons and a celebration message in song.

Family Talent Show

Ages: 4–adult
Time: 30–45 minutes
Materials Needed: This can be done live or on video (a tape can be sent out of town for a celebration you are unable to attend). Video equipment and tape. Loudspeaker system if the show is live and in a large gathering.

Advance Preparation: Arrange for family members to present their talents at the celebration. Prepare a narration.
Activity: Present a family talent show for the guest of honor and guests.
Variation: Put together a family band.

Coffin Brigade

Ages: 40 years
Time: 15 minutes
Materials Needed: Carpenter, wood, rope for handles, paint, friends for pallbearers, and red carnations.
Advance Preparation: Build a wood coffin 7 feet long and 2 feet wide. Drill holes in the ends for rope handles. Paint with a gray stain and decorate with funny captions, etc. Select the pallbearers and have them wear something outrageous. The head pallbearer may wear an outlandish mask!

Activity: Pallbearers walk up the street toward the honored guest's home! This works well in a surprise party setting where the guest of honor drives up and suddenly the coffin brigade comes walking down the street. Guests are all inside and come out singing "Happy Birthday." The guest of honor may choose to get in the coffin while everyone is singing "Happy Birthday," or have it filled with all the gag gifts.

"Eulogy"

Ages: 40 years
Time: 10 minutes
Materials Needed: Pastor/layperson, a eulogy adapted to a 40th birthday. End with, "Now you are entering the promised land."

Advance Preparation: Make arrangements for a person to deliver the eulogy.
Activity: Give the eulogy at the end of the party. It is important to keep it funny, clever, and light!

"This Is Your Life"

Ages: 40–80 years
Time: 30–45 minutes
Materials Needed: Stories, pictures, movie films, video, script, and a narrator.

Advance Preparation: Using varied media, drama, films, etc., create a life story about the guest of honor. Add music and script if using video.

Bus Bash

Ages: Adult
Time: 2 hours
Materials Needed: A British double-decker bus (if possible), hors d'oeuvres, and wine. A portable microphone.
Advance Preparation: Make arrangements for renting a bus or large van. Prepare the hors d'oeuvres and wine. Make a list of places important in the life of the guest of

honor. Write a short story about each location—birthplace, first job, schools, first speeding ticket, etc.
Activity: Party-goers make a pilgrimage about their town or country enjoying anecdotes, food, and drink along the way.
Variation: When appropriate, get off the bus and re-enact the events that happened there.

Memory Quilt

Ages: Adult
Time: Not applicable
Materials Needed: Letter giving directions for the memory quilt.
Advance Preparation: Six months before the celebration, send a letter to family/friends. The letter should

include clear instructions on completing a quilt square. Set a deadline for completion. All squares should be sent to the address of the person who will put the quilt together.
Activity: Present the memory quilt to the special guest. Stories about each square may be shared at this time.

Birthday Treasure Hunt

Ages: 6–teen
Time: 15 minutes
Materials Needed: None.
Advanced Preparation: None.
Activity: As guests arrive, they take great pride in find-

ing the most perfect hiding place for their presents. Secret hiding places can be located in designated places in the house or in the garden. The guest of honor must search for his/her presents.

Dancing

Ages: 16–50 years
Time: 1–2 hours
Materials Needed: Live band or recordings and disc/tape player.
Advance Preparation: Arrange for a band or select appropriate vintage recordings. Set up for dancing.

Activity: Dance and have funny dance contests.
Variation: Create a theme form a particular recording such as "Tara's Theme" from *Gone With the Wind*. This would make a nice 16th birthday garden party with dancing.

Roast

Ages: 40–50 years
Time: 30 minutes
Materials Needed: People and script for the roast.
Advance Preparation: Contact the people who will be doing the roast and prepare scripts. Keep the roast funny and light. Use discretion!
Activity: Roast the birthday person.
Note: Books on roasting are available at bookstores and libraries.

Ribbon Tree

Ages: All ages
Time: 10 minutes
Materials Needed: Beautifully wrapped birthday presents and lots of ⅝-inch ribbon.
Advance Preparation: Hang the presents with ribbon from a tree in the front or backyard.
Activity: Birthday person awakens to breakfast and a tree decked with lovely gifts.
Variation: If inside, use an indoor tree such as a Norfolk pine or ficus.

Crazy Soccer

Ages: 16–adult
Time: 45 minutes
Materials Needed: Nylon stockings, potatoes, soccer balls, and masking tape.
Advance Preparation: Create nylon stocking slings. Put a potato in the toes of two nylon stockings. Lengthen each stocking by tying a second stocking to it. Make a lasso-type noose on the end of the lengthened stockings. Each relay team should have a stocking sling filled with a potato. If the group is large create more slings for more teams.
Activity: Divide guests into relay teams of four. With a stocking slung around the neck, each relay member must "dribble" the soccer ball (potato) from the starting line to the finish line and back. The guests spread their legs and propel the soccer ball with the potato in the stocking (the body swings to propel the ball).

Publish Mother's/Father's Favorite Recipes

Ages: 60th–80th birthdays
Time: 6 months before the celebration
Materials Needed: Collect the birthday person's favorite recipes along with some pictures and stories. Special poems are also nice.
Advance Preparation: Gather recipes, pictures, and stories. Organize and type. Have an artist sketch the family home for the cover.
Activity: At the birthday celebration, give guests a copy of the birthday person's favorite recipes along with some special memories.

For a free information packet on family cookbooks write:

Cookbooks by Morris Press
P.O. Box 1681
Kearney, Nebraska 68848
800-570-1767

Memory Book

Ages: 50 years plus
Time: 3 months before the celebration
Materials Needed: Large picture album, a cover letter to go with the invitation. Tell guests to use black ink.
Advance Preparation: After you receive all the stories, pictures, etc., display them in a memory book.
Activity: Present the memory book to the guest of honor. See sample letter in "Book of Memories" in Anniversaries/Reunions chapter.

Countdown

Ages: 40–50 years
Time: Every day 2 weeks before the birthday
Materials Needed: Anonymous funny letters going out each day for a week before the recipient's birthday. Clip art helps expand ideas and creativity.
Advance Preparation: Prepare the letters. They can be done on a computer or with typewritten cards.
Activity: Send the countdown letters!

Zodiac Sign Celebrations

Ages: Teen–adult
Time: Varies
Materials Needed: Zodiac signs, pictures, prophecies, etc.
Advance Preparation: Send invitations to all who have birthdays under a particular zodiac sign. Remember these signs overlap months—for example: Capricorn is December 22–January 19. Invite celebrant's families. This is especially meaningful for Capricorns whose birthday often get lost in the holiday shuffle. Name badges should include day (but not year) of birth. People will be surprised to meet "twins."
Activity: Capricorns, etc. come together as a group and celebrate their birthdays.

Sweet Nothings

Ages: 40 and 50 years
Time: 20 minutes
Material Needed: Assorted candy bars, ribbon, recipe cards, pretty shopping bag, tissue paper, paper punch, and a sense of humor.
Advance Preparation: Create a story using the name of the candy bars. Tie the bars and cards together with ribbon.
Activity: Read the story one bar at a time.

This is "THE" BIRTHDAY! **BAR NONE!**
Just because you are 40 doesn't mean you are a **BIG CHEESE!**
You are now **TWIX.**
NOW & LATER you've lived life **GOOD & PLENTY!**
Now when you get up in the morning the bones **KRACKEL!**
You look in the mirror and feel a little **CHUNKY!**
SNICKER! SNICKER! (Purchase a package of bars)
Too many **WHOPPERS!**
SNICKER! SNICKER! SNICKER!
You are definitely feeling the **CRUNCH!**
Your **SUGAR BABIES** are almost in college, etc.
Your **BABY RUTH** is even in school!
You are feeling like a real **ZERO!**
You've even called your mother **WHATCHAMACALLIT!**
So buck up Gloria! We are your friends and not all of us are **NERDS**—just one or two of us!
Your **PAY DAY** is coming!
You are worth **100 GRAND** to us.
We are telling you, you are **SPECIAL!**
You are a real **POWER HOUSE!**
Some say an **ATOMIC FIRE BALL!**
KISSES to you from all of your younger friends. We love you!
We know the **SKOR!**
We are the **LIFESAVERS!** "CHERRY O!"

CELEBRATE!

Index